The Vietnam Experience

A War Remembered

by Stephen Weiss, Clark Dougan, David Fulghum, Denis Kennedy, and the editors of Boston Publishing Company

Boston Publishing Company/Boston, MA

Boston Publishing Company

President and Publisher: Robert J. George
Vice President: Richard S. Perkins, Jr.
Editor-in-Chief: Robert Manning
Managing Editor: Paul Dreyfus
Marketing Director: Jeanne Gibson

Senior Writers:
Clark Dougan, Edward Doyle, David Fulghum, Samuel Lipsman, Terrence Maitland, Stephen Weiss
Senior Picture Editor: Julene Fischer
Senior Editor: Gordon Hardy

Staff Writer: Denis Kennedy
Researchers:
Richard J. Burke, Steven W. Lipari, Anthony Maybury-Lewis, Nicholas Philipson, Janice Sue Wang, Robert Yarbrough

Picture Editors:
Wendy Johnson, Lanng Tamura
Assistant Picture Editor: Kathleen A. Reidy
Picture Researchers:
Robert Ebbs, Tracey Rogers, Nana Elisabeth Stern, Shirley L. Green (Washington, D.C.), Kate Lewin (Paris)
Archivist: Kathryn J. Steeves
Picture Department Assistant: Karen Bjelke

Production Editor: Kerstin Gorham
Assistant Production Editor: Patricia Leal Welch
Editorial Production: Dalia Lipkin, Theresa M. Slomkowski

Design: Designworks, Sally Bindari
Design Assistant: Sandra Calef

Business Staff: Amy Pelletier, Amy P. Wilson

About the editors and authors

Editor-in-Chief *Robert Manning,* a long-time journalist, has previously been editor-in-chief of the *Atlantic Monthly* magazine and its press. He served as assistant secretary of state for public affairs under Presidents John F. Kennedy and Lyndon B. Johnson. He has also been a fellow at the Institute of Politics at the John F. Kennedy School of Government at Harvard University.

Authors: *Stephen Weiss,* who has coauthored five other titles in *The Vietnam Experience,* is an American historian with an M.A. and M.Phil. from Yale University. Previously he was a fellow at the Newberry Library in Chicago. *Clark Dougan,* coauthor of three other volumes in *The Vietnam Experience,* has taught at Kenyon College in Ohio. A former Watson and Danforth Fellow, he received his M.A. and M.Phil. at Yale. *David Fulghum,* formerly a senior writer with the *U.S. News & World Report* Book Division, has coauthored two previous *Vietnam Experience* titles. A veteran of the U.S. Navy, he received his B.A. from Angelo State University in Texas and has done graduate studies at Texas A&M and Georgetown Universities. *Denis Kennedy* received his B.A. at Harvard and has previously been a researcher on *The Vietnam Experience.* Most recently, he was Assistant Editor of Boston Publishing's history of the Medal of Honor, *Above and Beyond.*

Cover Photo:

Operation Byrd, August 26, 1966. A soldier of the 1st Cavalry Division comforts a buddy after a firefight that took the lives of most of the men in his platoon.

Library of Congress Catalog Card Number: 86-070135

ISBN: 0-939526-20-4

10 9 8 7 6
5 4 3 2 1

Contents

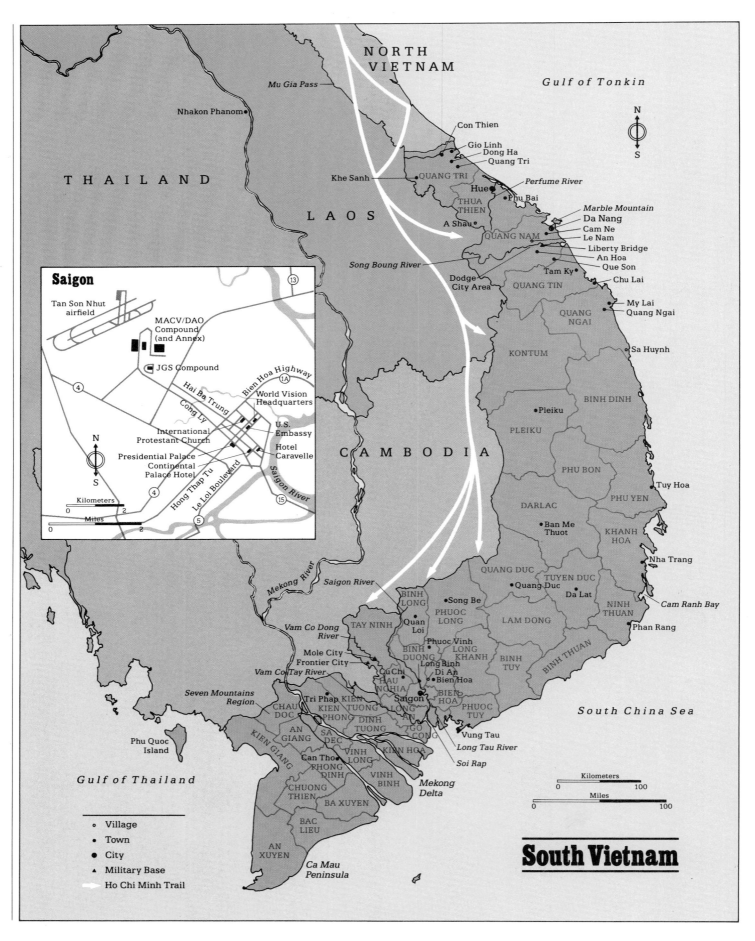

South Vietnam

NORTH VIETNAM

Gulf of Tonkin

Mu Gia Pass

Nhakon Phanom

THAILAND

LAOS

Con Thien
Gio Linh
Dong Ha
Quang Tri
Khe Sanh • QUANG TRI
Perfume River
Hue
Phu Bai
THUA THIEN
A Shau
Marble Mountain
Da Nang
QUANG NAM
Cam Ne
Le Nam
Song Boung River
Liberty Bridge
An Hoa
Que Son
Dodge City Area
Tam Ky
Chu Lai
QUANG TIN
My Lai
Quang Ngai
QUANG NGAI
Sa Huynh
KONTUM

CAMBODIA

BINH DINH
Pleiku
PLEIKU
PHU BON
DARLAC
PHU YEN
Tuy Hoa
Ban Me Thuot
KHANH HOA
Nha Trang
QUANG DUC
TUYEN DUC
Quang Duc
Da Lat
NINH THUAN
Cam Ranh Bay
LAM DONG
Phan Rang
BINH THUAN

Mekong River
Saigon River
BINH LONG
Song Be
PHUOC LONG
LONG KHANH
TAY NINH
Quan Loi
Phuoc Vinh
Mole City
Frontier City
BINH DUONG
BINH TUY
Vam Co Dong River
Vam Co Tay River
Cu Chi
Long Binh
Di An
Bien Hoa
HAU NGHIA
Saigon
BIEN HOA
PHUOC TUY
Tri Phap
KIEN TUONG
KIEN PHONG
DINH TUONG
LONG AN
GO CONG
Vung Tau
Long Tau River
CHAU DOC
AN GIANG
SA DEC
Soi Rap
Seven Mountains Region
KIEN GIANG
KIEN HOA
Can Tho
PHONG DINH
VINH LONG
VINH BINH
South China Sea
Gulf of Thailand
Phu Quoc Island
CHUONG THIEN
BA XUYEN
Mekong Delta
BAC LIEU
AN XUYEN
Ca Mau Peninsula

Saigon

Tan Son Nhut airfield
MACV/DAO Compound (and Annex)
JGS Compound
Bien Hoa Highway
Hai Ba Trung
Cong Ly
World Vision Headquarters
International Protestant Church
U.S. Embassy
Presidential Palace
Continental Palace Hotel
Hotel Caravelle
Hong Thap Tu
Le Loi Boulevard
Saigon River

Kilometers
0   2
Miles
0   2

Kilometers
0   100
Miles
0   100

○ Village
● Town
● City
▲ Military Base
➾ Ho Chi Minh Trail

4

Introduction

They came to Washington in boonie hats and bowling shirts, in jungle fatigues and three-piece suits. They came on chartered buses and commercial airlines, by foot and in wheelchairs, together and alone, 15,000 strong from every state in the nation. Ten years after the last American combat troops left Vietnam they came to dedicate a monument to those who had perished in America's longest war.

But the commemoration was not only for the dead. It was also for those who survived. "If I can touch the name of my friends who died, maybe I will finally have time to react," wrote a former Marine in the days before the dedication. "There just wasn't the emotional time in Nam to know what happened." From his VA hospital bed a wounded veteran declared: "All I ever asked for was a little thank you for the time I spent in my nation's service. Maybe this will be it."

Standing before the long black wall, their reflections falling like ghosts across the 58,000 names chiseled on the polished granite, many found a peace they feared had been lost forever. A former Special Forces trooper performed a quiet private ceremony above the apex of the memorial, giving away his most precious possessions to fellow Green Berets. Another veteran approached the wall and took out a bottle of whiskey and twelve shot glasses. Standing in front of a name he saluted, filled all the glasses, drank them rapidly, saluted again, and left. "When you touch a friend's name on the stone," explained one vet, "for a magical moment you are suspended halfway between

heaven and earth, with them again." Some stroked the names as if trying to pull life from them; others slammed their fists against the wall; many were in tears. "We waited fifteen years to get here, man," said one vet who had served in the 101st Airborne Division. "But it's not too late. I'm just proud to be here. We made it. It's like coming home."

Although the controversy surrounding it mirrored the bitter rhetoric of the war itself, the emotions released by the dedication of the Vietnam Veterans Memorial on November 13, 1982, inspired a process of healing and reconciliation. As if awakening from some collective amnesia Americans at last began to come to terms with the most divisive event in the nation's history since the Civil War, belatedly expressing appreciation for those who had served and the sacrifices they had made.

In the years that followed memorials to the war were erected all over the country, some of them with public funds, many by veterans themselves. By 1985 monuments honoring Vietnam veterans existed in twenty-nine states. In May of that year New York City dedicated a translucent glass wall inscribed with excerpts of letters written home from Vietnam, the celebration attracting 1 million people who thronged the parade route in enthusiastic approval of the 25,000 veterans who marched before them. Mayor Edward Koch spoke for many of the spectators when he acknowledged that the nation had failed "to recognize the contribution of our relatives, neighbors, and friends who sacrificed so much." Eager to put behind them the rancor and turmoil of those

years, Koch said, "many Americans wanted to forget about the war once it was over, but in the process they forgot about those who were sent to fight it."

Yet, the story of Vietnam is not only the story of those who fought. To remember Vietnam is also to remember those who cared for the wounded and ministered to the victims of war, those who helped shape U.S. policy and those who called that policy into question, those who went to help and those who watched them come.

In the pages that follow are the personal accounts of twenty-five people whose lives were shaped by the Vietnam experience. Hawk and dove, soldier and civilian, proponent and protester, American and Vietnamese, they speak in their own words of the things they saw in the way they saw them. Their perceptions differ according to time, place, circumstance, and personality. Their stories are "representative" only of the personal reality which finally illuminates the meaning of history.

This is not a book of war stories, but a book about people caught up in a difficult struggle and its troubled aftermath. It is not intended to stand for the totality of what took place in the long years of American involvement in Southeast Asia, but to preserve in some small measure the individual legacies of a crucial era in the nation's life. Their stories are reminders of what was endured by the men and women who took part, and what was sacrificed by all those who never returned. It is to them, who can no longer speak, that this book is dedicated.

War and Remembrance

"We erect monuments so that we shall always remember and build memorials so that we shall never forget," one observer commented after viewing the Vietnam Veterans Memorial in Washington, D.C. Among the testaments to America's Vietnam veterans, there are no arches, obelisks, or towers rising in triumphal splendor, but unadorned plaques, quiet parks, austere walls, and simple statues. Scattered across the country, they bear witness to those who died and honor those who served. But they serve as well a larger purpose, calling upon every American to reflect upon one of the most divisive eras in the nation's history. In so doing, suggested one VA psychologist, the memorials "open the experience to all Americans. All are carrying around some trauma from the war. In that sense, everybody in this country is a Vietnam War vet."

Visitors view the New York Vietnam Veterans Memorial at its dedication, May 6, 1985. The inscription at the top, taken from a serviceman's letter home, reads: "One thing worries me—will people believe me? Will they want to hear about it, or will they want to forget the whole thing ever happened?"

7

Many Vietnam memorials, such as these in New Orleans (above) and Wilmington, Delaware (below), depict the anguish and vulnerability of American soldiers.

Left. *In Nashville, Shriners take part in the parade preceding the dedication of the Tennessee Vietnam Veterans Park on November 10, 1985.*

Designed by a local veteran, the Somerville/Cambridge, Massachusetts, memorial stands in Union Square, Somerville.

Memorabilia (above) left by visitors to the Vietnam Veterans Peace and Brotherhood Chapel in Angel Fire, New Mexico (right). Victor Westphall created the chapel in memory of his son, who was killed in Vietnam.

Three veterans embrace at the Vietnam Veterans memorial in Washington, D.C. Every day, over 10,000 people file past the black granite walls that bear the names of the 58,022 Americans killed or missing in Vietnam.

Commitment

From the beginning it was a curious alliance—
a small, fledgling republic on the Southeast
Asian peninsula joined in common cause with
the world's most prosperous and powerful nation.
Yet from the American point of view, the pledge
to defend South Vietnam from Communist ag-
gression assumed global strategic significance.
Committed to a bipartisan policy of "containment," Presidents Eisenhower, Kennedy, and
Johnson successively reaffirmed the decision to
take a stand in Indochina, backing their words
with money, materiel, and men. Each expressed
confidence that the United States would accomplish its chosen mission, but as the fighting
dragged on and U.S. military involvement deep-
ened, victory remained elusive. By the end of
1967 there were nearly 400,000 U.S. troops in Vietnam, and more were on the way. The majority of
Americans still supported the war and believed
that in the long run U.S. military might would
prevail. But the easy optimism of the early years
had begun to wane as the perception dawned
that the Vietnam War was at best a stalemate.

*Lyndon Johnson and John Kennedy, from 1961 to 1968 the archi-
tects of American involvement in Vietnam.*

Bui Diem

*South Vietnamese Ambassador
to the United States
1967–1974*

Sunlight glinted from the canopies of the strange double-fuselaged aircraft that broke formation over Hanoi one day in 1944, the third year of World War II in Indochina. Bui Diem, a scholar who used his student status to conceal his activities as a Vietnamese Nationalist, saw the planes begin their dives and heard the twin engines scream as the Lockheed P-38s hurtled down toward the capital city. Diem leapt from the roadway into a nearby ditch to escape the .50-caliber bullets spraying the Japanese military traffic. The young man raised his head enough from the shallow refuge to see white stars on the airplanes. It was his first view of American forces.

In 1949, Emperor Bao Dai signed an agreement with the French recognizing Vietnam's independence and giving birth to the new State of Vietnam. Many non-Communists like Bui Diem chose to serve this government and left North Vietnam. Diem was cabinet secretary in the defense ministry in 1950 and 1953. He then served as secretary of state to Premier Phan Huy Quat in 1965 and later to Premier Nguyen Cao Ky in 1965–1966. He was appointed ambassador to Washington in 1967 and is now a resident scholar with the American Enterprise Institute in Washington, D.C.

I was a student at the university in Hanoi and, as you know in every emerging country, the students played an important part in advancing the ideas of revolution. All of us students joined one party or another due to the fact there was a general enthusiasm for any kind of political activity. But during the early days of the fight against the French and during the Japanese occupation, the focus was on the independence and not on the difference between parties. It was a large front, grouping all the nationalists fighting against the French. During this whole period of four years, all of us participated in clandestine activities.

I was approached by many Communist cadres involved in these clandestine organizations. I remember very well that many of their cadres came to me and gave me splendid magazines about the Soviet Union. They gave me *The Capital* by Karl Marx to read over. Vo Nguyen Giap, who later became the victor at Dien Bien Phu, was by then my professor of history and a colleague of my father, who was also a professor. He came to the house quite often and gave me material about communism, too. In the history course he taught, about the French revolution and the period after, Vo Nguyen Giap skipped over much of it, instructing us to read the book. Giap said instead, "I would like to give you my full course on the Napoleonic Wars." It was fascinating. We spent the whole year studying the maps he had on his desk and listening as he used his fingers to show the troop and logistics movements of the French, particularly in the retreat from Russia. Perhaps he didn't know yet that his future would be in the military, but he liked it already. It was no surprise to me to see him as commander in chief at Dien Bien Phu fighting against the French.

But somehow I was not attracted by communism at all. I resented the kind of uniformity of views among them and the kind of strict discipline they imposed on people. And they did not tolerate any discussion about what would be the best way to achieve independence. The Communists said, "That is the line of the party and you have to follow it." I resented it, you see. That is the first natural reaction on my part. I joined a Nationalist party, the Dai Viet, although at that time not many people realized that there was a difference between nationalism and communism. In terms of appearance there was a large front grouping all the nationalists fighting against the French. It was only when the Communists came to power in 1945, after their revolution of August 18 and after the proclamation of the Democratic Republic of Vietnam in September by Ho Chi Minh, that the Nationalist parties began to identify themselves as against communism. Only after the revolution did the split of those for and against communism become clear.

It was a very difficult position for the non-Communists because after achieving their goals in taking power, the Communists took for themselves the monopoly of the fight against the French. We were put in a very awkward position in spite of the fact that we fought against the French exactly the way they did. And the Nationalist parties suffered as much as the Communists in the common fight. But somehow the Communists got the upper hand. Many of the Nationalists, like myself, were compelled to be on their side in spite of the fact that we knew by then if the Communists succeeded we would be squeezed out.

I was assigned by my party to organize an external front. In that role I made many visits to China after 1945, bringing out non-Communists from North Vietnam and getting in touch with the Nationalist Government of China under Chiang Kaishek. The Communists knew me very well by then, that I did not like the idea of communism very much. But my father was a member of the large patriotic front in North Vietnam. So a kind of tolerance was assumed due to the fact my father was a high-ranking officer. But the Communists found out about my activities—going to China and back. I didn't dare appear publicly. I had to go to a remote area along the Laotian border to stay in small villages for nine months watching, watching and acting like a poor peasant. Gradually I made contact with my father and asked him if I could come back, so he talked to the Communists and paved the way for me. I agreed to get involved in some of the activities of the patriotic front by going around the country mobilizing the masses of the people.

Many of my friends did not survive. During 1945 we non-Communists went up to Lao Cai Province near the Chinese border, where the Dai Viet party began to organize using Japanese officers to train a cadre of Vietnamese military leaders. I was called back to Hanoi to go outside China but my classmates stayed. There was a long fight against the French troops and some of them were killed in the fighting, but many others were liquidated by the Communists. Later on, in Hanoi for instance, many were arrested and disappeared completely. It was a brutal policy aiming at exterminating the Nationalist parties.

I had discussions with some of the moderate people among the Communists and asked them how can they do this to their own people? They were somewhat self-righteous. Most of the time they said it was not the time to argue. It is the time to fight against the French. We will see to it that the problem would be solved later. In our situation, in the Communist zone, we had to follow them or get out. There were no more alternatives.

During this period I met the Americans for the first time. The Communists had organized a friendship association between Americans and Vietnamese and I went to one of their receptions. All of us in the reception room tried to get close to the Americans as if we would like to touch them. They were the liberators who beat the Germans, who beat the Japanese, and who opposed French colonial power. We had high hopes because during the war we heard that President Roosevelt was very much for the idea of a trusteeship for Vietnam. We approached and told them we welcomed the idea from the American administration of a trusteeship. It was a very good first impression that we had of the Americans. We hoped the Americans would come to our side and help us in our negotiations with the French, and we had high hopes because our perception was that the Americans were against colonialist regimes. And if our view was shared by the Americans, it

A team from the U.S. Office of Strategic Services trains Vietminh forces to fight the occupying Japanese in the jungles of northern Vietnam on August 17, 1945.

Grumman Avenger torpedo/bomber planes from the U.S.S. Essex approach the coast of French Indochina on January 12, 1945 en route to bomb Japanese-held airfields and shipyards around Saigon.

would be a tremendous help for us in our political struggle with the French.

I stayed with the Communists for many years after the war broke out with the French forces, up until the time when there was the beginning of the Bao Dai solution on the Nationalists' side. I remember very well, we discussed during long days in the Communist zone, those of us who were not Communists, that the Bao Dai government is not the ideal solution and Bao Dai is linked to the French, but it offers a chance for us to get out of this dilemma. On the one side, we want the independence of the country and on the other side we don't want to be squeezed out or exterminated by the Communists. Because Bao Dai came to power there in the southern part of Vietnam, there was the beginning of the State of Vietnam. We suffered a lot in terms of identity because we knew that we ran the risk of being characterized as the collaborators of the French. But we fought fiercely against the French, diplomatically and politically, to achieve the independence of Vietnam through negotiations. We were very aware of the fact that if we could not get independence from the French, we would be in a very difficult position.

We stated clearly that we wanted complete independence with only a symbolic association with France. But the American officials in the Saigon embassy

cautioned us against any radical solution of this sort. The United States wanted France to join in the European defense community. They wanted to keep the French on their side. That is the reason for the ambivalent attitude toward complete independence for Vietnam. We were cautioned by the Americans to go slowly. We were very much displeased.

To be very candid with you, we understood very little about Americans. Our views of the Americans were, most of the time, very idealistic. And by the time we learned that the Americans didn't go completely along with our idea, we were displeased and perhaps had the beginning of a doubt, you see. We were very ignorant about America in general. The thing that we knew about America was first the very moralistic and strong anti-Communist stance, the fight in Korea, and later the memorable inaugural address of John F. Kennedy, saying that we would bear all the burdens, help any friend, fight any foe for the liberty of the free world.

The American system—election day every four years, Republican and Democratic parties, politics and public opinion, the balance between the legislative branch and the executive branch—we knew practically nothing about it. And I think that it is one of the tragic things about the war in Vietnam, that two people who knew nothing about each other were thrown together by international circumstances in a conflict against a common enemy. And the kind of misunderstandings between a big nation and a small people developed into mistakes and errors. These mistakes and errors combined together, both from Americans and from Vietnamese, constitute a kind of mixed bag of responsibility that we have to share.

In spite of the fact that I opposed the policy of President Ngo Dinh Diem during the nine years of his regime, I have to recognize the fact that his success was the establishment of some sort of stability in South Vietnam. We understood by then that the Americans were already trying very hard to help Mr. Diem, and it was quite a success in the beginning. But later on, when Mr. Diem got into political trouble, we realized through our contacts with the Americans there was a lot of controversy about what policy should be pursued in Vietnam. On one side there was the problem of stability of the regime, and on the other side there was a problem of having as large as possible participation from all the elements in the country in the fight against communism. And so we realized by then that there was a kind of constant controversy and contradiction in American policy.

I'll say that in 1963, when the coup against Mr. Diem happened, the Vietnamese people didn't blame the U.S. for intervening. The problem was not really to intervene or not intervene, but the problem was rather how to do it. If you intervene the right way, people will praise it, but if you intervene the wrong way, people will put the blame on you. It was only later, with hindsight, that people realized that the coup against Mr. Diem provoked a period of instability, of upheavals, of coups in South Vietnam, which was the main reason the Americans felt compelled to intervene directly in the war in 1965.

I understood through my own contacts with the generals who prepared the coup that relations were maintained with the American side. I think that here we can say that it is the first sign of what we can call an American mistake. The Americans helped a group of generals to overthrow Mr. Diem, but they did not know exactly what the generals had in mind. The Vietnamese generals said that they started a revolution against Mr. Diem, but in fact it was not true at all. They started a coup. They had no idea at all about what they would do later. And that was the main cause of the trouble during the years of '64 and '65. They were military men without vision, without conceptions of how to reform the society.

It was a complete failure from the American side, a complete disappoint-

Vo Nguyen Giap (right), commander of the Vietminh army, with Ho Chi Minh at Dien Bien Phu, site of the Vietminh's historic victory over the French in May 1954.

ment. From one government to another, the Americans dealt with the government in power, trying to salvage it, trying to boost it up. Unfortunately, America didn't succeed in the enterprise and the problem became more and more difficult to deal with later on because as the government in Saigon reshuffled, the situation in the countryside deteriorated. When in early '65 there was an offensive from the Communists to try and cut the country into two parts from the highlands down to the sea, the Americans got alarmed and saw but one alternative, to take over the war.

On March 18, 1965, early in the morning, Quat called me and said, "Diem, you have to come to my office. There are urgent matters." I came to his residence and I found there an official from the American embassy. Quat said to me, "You have to sit down and write a communiqué about the landing of the Ma-

rines in Da Nang." I was surprised and took Quat aside and said to him, "Is the military situation that bad that we need the Marine battalions right now?" Quat said, "Go ahead and draft the communiqué, and I'll talk to you later after the session about it." After we finished the drafting and the American official left, I talked alone with Quat. He said to me, "Ambassador Taylor talked to me a few days ago about this problem but he was himself taken by surprise by the very heavy pressure from Washington, and he reassures me that it is a very limited move with the strict purpose of protecting the Hawk missiles in Da Nang. But the decision from Washington came so fast that we didn't have any time to react to it. By the time you finished the communiqués, the Marines were already on the beach."

That is the very strange story of the process by which the two governments

The Vietnamese government established by the Franco-Vietnamese treaty is installed in Saigon on December 30, 1949. Emperor Bao Dai is standing behind the desk (left center).

got together for what we called at that time "concurrency." Literally, we cannot say that there was no consultation between the two governments, but in fact the decision most of the time was from Washington and was put before the authorities in Saigon, whether Vietnamese or American, as a *fait accompli*. The decision was taken to land the Marines and the Marines are there. Most of the time it was that way.

The Americans felt in all honesty, I think, that they could finish the task in a short period of time and hand back the country to the Vietnamese. The government in power didn't have enough vision to say candidly to the Americans, "Look, you come to help us, that is all right. But we have to sit down together and work out a process through which you can help us effectively." But instead the Vietnamese left it to the Americans to do the things they wanted and it was like a bulldozer rolling. With the impatience quite natural from the Americans when they saw things go slowly, they have the tendency to take over and say, let me do it. And so that is exactly the way it happened. Gradually the war became completely Americanized.

We on the Vietnamese side had a lot of doubts about the landing of U.S. ground troops in Vietnam. Dr. Quat was prime minister and I had come to help him, and I remember we had a lot of discussions about the problem of the presence of the American troops. We were aware of the negative aspects. It could be a handicap in our fight against the Communists because they fought against every foreign domination, and if we asked American troops to come in we felt that it would diminish the legitimacy of our cause.

It is difficult to say what I would do differently because I was but a man in the machinery on the Vietnamese side and my voice was not a determining voice. But in hindsight I would say that I regret that I did not point out in a more forceful way the Vietnamese point of view to the Americans. I feel that Vietnamese in general have to accept this responsibility for failing to convey their points of view, for instance, the strategy against North Vietnam, for instance, the number of American troops in Vietnam, for instance, what was the best way for the Americans to help us?

I have no doubts the Americans would

have listened to the good arguments of the Vietnamese. But the Vietnamese were much too passive. They let the Americans run the war. Unfortunately the United States didn't succeed in doing what they tried to do within the period of time during which they still had the tolerance of the American people. The Americans did not understand that for the North Vietnamese Communists, it cost practically nothing for them to go further in the war. The policy for them is to try to survive and to wear out the Americans.

It is too presumptuous on my part to talk in terms of lessons for the Americans. But as a Vietnamese, I would say that I hope next time the U.S. has to confront an international problem like the one you had in Vietnam in the sixties, please do consider more carefully the pros and cons before getting in. Please do try your best to achieve a consensus among U.S. public opinion before getting into a venture like Vietnam. If you have taken a decision to do something abroad, please stick to it because people in the world believe in the words of the U.S. At worst, for the Americans the Vietnam tragedy is a bad chapter in U.S. history and you can turn the page. While many of us hope for and expect the eventual freedom of our country, for millions of South Vietnamese there are no more pages to be turned. ∎

In March 1964, in a display of continuing U.S. support for South Vietnam, Secretary of Defense Robert McNamara and Army Chief of Staff Maxwell Taylor join hands with the GVN's premier, General Nguyen Khanh, at a rally in Hoa Hao. Three months before, Khanh had assumed power in a bloodless coup.

Anthony Lake

Foreign Service Officer
1963–1970
Special Assistant to Henry Kissinger
1969–1970

Born in New York City in 1939, Anthony Lake joined the foreign service in 1962, a year after his graduation from Harvard. Between 1963 and 1965 he served in Saigon in the consular section and then as staff assistant to Ambassador Henry Cabot Lodge before assignment to Hue as American vice consul. After his return to the State Department he continued to devote his attention to Indochina, first on the Vietnam desk and the Far Eastern Bureau, and finally as an assistant to the undersecretary of state. In 1969 Lake joined the staff of the National Security Council only to resign a year later at the time of the Cambodian invasion. In 1977 he returned to the State Department where he served for three years as director of policy planning. Today Lake is a professor of international relations at Mount Holyoke College in western Massachusetts, where he also operates his own farm.

In November 1960 I was one of thousands of people who jammed the streets of Boston in an election eve rally for John Kennedy. Huge, huge crowds, lining the streets, engulfing the cars carrying the Kennedys. The people were so enthusiastic that at one point I was shoved almost into the back seat of his car. I'll never forget it. Kennedy exuded power and confidence. There was no hesitation in him as he rode through this hysterical scene, completely in control of a moment that was packed with enormous emotion. For a young college student, a member of the Young Democrats at Harvard, it was very powerful stuff. As the car drew away I desperately wanted to follow it. And I guess, metaphorically, that's kind of what I did.

During the following year, while I was studying at Cambridge University in England, I decided that I wanted to join the foreign service instead of going back to graduate school. And I wanted to go to Asia. I wanted to serve in Vietnam and promote democracy and do all the things that the Kennedy administration was trying to accomplish. Like so many Americans then, I believed my country could do anything. That was what Kennedy had captured, this feeling that if you just try hard enough, anything is possible.

So I joined the foreign service and took the basic foreign service officers' course that trained us to be diplomats. But we were also trained in counterinsurgency.

This was just after the book *The Ugly American* came out. People forget that the "Ugly American" was the hero of that book. He wasn't the tourist with the camera yelling in a loud voice in English so the ignorant natives will somehow understand what he wants. He wasn't one of the diplomats isolated in the capital city. The "Ugly American" was a man who went out in the countryside, spoke the local language, and got mud on his shoes helping the people. That's what we wanted to do, to go out to developing nations threatened with Communist subversion and be modern diplomats and get mud on our shoes and work in this new thing called counterinsurgency.

Some of what we were learning might have told us something if we'd stopped to think. Most of the theory of counterinsurgency as it was taught at that time came from the French who had, after all, lost in Vietnam. Then toward the end of the course we had a training exercise on how we could organize a counterinsurgency effort in a mythological country in Southeast Asia. It was called "Modernization at the Mekong." We all played roles—some people played the guerrillas, some people played the USIA or the Peace Corps or the military, and so forth. It didn't occur to me until many years later that there was no role for the local government and the local people, which says something about the way we were approaching it all. But it was an omission none of us seemed to be aware of.

So when I went off to Saigon in the spring of 1963 I was confident we would prevail, though even in the early sixties Vietnam could be a dangerous place. Almost every other night you'd hear a whump somewhere, and you'd know it was a bomb going off. The VC killed a number of Americans in terrorist incidents during those years. We all had big walls around our houses. There was fighting near our home during the coup against Ngo Dinh Diem in November 1963. And during '64 it was coup after coup, military against civilians, just political chaos. At one point there was real anarchy in Saigon for a few days—no government, no police. The city was turned over to mobs of young Buddhists and young Catholics who were killing each other with sticks.

It was often scary, although nothing like as tough or dangerous as it would be for our combat troops. But it was also exhilarating. There was the excitement of participating, if even in a small way, in the ferment of great events or riding in a military jeep at fifty miles an hour through an ambush area. In Hue my job was not only to cover the troubles with the Buddhists, who were staging increasingly violent demonstrations, but also something called provincial reporting. I'd travel around in the countryside and stay with American military advisers in the field or drop into villages and talk to the people to try and figure out how the war was going and report it back to Saigon. Six months later the area I was driving around outside Da Nang would be the scene of heavy fighting between the U.S. Marines and the Vietcong.

But even before the American troops arrived, the incredibly naive optimism of my first months in Vietnam began to turn to skepticism. I remember vividly one afternoon in early 1964 while I was working for Ambassador Lodge. We got a report of a battle down in the delta where a Vietcong battalion had ambushed a South Vietnamese unit. After carrying out the ambush they had slipped away into the jungle. But air strikes had been called in, according to the report, and there had been tremendous casualties inflicted on the enemy. After I passed the report on to the ambassador, Neil Sheehan, then a UPI reporter, came into the office to see Lodge on a previous appointment. Sheehan had been at the ambush site and told me what had really happened. The Vietcong had gotten into the woods, the bombing raid had been carried out, but nobody had gone into the woods afterwards. They had no clue as to how many casualties they'd actually inflicted. I was told later that they'd determined the casualties by figuring how many enemy soldiers would be killed per ton of bombs dropped, figured how many tons they dropped, and thereby calculated how many enemy they'd gotten. Meanwhile, Sheehan said, the ARVN unit had been really chewed up.

It made me wonder what was going on, but it wasn't until I was traveling in the countryside in late '64 and early '65 that I began to think that the formula wasn't working. There was too much "negative progress" showing up on American advisers' progress classification maps. As the months went by it was becoming clearer and clearer that the South Vietnamese army was getting the hell kicked out of it. There were some very good soldiers, but for the most part they didn't seem well led.

By the time I came back to Washington in June 1965, my skepticism was turning to real doubt. I hadn't brought myself to a belief that it was inevitable that we would lose, but I was beginning to suspect that maybe we couldn't win. Psychologically I think that was the case for a lot of people. It's very hard to tell yourself that what you're doing can't work. So you go through a kind of self-hypnosis to persuade yourself that it all makes sense somehow, even when you know it doesn't.

Yet the flaws of American policy in Vietnam were there for anybody to see. We had failed at the beginning in not looking at Vietnam itself, in not asking ourselves what is this country that we're getting involved in? If you look at the *Pentagon Papers* you'll see that in the late forties and early fifties the experts at the State Department were saying, "Watch out. The French are losing Indochina, the Vietnamese are a very nationalistic people. If we get involved in this we're going to be getting into a terrible problem." But most officials didn't pay any attention because we were in the grip of a doctrine, the doctrine of containment.

Wherever Communists or radicals or people who were anti-American threatened to come to power, then automatically the United States would react. Automatically. Because of the Munich analogy. Because of the idea that if you let them get away with it anywhere, then they'll be encouraged to try it elsewhere. And because of the China analogy. In 1949 Harry Truman "lost" China. China wasn't ours to lose, of course, but we had spent a lot of money in behalf of Chiang Kai-shek, who then proceeded to lose to the Communists because his regime was corrupt and he was inefficient and he was losing legitimacy.

Chiang's performance should have told us something about Vietnam later, but at the time the popular perception was that Harry Truman had "lost" China and all hell broke loose in Washington. This was really the beginning of McCarthyism. It was the beginning of the argument that we shouldn't just be containing the Soviet Union, we should be "rolling back" the Iron Curtain. So the political atmosphere in Washington was one of, to put it mildly, prejudice against being soft on communism. Within a year the decision was made to send major amounts of aid to the French and get ourselves involved in Indochina. The problem wasn't trying to contain communism. It was doing so rigidly and blindly.

Because for the Vietnamese, neither the French nor later the American war had a great deal to do with ideology. They had a great deal to do with nationalism. The appeal of the National Liberation Front was first, and overwhelmingly, nationalistic. That's what they would hammer on, that's what they would put on the signs you would find left on buildings—that the Saigon government was a puppet of the Americans. And the Communists were very good at appealing to traditional Vietnamese sentiments. The irony is that we thought of the NLF as radicals, as Commies, which most of them were. But in Vietnamese terms, we were the radicals. Democracy was a much newer concept to the Vietnamese than the idea of collective organization or highly disciplined political structures.

Now the peasants, the villagers working in the fields, probably would not have passed an exam on Marxist theory vs. democratic theory, but they certainly knew something about Vietnamese history. They knew who the Vietnamese heroes were, and they knew they didn't like foreigners. It is extremely important to understand that there were a lot of southerners who joined the NLF, who fought fanatically, undergoing incredible danger and hardship not because they were Communists, but because they believed they were fighting for an independent, unified Vietnam.

This was a war, as the cliché had it, for the hearts and minds of the people. But if you talked to almost any American about it you'd find out that what they were really talking about was winning the hearts and minds of the Vietnamese people for the Americans, not for the South Vietnamese government. And that was a basic trap. Because the more we became involved, the more we did for the government in Saigon, the more the people in the countryside saw government officials working side by side with Americans, the more they saw government soldiers dependent on American helicopters and artillery for their support, the more they saw a series of political events in Saigon that seemed to be manipulated by the Americans, then the more they saw the government as being the agent of the Americans and therefore illegitimate in Vietnamese terms.

At the same time, the more the war became politically important within the United States, the more we could not lose. And the more we could not lose in our own political terms, the more the South Vietnamese government knew that we didn't dare get out. So they didn't have to listen to us when we would go to them and say, "Look, you have to reform. You have to start promoting the young colonels who really know how to fight the war. You have to clean up the corruption. You have to do all these things." They could simply turn around and say, "Well, if we don't what are you going to do to us? The only thing you can do is cut off the aid, and you can't cut off the aid because the war's become as important to you as to us." We lost our leverage, and the less leverage we had the less we could get them to pursue the war in the only ways that might be effective. It was a giant political trap.

Meanwhile, we convinced a lot of good people in South Vietnam to raise their flag to our mast. In late '64 I had a friend who was in the Vietnam Information Service. He was an extraordinarily brave and effective worker who would travel on his Lambretta with a little tape recorder and some loudspeakers,

spreading the gospel in the villages. Some of the places he went were really dangerous, he ran huge risks. And I remember one night admiringly asking him why. What was motivating him? First he said he hated the Communists because they had killed his brother. And then he said, "Because we're going to win." So I asked him, "How do you know you're going to win?" And he said, "Because if we, the South Vietnamese government, lose, the Americans will come and they will start at Ca Mau, and they will drive the Communists back up across the seventeenth parallel and out of South Vietnam." The man was betting his life on our power, on his certainty that we could win the war.

But we could *not* win the war. And the reason we could not win the war was not because American soldiers fought badly. They fought well and deserve much more credit for this than they have been given. And it was not because of a failure of military tactics, although perhaps we could have pursued better tactics. Studies at the time showed that even more bombing would not bring victory, and that the enemy could replace all the casualties we inflicted. And it wasn't because of a loss of political will in the United States. If you said in 1960 that this is going to go on fifteen years, more than 55,000 Americans are going to die, $150 billion are going to be spent, you are going to tear American society apart, anybody would have said that's a helluva lot. Yet that was the price we paid. The reason we could not win was because it was not just a war of territory or interdiction or attrition, it was a political war. Those who ruled South Vietnam never had the political strength among their own people to succeed, and our presence only made the political situation worse. We could not win the war for them, which is a bitter thing to say for anyone who was there, and it was a bitter thing for me to realize.

During '66 and '67 I was working in the Far Eastern Bureau and then for the undersecretary of state. By that time there were plenty of people in the government who were skeptical about the war. But for a variety of reasons most of us could not bring ourselves to say it was hopeless. If you did admit it, and you said it, then you condemned yourself to not being listened to because that was a rejection of the basic assumption.

For dedicated young foreign service officers, the early years of U.S. involvement were filled with optimism. At a school outside Hue, Lake befriends some Vietnamese children.

If you wanted to have any impact in Washington in the late sixties, you didn't say this is basically a loser. You argued for better tactics in the field, you argued for a better negotiating position. You continued to maintain that we could win it if we did it right. And that was what everybody in Vietnam kept telling you. That the war was going pretty well. That there were problems, but they were all technical problems. That if you only got more barbed wire to the delta, if you only got precise bombing runs, if you only managed the pacification program better, if you only could put all the pieces together. ... There were seldom conversations in Washington about who were these Vietnamese? What are their political loyalties? Why are so many either sitting on the fence or going over to the National Liberation Front? You just didn't talk about the more basic questions.

And as the public grew more and more disenchanted, a lot of the work on Vietnam within the State Department became public relations, drafting speeches and testimonials that would help Dean Rusk and Lyndon Johnson convince the American public that the war was right. If you're a bureaucrat and you're writing those speeches and press conference statements and trying to justify the war externally, there's a tremendous impulse to justify it to yourself internally, to persuade yourself that what you're writing is true. Because if you don't, you're saying to yourself, "I'm writing lies." And it's not because bureaucrats are cynics that they do this. It's precisely because they don't want to believe that they're writing lies every day that they persuade themselves and deceive themselves so they can feel good about themselves as they write this stuff.

I refused ever to give a speech myself on Vietnam because by then I really did have very strong doubts about it. I would help draft the testimony and the speeches, but I wouldn't give them. It's a fine line, maybe too fine. But I'd gotten to hate the problem so much. I felt so trapped between all these conflicting feelings—believing that we couldn't win but certainly not wanting to lose—the way most Americans felt. It became a terrible kind of balancing act: arguing within the government against our policies during the day and then in the evening arguing bitterly with my friends in defense of those policies, never quite saying that they were

wrong to be against the war but always pointing out why their reasons were wrong.

I finally got so sick of it I asked to take an academic leave. Between 1967 and 1969 I studied at Princeton and did more reading on Vietnamese history and society than I'd ever had time for while I was actually working on it, which convinced me all the more that we had made a mistake. It was at Princeton, where the discussion tended to be not so much tactical but much more about the basics of the war, that I became convinced not only that we were prosecuting it in the wrong

Top. *"After being Ambassador Lodge's assistant for several months I asked to go outside Saigon somewhere. I was assigned to Hue as a vice counsul. It was a two-person post and we were both very young."*

Above. *Caught up in the Buddhist demonstrations that rocked Vietnam during 1965, Lake soon found himself attempting to keep protesters from burning down the USIS library, shown here after the attack.*

way, that it was hopeless the way we were going about it, but that it was just hopeless period.

Then, when it was time for a new assignment, I got a call from Henry Kissinger. Kissinger had been a consultant to the State Department on the peace negotiations in '66 or '67, and we'd gotten to know each other a little. Now he was Nixon's national security adviser, and when his special assistant, Larry Eagleburger, became ill, they offered me the job. My initial reaction was "no." I knew it would involve a lot of work on Vietnam, and I didn't share the new administration's attitude toward the war.

So I went down to Washington to tell Kissinger I didn't think I was the right person for the job, but he convinced me I should take it. I told him what I thought about Vietnam, that we should get what we could and get out, and that I wanted at least a chance to argue with him on these things. He said, "Fine, argue." And he was very good about it. He encouraged me to argue, and we did argue for the year I was there. Very openly, in a way I never had before. I think he found it useful to have somebody like me around not only because he knew he would still win all the arguments—which he did, even when he was wrong he won the arguments—but because I would kind of reflect for him what the liberal establishment was arguing on the outside, something he wanted to keep track of.

I thought we missed an opportunity, that first year of the Nixon administration. I think if we had made proposals to Hanoi along the lines that Clark Clifford and others were suggesting at the time, which were very close to what was actually negotiated four years later, we could have struck a deal.

Nixon, however, was as firmly wedded as Johnson had been to the proposition that we could not lose in Vietnam. He felt that the United States had been right to have become involved in the first place and that we had to end it on what he called honorable terms. Kissinger was much more skeptical about whether we should have gone in, but he believed that once we had gotten involved we could not get out on terms that would damage American prestige and credibility. I don't think either Nixon or Kissinger thought the war was winnable militarily, but they thought that through military power and

through threats they could gain enough concessions from the North Vietnamese so that it wouldn't be a loss, that some sort of compromise could be arrived at that would make it peace with honor. And of course they later tried to argue that that's what they got.

By that time, though, I had long since departed. A week before the Cambodian invasion in late April 1970, Kissinger called a few of us into his office. He said he wanted to meet with his "bleeding hearts." He told us that they were planning an incursion by South Vietnamese forces with some American forward air controllers and what did we think about it? So we argued with him some from a tactical point of view that it wouldn't work. And a couple of us tried to argue from a political point of view that the South Vietnamese army was going to run into trouble on its own and that if you send in American forward air controllers you're going to have to go in and rescue them. And that meant American troops going into Cambodia and all hell would break loose.

Kissinger listened to our arguments obviously unconvinced, and at the end as we walked out he said, "Well, Tony, I knew what you were going to say." And I remember thinking to myself, "If you knew what I was going to say then there isn't much point in my saying it anymore." I had lost my effectiveness. I had become so predictable that I didn't have to be there. And since I didn't have to be there I could do what I felt I couldn't do before, which was to leave, something I had already begun to talk about with my friends.

Everything just kind of came together. It seemed to me that Cambodia was another step down a road from which there was no turning back. I felt that the Nixon administration, which had once had some flexibility, had now trapped itself in the same pattern that Lyndon Johnson had. If I stayed, I was going to have to work on speeches attacking the critics of the administration—people I actually agreed with—and I just couldn't.

Some people seemed to think that resigning was very difficult because I was giving up my career or that I was some sort of hero for having resigned on principle. In fact, the resignation was easy. It was easy to leave a job that I had come to hate, working on policies that made no

sense to me. What was difficult was the guilt I felt. Because I believe in the effectiveness trap: that if you can work within the government on policies that you care about, then even if you hate it you ought to be there rather than on the outside.

I don't believe that everybody should resign whenever they disagree on an issue because then the people who you want to have there, raising other sides of the question, will all have left. What happens, is a lot of people convince themselves that the nation is so dependent on their own presence in the government that they can *never* resign, or they are simply unwilling to risk their next promotions. But then they don't fight from within, either, for the sake of their "effectiveness" on other issues. And that's how it becomes a trap. What little pride I have in all of this, and it's not a lot, is not in my resignation. It's in having argued with Kissinger flat out during the year I was there.

I think that the critics of American policy in Vietnam tended to overstate American power for evil and to blame too much on the United States, just as the supporters of the war gave us too much credit for being able to win it. And we still have trouble thinking in mature ways about our foreign policy. I've seen communism, and it is the opposite of everything that you would wish on a society. What I object to is the *doctrine* of containment, of contesting communism in an automatic way so that we tend to do the same thing in every country and it doesn't matter what that country is because we know what we have to do. We know all the answers before we ask the questions. We competed with communism in Vietnam in the same way that we would in Europe or Central America or any other place. But the world is much more complicated than that.

Instead of making foreign policy out of doctrines or analogies or because of domestic political pressures in the United States, we ought to be making foreign policy based on cases. We should be looking at the countries we are dealing with and asking some important questions. What are our interests in this country? What are our economic ties? How can we most effectively compete with the Communists there? If we're talking about military intervention, how many forces are we talking about? What are the costs in human lives among the civilians, among our own military? What do our allies think? What does international law say about all this? Do we have a right to be intervening there? Have we been asked in by a sovereign government that can pull its own weight? And most importantly, if we're not quite sure that we can win, is our exit clear? In England, I'm told, there used to be a little box painted on the road at intersections that said, "No Entry Unless Exit Clear." I think that box ought to be put up as a poster in government offices so we never forget to determine how we're going to get out before we get in. In short, ask questions. Don't assume the answers in advance.

And we need to learn to live with the fact that we are the greatest nation on earth, but we're not as powerful as we thought we were. I think that's a lesson of Vietnam we're missing. We're still not really sitting down as a nation and thinking through what are those things we can do and what are those things we can't do. What are those areas of the world where we can pursue one type of strategy, and what are those areas of the world where we should pursue another? If we don't use force where it will work and avoid it where it won't, people will react by believing—as some did after Vietnam—that you can and should never use power at all, even when it is justified. We still haven't politically been able to say, okay, in the short run this situation is a loser. Let's just face that fact and see if we can't find a long-term strategy to still achieve our goal.

We could have done that in Vietnam. You can think back to the independence celebration in Hanoi in 1945 when Ho Chi Minh read the Vietnamese Declaration of Independence, which was almost a direct translation from our own. Just as he finished, an airplane flew over and the crowd grew very quiet. They were probably scared because they thought it might be a French plane or a Chinese Nationalist plane or some other hostile aircraft. Then they saw that it had American markings, and when they saw the American markings they cheered. Tens of thousands of Vietnamese. They cheered. And it breaks your heart. Because you think of the political opportunity that those cheers suggest that we missed, the people who died as a result.

I'm not saying that we could have turned Ho Chi Minh into Thomas Jefferson

At an anti-American demonstration in Hue, protesters carry a sign reading, "Down with [U.S. Ambassador Maxwell] Taylor."

and that if we had only been nice to the Communists in Vietnam that they would have all become democrats. What I am suggesting is that the Vietnamese were above all nationalists who at that time perceived the United States as a champion of anticolonialism. What I'm saying is that we could have put pressure on the French not to go back in and try to seize their colony.

Vietnam would not have become Great Britain or France or West Germany, but Vietnam could have become Yugoslavia. Vietnam would still have become a Communist state but one that was neither pro-Chinese or pro-Soviet and not threatening to American foreign policy interests. Perhaps not great for the Vietnamese, but better than what actually happened. And perhaps in time, because the Vietnamese are very practical people and you can see it happening now in Vietnam, there would have been pressures for reform and some liberalization away from strict communism.

But we missed that opportunity. We missed it because of a doctrinal anticommunism, a stupid, automatic response to a complex world. We missed it because of a belief that we could do everything, that there were no limits to our power. And we missed it by not doing what we ourselves believe in, which is giving people the right to choose their own futures. We made a terrible mistake in Vietnam. It didn't have to happen the way it did. ∎

In the wake of Communist attacks against American military installations in early 1965, Lake's wife Antonia and one-year-old son Timothy await evacuation to the United States.

William R. Melton

---

*Squad Leader, Company D
1st Battalion, 9th Marines
1965
Platoon Commander, Company F
2d Battalion, 5th Marines
1968–1969*

Bill Melton was born on September 9, 1937, and grew up in the small farming community of Wheatland in northern California. At the age of eighteen, following graduation from high school, he enlisted in the Marine Corps.

After ten years of duty in California, Okinawa, and Japan, Melton was among the first American combat troops to arrive in Vietnam in 1965. Wounded in action four months after his arrival, he was sent back to the United States to take up duties training new recruits. In 1967, Melton received a combat commission as a second lieutenant. Within a year he was back in Vietnam as a platoon commander. During his two tours of duty he was awarded the Silver Star, Bronze Star, and Purple Heart decorations. In 1975, Melton returned to Vietnam for a final time, taking part in the evacuation of Saigon. Today Major Melton is executive officer of the Weapons Training Battalion at Quantico Marine Base in Virginia.

I've never been a civilian. I came right out of high school and joined the Marine Corps and I've been here for thirty years. It seems kind of unbelievable, but here I am.

I guess what really caused me to think seriously about joining the Corps was World War II. All my uncles and cousins who joined the service were in the army, the army air corps or the navy. And they all agreed they didn't like the godamned Marines. "They think they won the war by themselves, they're always seeking glory, I can't stand any of them!" Well, that sounded pretty good to me. And the more I thought about it, the more I read about it and heard about it, the better it sounded. Because I understood that the Marines were good fighters, took great pride in bringing out their equipment and their dead, left nobody on the battlefield. So I thought that's a pretty good outfit to be in.

By 1965 I'd been in the Corps for ten years. I'd trained a lot but I'd never been to war. The military must teach the psychology of killing, and after awhile you're combat ready and you want to test it. I was scared to death that I'd be like the boxer that trained and never got in the ring. Company D was filled with Marines who had from three to over twenty years in the Corps. The staff NCOs were Korean War veterans; one had even fought in World War II. So when we got orders to go to Vietnam we were all pretty much relieved. The company was ready, the battalion was ready. We were really in a high state of motivation and enthusiastic about what lay ahead.

We did some counterguerrilla warfare training on Okinawa and then in June we left for Da Nang. On the ship over there was a lot of talking. There was also a lot of nontalking, sitting around and looking into the never-never and wondering about it. We talked about hunting the guerrilla. Most everyone in the company, myself included, had hunted deer and different game. Now we talked about hunting men. Some of us worried it'd be all over by the time we got there, but we found out later that you got just about all you could handle.

Once we arrived in country we operated in the area south of Da Nang and later around Marble Mountain to the northeast. It was pretty much water everywhere. There'd be a rice paddy and then some jungle tree islands where the villages were, and then more rice paddies. Off to the west were the mountains, Indian country for sure.

The villages were very primitive. The houses had dirt floors and thatched roofs, and some had little holes dug out near the entrances where the people could get in for protection in case of firefights or bombing. In the center of the floor was a black pot that'd probably been cooking rice for centuries. The people worked the ground with water buffaloes and wooden plows or supplemented what they could get from their farms by fishing. They probably ate two meals a day, and you'd see them sitting and smoking what looked to me to be cigars, the women chewing betel nuts. For the villagers it was a very small universe. Life was rather simple, not much more than being born, living, and dying.

For us it was a little more complicated. The war in 1965 was a squad leader's war. The platoon commanders, the platoon sergeants, and those in higher billets usually stayed back while the squad went out to fight the Vietcong guerrilla. You might have a day patrol and then you might have one in the wee hours of the next morning, generally maybe two or three patrols in twenty-four hours. You'd get an area that you're going to, lay out a route—three or four "legs" each along a certain compass heading that would eventually bring you back to your perimeter—check your gear, and get going.

Our job was to see if we could locate the enemy, find where they might be massing to make an attack, and determine whether it was a company or a battalion or whatever strength. Except that didn't seem to be what was going on. We never met large bodies of the enemy. The most we ever ran into at one time was maybe four or five guerrillas. The first couple of months it was very difficult because we'd have contact, but we never really got to see the guy we were fighting. Or you would see them, you'd see the enemy fall, but afterwards there'd be no indication of any wounded or dead. You might see drag marks or even blood trails, but there'd be nothing there, not even an expended cartridge. I mean, you saw them go down with your own eyes and then there was nobody there. More often than not you wouldn't really see them at all. There'd be sniper fire from a distance, one of our guys would get shot in the arm or some other minor wound, you'd return fire, and they'd disappear.

We spent as much time looking for Vietcong suspects as we did fighting the guerrillas. I remember one time we came up to this village on a night patrol and there's this fellow standing in the village square giving a speech. We crept up and watched and I heard him saying, "American," so I asked the ARVN interpreter who came along with us what he thought and he tells me this guy's a Communist, he's speaking out against so-called American democracy. Now I had not been instructed on intervening in any political activity, but I had done some reading on guerrilla warfare on my own—Che Guevara, Mao Tse-tung. They taught that the people are the ocean and the revolutionaries are the fish. The fish have got to get along with the ocean if they're going to swim in it, so they've got to take care of the people, dress like the people, and talk their language to win them over, and that's what it looked like to me. So we went in and grabbed him—the guy put up one helluva fight and all the time the villagers never did a thing—broke off the patrol, and brought him back to camp. And I recall a staff sergeant who got all upset. "You mean you brought this old man back? He must be fifty years old." But we found out later that this guy was pretty important in the Vietcong political structure. He may not have been a warrior, but we made a good catch.

Basically we didn't have much problem dealing with the villagers. In the daytime we'd try to be friendly to them. But anybody out and about after eight at night, they were open game because they were not supposed to be there. If they were in their house they were safe, if they were out there you had to worry about them.

We had a sad occasion I'll never forget. I had sent one of my fire teams out at night to set up an ambush, and they heard a pair of Vietnamese talking and they fired. Turned out they shot a poor old man who'd come out of his house with his wife looking for a water buffalo that had wandered off. Really was a sad case. They were not supposed to be out but there they were, looking for a water buffalo.

Sometimes we would take interpreters and give the villagers a spiel on what we were there for and who the bad people were. Or we had what were called "County Fairs" where we tried to show the people our way of life, try to tell them we're on their side. We'd gather them into the center of the village and give them talks, and sometimes I'd take a corpsman out and he would treat people who were sick or hurt. But it just didn't seem to be getting us anywhere. I thought it was bothersome to the people and I imagine it turned them off. They had more important things to do; there was rice to plant and fish to clean. They just seemed to be more

Below. *Private First Class Bill Melton (center) and two fellow Marines take a break from maneuvers in Japan in 1956.*

Bottom. *After three days of training exercises, nineteen-year-old Melton discovers the luxury of a helmet bath.*

29

Top. *Homemade death. Vietcong booby traps, which often employed crude grenades like the ones shown here, accounted for between 20 and 40 percent of Marine KIAs during 1968 and 1969.*

Above. *June, 1965. Sergeant Melton stands guard over the wife and child of a Vietcong suspect about to be led away for interrogation. Her husband was later executed by South Vietnamese Rangers.*

interested in going about their daily lives than listening to us.

I think it was a good idea to try to pacify the people and win them over to our side, but it's not something a Marine is trained to do. I think it got in the way of our primary mission. I don't think you can do a little of each, a little fighting and a little pacification. You just can't do that. You can't be an ambassador and carry a rifle too.

Take what happened at Cam Ne. At the beginning of August we got word that Company D was going to a known Vietcong village called Cam Ne (4). It was the

same area where another company had been a little earlier and run into some real trouble. To get to the village we came up along a river on amtracs and debarked a short distance away. Just as we formed for attack the enemy took us under fire, wounding four men from another platoon. So we went in there and destroyed the village. Those were our orders. In fact, I had asked our platoon commander before we set off, and he said if they fire on us we can destroy the village. The unfortunate part of it was that one of the men in our platoon used a Zippo lighter to set fire to one of the houses, and that got on television because we had Morley Safer of CBS News with us. Boy, he did us a job.

Afterwards the commanding general of the Fleet Marine Forces in the Pacific ordered an investigation. They were trying to find out who was the guy with the Zippo lighter, and I was told we had to pay back the villagers for the rice that was destroyed by the amtracs. I found it very curious. I thought, "Now what is this all about? Just what did we do wrong?" Anyway, whoever the guy was with the lighter, he kept his mouth shut and a few days later we were back out in the field.

From that point on we had a lot more contact. We were getting into their area. We were pushing out from the Da Nang air base and starting to cause them some problems. I thought they were very good, the Vietcong. They were familiar with the area, they could get around and pop up in places you didn't expect them to be. But I also realized they weren't perfect. One time we killed a guerrilla whose brother was one of the South Vietnamese soldiers working in our company. And he was very upset because he had to identify the body. He said he'd told his brother to get out of it. Now that the Americans were here it wasn't just an adventure anymore. But his brother had refused to quit. He said, "It's fun, what else is there to do?" So I kind of thought they were playing their game and we were playing ours. It was good training. It was what I wanted to do, going out and pitting my squad against whoever was out there, doing my job and getting back, not getting anybody hurt, and killing the other man.

We began to develop our field craft, and we found out that Marines could operate in the jungle as well, in some cases better, than the Vietcong. After World

War II everybody believed the Japanese were the ultimate in jungle warfare, that those guys could go out with no food, nothing, and stay there forever, and that the Americans knew nothing about field craft in the jungle. That was the way it was portrayed by Hollywood, but we found out it's not true. Americans, or anybody who spends enough time out there, is going to learn how to deal with it, how to live in it, and how to move through it without being spotted. And we began to learn those things. How to camouflage yourself, how to operate, how to maneuver, how to survive.

You learned to stay in the shadows, not to cross the paddies if at all possible. Sometimes the long way home is the safest way. You learned not to talk. You got anything to say, you used your hands—you had signals for "we're coming to a house," "be quiet," "there's a river ahead," and so forth. You learned never to walk through an opening in a hedgerow. You watched the villagers. If they walk through the opening it's ok. If they don't, if they're standing around watching you, they're probably waiting to see how many pieces you're going to blow up into. You don't kick boxes or cans. You walk around them and you make sure that you really observe where you put your feet. The key was discipline—no talking, no smoking, no nothing. And patience.

My squad had more kills than all the rest of the squads in the company, and we were proud of that. We were proud of our ability to get through the jungle and not be seen or heard and be able to watch people. We were beginning to slip around in the villages and pull a few ambushes ourselves. We were beginning to catch *them* not being alert. By October we'd had some real good contacts. We

Sergeant Melton (third from left), members of his squad, and a Marine public affairs writer (far left), survey the corpses of three Vietcong guerrillas killed during Operation Golden Fleece, near Da Nang, October 1965.

didn't seem to hold onto any real estate, but we were killing the enemy.

Then I got shot, wounded in the knee, and was evacuated to Okinawa. For a while I thought I'd be able to get back to my unit, but the wound didn't heal fast enough so I went home. I really felt let down because I figured I'd lost my chance to be platoon sergeant. I had no idea I was going to be commissioned and return to a platoon of my own. But three years later I was back in Vietnam. The only thing was that the first time I went it was a big adventure. The second time was a hard day's work every day.

In August 1968 I joined Company F of the 2d Battalion, 5th Marines, operating out of Liberty Bridge in the An Hoa Valley about twenty-five miles southwest of Da Nang. Despite the physical changes— more buildings, bigger installations—we were still playing more or less in the same terrain as when I left and that got my attention. One difference was that the Marines now had the M16 instead of the M14 we'd used in '65. But the big change was that now the North Vietnamese Army was there, we weren't operating against the Vietcong alone. It was a different kind of war because you didn't always have to sneak around. You knew where they were and you went out and fought them. Battalions were on the move out there now, even regimental operations. It wasn't a squad leader's war anymore.

The company's job was to walk the road from Liberty Bridge halfway to An Hoa each morning and clear it of mines and booby traps. We'd clear it in the daytime, and during the night the Vietcong would booby-trap it again. These people were blowing Marines to pieces. When I got there I was the number three lieutenant. In a matter of a couple of days I was the only lieutenant. The others had been hurt by the booby traps along that road. In the one month we stayed at Liberty Bridge, the company lost between forty and fifty people.

On the second or third of September we got orders to move out to an area called the Phu Nhuans. When I told my squad leaders they looked sick, but that's where we were going. By four in the afternoon we'd set up our new position and the company commander wanted to see all the platoon leaders. I took a squad with me for protection but we never made it. My point man violated all the rules. He

walked through an opening in a hedgerow and stepped over a booby trap and the second man set it off. It was an 81 or 82MM mortar round with a pressure release. You step down, it goes down, and when you step off it comes back up and explodes. Blew both his legs and one hand off, a big sturdy black Marine.

By the time I got there he was lying just in front of the point of explosion, staring at his legs in disbelief. One has a big flap on it, the other one is neatly trimmed, what you'd call a traumatic amputation. His rifle with the bayonet on it is sticking in the ground, quivering. Over to the right is a boot laced up perfectly. The other boot's over on the left side just blown to smithereens. And here's this guy lifting his legs and he can't believe it. So we get a corpsman to him, apply tourniquets to his legs and wrap his hand, and he looks up at me and he says, "I'm sorry sir. I've only been here two weeks, and I didn't even get to kill anybody. But don't worry about me, I went to boot camp and the Marines teach you to be tough." He started lecturing me on the Marine Corps, and every now and then he'd scream and ask for water, but he kept talking about boot camp and how tough the Marines were. And he lived. This guy wanted to live, he wouldn't let himself die, he just talked his way out of it. A damn good man and Marine.

But every time you turned around people were losing legs, arms, eyes. It was a terrible thing. The Vietcong would string a wire with a hand grenade on each side or take an artillery shell and rig it to blow up, or use TNT or C-4 plastic explosive to make box mines. It was just ridiculous, the casualties we were taking from booby traps.

The NVA were like us. They didn't know the ground, they didn't put out booby traps, you met them and they shot at you and you could shoot back. About a month after we moved into the Phu Nhuans, for example, we had a very successful battle at a place called Le Nam. The NVA had fortified the village with bunkers and were using it as a base of operations so we went out there to find them. Now the only way to get at them was through a natural opening in the hedgerow that surrounded the village. We didn't have all day to hack our way through because we knew the enemy was just on the other side. So when the

captain gave the word I got up, pulled my pistol, cocked it, and screamed "forward charge" as loud as I could.

The platoon came together, went through the opening and spread out, and immediately came under automatic weapon and small-arms fire. We chased some of the enemy into a large command bunker, but when we got up next to it they started throwing out hand grenades. I've never seen so many hand grenades in the air in my life. We had to turn around and run back for cover. But we were catching a lot of fire from that bunker and taking casualties. I had one of my men lay down covering fire while I worked my way back to the bunker with a couple of hand grenades that I managed to throw inside. Once that bunker was knocked out we had them on the run. In fact, it was exhilarating. I lost one dead, but the company ended up killing twenty-seven of the enemy and capturing three.

So fighting the NVA, that was all right. But when the dust and smoke clears from a booby trap you lick your wounds and look around and there's nobody to shoot at, nothing to do but stand there and grit your teeth and hope to hell you don't step on something. That Vietcong guerrilla in '68, I think I could probably stand by while you skinned one alive and I wouldn't say a word to try and stop you at all because of the number of booby traps that they put out and the number of Marines that I saw with legs blown off and hands blown off and their eyes put out. I really hated them.

It took a terrible toll, and not just physically. The war was winding down and the men knew it. All they wanted to do was to get out of that place. Rumors were flying in late 1968 that the 3d Marine Division was going to withdraw from Vietnam. There were preparations being made and there was a lot of talk that we were going to disengage. And who wants to get killed when you've got one foot on a ship and the other on land?

In my unit there was never any indication that it crossed anyone's mind to disobey their officers and not fight. But right away I learned that my platoon wouldn't always move unless I got up and moved first. You had to go out and show the way. If it was time to get up and charge, you got up first, it wasn't a matter of falling back from the situation so you could observe and direct it like I had been taught. The traditional Marine leadership techniques weren't enough. You had to be aggressive, you had to be threatening sometimes. You always had to be positive and explain to everybody what was happening.

We had people who didn't even have two years in the Corps. A lot of the younger ones just got out of boot camp and went to infantry training and they were over there. They learned rapidly, but there was something missing. For example, being an NCO didn't mean anything to them. Noncommissioned officers have certain prerogatives, but they weren't aware of them and they didn't care about them. All they wanted was to do a job and go back home. About a month after I got to An Hoa, three of my men were wounded by a booby trap. I walked up to one of them who was crying and I said, "Take it easy, it doesn't hurt." And he said, "Sir, it doesn't hurt at all. I'm crying 'cause I'm getting out of this place."

The men who had been there for a while had fought and bled and felt it was for nothing. It was extraordinary for me to hear young men talking about there shouldn't be a war, we shouldn't be fighting this war. But even some officers were upset about the way the war was being fought and their participation in it. They felt the American military forces were killing people for no real reason. I guess I've always been able to say I'm a professional Marine. I do what I'm told and that's it. I believe it's the role of the officer and the NCO to make sure there are no My Lais, to make sure that innocent people aren't murdered. But war is not an exact science. There are accidents, you make mistakes, people get killed that shouldn't be killed. It happens. That's the way war is.

I applied my trade in Vietnam and I thought I did a good job. I'm not ashamed of what I did over there. Being a lieutenant platoon commander was a very satisfying experience for me. I think the Vietnam veteran in the Marine Corps is proud of his service because we fought and fought well. But I do have to say that the overall picture was a little blurry. Even though we were successful at doing what we were assigned to do, the American presence wasn't getting the job done the way I understood it at the outset. We weren't winning. We weren't preventing the VC and the NVA from roving through the countryside because we didn't take serious steps to stop it.

My war wasn't the best war we ever fought, but it's the only one I've got. And it can't be all bad in my mind because I got a combat commission. I went from enlisted rank to officer, so I did okay. Let's face it, I had a dream that I wouldn't even mention out loud of just being an officer and a platoon commander. But I came from a very modest background so I never thought there was a chance. It turned out there was, it happened, but it took the war to do it.

What disappoints me is that this country hasn't recognized the Vietnam vets. I think it's particularly sad when you're sent to fight by your country and then you have to welcome yourself back, you have to build yourself a monument, dedicate it to yourself, and tell yourself you've finally come home. But don't call me a victim. I'm a professional Marine. I was in the Marine Corps before the war, I was in it during the war, and I'm still in it. Now if you say that Johnny Jones, who signed up to go fight and found out it wasn't his fight and he didn't know what he was fighting for, okay, you can call him a victim. But don't call me a victim. I'm a professional, and I went to fight a war. ■

In April 1975, Bill Melton returned to Southeast Asia, but with a new rank and a different mission. Now a captain in command of his own company, he poses with his platoon commanders on the deck of the U.S.S. Vancouver. Just hours later he and his men will take part in the evacuation of Phnom Penh, Cambodia.

Robert Nylen

Platoon Leader
1st Cavalry Division (Airmobile)
June–September 1968
Adviser to South Vietnamese Regional
and Popular Forces
Quang Ngai Province
September–November 1968

Born in Oak Ridge, Tennessee, in 1944, while his father was working on the Manhattan Project, Robert Nels Nylen grew up in a suburb of Wilmington, Delaware. After graduating from Bucknell University in 1966 with a B.A. in English literature, he enlisted in army OCS, earned a commission as a second lieutenant, and then worked for a year teaching "speaking, writing, and patrolling—yes, speaking, writing, and patrolling"—at the Ordnance Center and School at Aberdeen Proving Grounds in Maryland. Ordered to Vietnam in 1968, he was twice wounded while serving as a platoon leader with the 1st Cavalry Division. Upon completing his term of enlistment in 1969, he earned an M.B.A. at the Wharton School in Philadelphia before embarking on a career in publishing. Currently the publisher of New England Monthly, *a magazine he helped to found in 1982, he lives in a Berkshire Hills town with his wife and daughter.*

I'd like to pretend that I was cynical about it or blasé about it now, but the truth is that going into the military was something I really wanted to do. I wanted the challenge, and I was attracted by the adventure of combat. I was slightly troubled, and I mean only slightly troubled, by the controversy concerning Vietnam. Times were different in 1966, you know. Embarrassing as it is to admit, I was more concerned with proving myself. Like many young men who are confused about their future, I wanted to go through the same rite of passage that other men had gone through in times past.

I had been a poor student in college. In fact, I had to go to summer school just to scrape by. I was immature and spoiled in the way that a lot of semiaffluent kids are spoiled. My dad had enough money to send me to college, and I treated that as a right. I was even ungrateful. I spent a lot of time fooling around and very little time with my books.

So by 1966, my senior year, I was ready for, wanted, and needed a tough challenge. My first choice was to be a navy flier. Why, I don't know. I had never flown a plane before and haven't since. Perhaps it was the swoosh of jet engines or those neat dress whites; it sure wasn't a rational plan. But I decided that was what I had to do, so I applied for the Naval Air program, took the exams, and was promptly disqualified for varicose veins in my left leg. Undaunted, I went to the trouble of having an operation for the ligation of varicose veins, only to be disqualified again because of the scar tissue left by the surgery.

I was devastated by that. I thought, what do you mean I can't serve? It doesn't take incredible skills or superhuman intelligence to do that. You can't keep me out! So I became obsessed by the need to overcome rejection. I pursued the Marine Corps—no dice, navy doctors again—and then the army, which had no compunctions about varicose veins. And in mid-August 1966—two and a half months after graduation and six days before my draft notice arrived—I volunteered for army OCS. In a way, the army rescued me, because my job at the time was as crummy or worse than permanent kitchen police work; I was a plastics grinder on the two-man graveyard shift of a small company. I passed my physical. I was proud. I was going to become an infantry officer.

I did my basic and advanced training at Fort Dix, New Jersey, for four months and then off to Fort Benning, Georgia, for OCS. I gather that Fort Benning deteriorated until the fabled time of Lieutenant Calley, but when I was there it was still a classic and honorable military institution. Not the Yale or Harvard of the military educational system but more like the University of Texas—big, put a lot of people through, did a basically good job without a great deal of pretension. And a thousand million zillion times better than ROTC.

I remember it as a riveting time—bracing and invigorating and demeaning all at once. The process of becoming an officer is one in which a great deal of pressure is placed upon all candidates to ascertain how they will stand up under fire—to find out whether or not they're team players, whether or not they can follow orders, whether or not they're physically and mentally strong enough to lead other human beings into mortal danger, and, I suppose, to make sure they're crazy enough for the work.

Part of it is positive and constructive. You run, jump, push, climb, and low crawl to the point of utter exhaustion so that you extend the limits of your endurance past reason. And part of it is stupid, humiliating, and silly. I vividly remember one night when we were called out in the rain with our uniforms on backwards and forced to carry our footlockers on our backs because of some imagined malfeasance. Grown men being ordered to act like fools, though of course we did it without question and even enjoyed it with the perverse pride that soldiers take in their own sufferings. With very few exceptions, we felt a common terror of being "paneled," as the army called it, and shipped off to become grunts. We insisted on becoming Officer Grunts, a distinction that turned out to be thinner than we thought.

On the whole the training was very effective in doing what it was intended to do, which was to separate the competent from the incompetent and to prepare those who made it to lead other men on the battlefield. The dehumanizing aspects of it galvanized us and taught us that what happens to the group is what is important. Once this fact is established, then in the time of gravest danger what happens to one person isn't important. The inconsistency of the decisions we were subjected to prepared us for the crazy illogic of virtually all orders in war, such as "Run up that hill and take that position!" … "But, sir, there are people shooting at me." Even the fear of being unfit prepared us in a way. Because in combat the fear of embarrassing yourself in front of other people while simultaneously being driven to help other people out—people who are close to you—is a great source of motivation. It makes it possible for you to expose yourself to death.

But no training can convey the reality of war or the reality of Vietnam. You can't simulate death and dying in any realistic way. OCS can't ensure that you will still function when chunks of human flesh are flying about, perhaps some of it your own. You can't really prepare someone for a climate which is hot to the point of torpor, so hot that a simple two-mile march becomes a grueling, awful affair and the heat itself becomes an oppressive enemy as strong as any we faced. And you can't readily prepare American soldiers to deal with a culture that is totally alien to them, a strange Third World country in which they are themselves strangers and the natives are simultaneously enemy and friend. The overwhelming majority of American troops had never been out of the country before; in fact, most had never been out of their own states. They were naive, innocent kids. So when they confronted these Orientals who looked physically unlike themselves, who spoke a language that sounded like chickens clucking, who lived with barnyard animals under their ramshackle roofs and had no idea how to use toilets or toilet paper, it was difficult not to think, "These people are somehow less than us, they have less so they are less, their lives count less."

I remember that when I arrived in Vietnam in June 1968, the 1st Cavalry Division made a special effort to acquaint its incoming officers and soldiers with the vicissitudes of the battle the Cav was fighting in I Corps. This took place at Camp Evans, the division's forward base. They told us about the nature and history of the 1st Cav, the nature of the terrain, the nature of the enemy. And one of the briefings we got was from a very intelligent psychological operations officer who impressed upon us the need to attempt to distinguish between the enemy we were fighting and the nation we were attempt-

ing to save. He said, "It's as much your job to treat village elders with respect as it is to watch your ass on patrol." He described the Chieu Hoi program, introduced us to two Kit Carson scouts, and cautioned us against "calling these people gooks or slopes or zipperheads or dinks or zeroes."

As soon as that lecture was over, we were trucked to a class on ambushes and a practical exercise in patrolling, both conducted outside the camp perimeter. The instructor was a tall lieutenant with a three-day growth of beard, a field-experienced officer who had seen the worst of it. I remember he had inscribed on his helmet the names of the places he'd fought—Que Son, LZ Peanut, Hue, A Shau, Khe Sanh—and in front, in bold block letters, GEORGIA. And the first words out of his mouth were, "Men, one of the things you'll learn here after you've been out in the field for a while is that these gooks are goddamn good at ambushes. It's their best tactic and the one they use most often. Gooks are more patient than we are."

At the time I thought, "Experience 1, Psy Ops 0." But in fact those two lectures presented a conundrum that I, for one, never really solved. Rationally and humanistically, I knew that we had to befriend the Vietnamese, to understand them, that we had to treat them as human beings, yet at the same time I knew they had to be distrusted because their own

Second Lieutenant Robert Nylen (left) displays an official letter of commendation received for his work as an instructor at the Aberdeen Proving Grounds Ordnance Center and School in Aberdeen, Maryland, in May 1967.

personal family alignment was with the enemy. During the daytime virtually any Vietnamese we saw was likely to be friendly to us. And at nighttime they weren't. I know that's a cliché, but it's nonetheless true. In the daytime kids would press around us, jostling, speaking in pidgin English: "GI Number One," "You give me candy," "You give me cigarette." Smiling kids, beatific expressions, great interest in the riches and the pleasantness of the American GI. And at night these same villages would be the points from which the enemy would assault us. We had to be suspicious, not only of anyone of military age who wasn't black or white or wearing an American uniform but of *anyone* who was in a position to do us damage.

My own abbreviated tour brought me face to face with both sides of the problem. During my first three months I was a combat platoon leader. My job was to make contact with the enemy and then kill as many of his troops as possible. A simple, brutal, clear job. Then I was assigned to be an adviser to the South Vietnamese Regional and Popular Forces, the "Ruff-Puffs," where my task was to win "hearts and minds." Less dangerous but much harder.

If you subtract the week I spent in camp being acclimated and the three weeks I spent in four hospitals recovering from wounds, my actual functioning time with the Cav in the field was probably less than two months. Yet in that space my platoon lost six men KIA and I don't know how many more wounded in every conceivable way—sniper attacks, booby traps, ambushes, mines, our own helicopters, short rounds, and even by moronic practical jokes with live weapons. And we had a good unit!

I still remember how gleeful we felt whenever we had an opportunity to strike back at the enemy we so seldom saw. There was one occasion in particular, after we had been ambushed and lost four men—one killed, three wounded. We pulled back and called in an air strike. Ten minutes later an air force jet, an F-4 or maybe an F-105, swooped in over the ridge and dropped napalm where we thought the North Vietnamese were escaping. We laughed and cheered and imagined the direst possible end for the bastards who had just laid waste to four of our people—shouting "It's crispy critter

time!" God help us, we wanted them barbequed, sautéed, and cooked any way the Geneva Convention permits the roasting of the other side. We wanted to hear the crackling of their fat.

Alongside that memory is the memory of a day several weeks later when the top sergeant and I were invited by the elders of a little hamlet to share a meal. We didn't know why we had been invited, but since the village was only a few meters from our base perimeter it seemed safe enough. In fact, we didn't even take along our weapons because it was daytime. We learned the reason for their hospitality after we arrived. An American unit that had previously been positioned there had apparently mistaken the unfamiliar sounds they had heard one night for an enemy attack and had shot up the village. Fearful that this would happen again, the villagers wanted to meet us and let us know they weren't bad guys.

It turned out to be the warmest experience I ever had with the Vietnamese. They offered us some powerful rice whiskey—very raw and intoxicating. After three or four we were both knocked for a loop. In the meantime their children congregated around us, like a flock of little fawns, and began caressing our arms and legs. They were amazed that hair grew on our bodies and perhaps even more so by its unusual blond color, which was accentuated by the bleaching of the tropical sun. So we sat there drinking this whiskey and attempted to communicate with them, and they attempted to communicate to us in pidgin English what was most on their minds, which was "Don't shoot us, please."

The food and the entreaties lasted until a couple of hours after dark. And even though I'd had a strangely wonderful time, I couldn't help but think as we were stumbling our way back to our camp what an evil plot it could have been if they had just wanted to get us out and then shoot us on the way back.

Not long after that we had a different kind of encounter with Vietnamese villagers. Our company had arrived at a base camp called LZ Nancy, after spending a week in search of an invisible battalion of North Vietnamese regulars that intelligence sources had pinpointed in locations ranging from the coastline to the fringes of the central highlands. Nancy was an immense two-mile oblong de-

signed eventually to hold the entire second brigade of the 1st Cavalry Division. Unfortunately, an entire brigade was not occupying the base at the time. Instead we had only four companies—three engineering companies plus our own infantry company—to defend the entire perimeter, which in some areas consisted of a single tangle of concertina wire. My platoon's sector extended over an area about 700 meters long. To cover it, we had exactly thirty-four men—the strongest it ever got as long as I was in it. That meant that in every case more than 50 meters separated our bunkers. We were very vulnerable, and we knew it.

Our positions overlooked two small villages that were nestled against the wire. During the day the village children would come out and play and exchange pleasantries and taunts with our soldiers. By taunts I mean an occasional "Fuck you, GI," but nothing out of the ordinary.

Then one night—I think it was the third, maybe the fourth night after we arrived—we were hit. It began with a barrage of mortar fire from a position in an abandoned part of one of the villages, followed by a sapper attack through the wire. We returned fire toward the mortar position and then fired into the fringes of the villages themselves. I had no compunctions about that because it was clear that the villages had been used as staging areas for the attack.

It was a savage night. They nearly overran our positions, but in the end we held them off. In the morning we found seventeen bodies in the wire, including three sappers just outside our bunker that I had apparently killed in the middle of the night during a bizarre and macabre baseball game consisting of their dynamite coming in and then my grenades going out, alternately—in, boom, out, bang; in, boom, out, bang, and so on. This dead trio was stripped to the waist and daubed with camouflaging charcoal, wearing loincloths and headbands, and festooned with bangalore torpedoes and satchel charges they had been unable to use. American casualties were just as bad, something like eighteen killed and fifty wounded, including two KIA from our platoon.

I was one of those wounded. It wasn't very serious—I had a concussion from one of the satchel charges that exploded near my bunker, blinding our medic, Doc

Froemming—but it was enough to land me in the hospital at Da Nang for a few days. One day while I was there, a very young Vietnamese girl, perhaps nine or ten, was brought into the ward accompanied by her grandmother. Allegedly she had been molested by an American who had inserted a Coke bottle into her vagina, but that was only hearsay. True or not, it was the *only* incident I heard about of any atrocity performed by an American on a living Vietnamese during the time I was there. And I saw a fair amount of combat and worked closely with the Vietnamese population.

In any event, it turned out that the girl's grandmother was much sicker than the girl herself. And during the night, as the child slept, the grandmother died. All the other Vietnamese in the ward paid no attention either to the cadaver of this poor old lady or to her granddaughter. They totally ignored them. At first the granddaughter was stoic, and then she began to cry. And immediately the Americans in the ward—black and white, all ages and ranks—gathered around her and tried to comfort her, little reflecting on the fact that an American was supposedly responsible for putting her there and that she might still be terrified of us. They weren't thinking about that. They saw a child who was suffering, and they wanted to help her out. And the fact that the other Vietnamese, her own people, didn't seem to care, made us angry. So one of us asked a Vietnamese nurse's aide who spoke very good English, "Why don't these people care? What's wrong with them?" And her answer was, "They are not her family. They do not know this child. It is up to her family to comfort her and care for her. These people have seen so much tragedy and death, they cannot be bothered. This is nothing to them." So whether that child would be well taken care of, or not taken care of at all, was entirely dependent upon the circumstances of her family, if in fact her family was still alive. It was something most Americans just could not understand and another example of the profound gulf that separated our cultures.

Several weeks after I got out of the hospital, in September 1968, I learned that I was to become an adviser to the South Vietnamese "Ruff-Puffs" in Quang Ngai Province. I remember the shock of realizing that I was going to be spending the next eight months with 150 South Viet-

namese of uncertain reliability and only five other Americans in a camp that I learned had been overrun the year before. It turned out that the camp was in a district that had been a Vietcong stronghold for decades, fifteen miles from the Pinkville area made infamous by Lt. Calley, though of course that meant nothing to us at the time. Even so, the thought of being in a fixed position, with a headquarters whose location was on every VC and NVA map from here to Hanoi, was more unsettling than being part of a rabidly aggressive cavalry unit.

Top. *Local villagers view the bodies of Vietcong sappers killed in a raid on the Binh Son District Headquarters in mid-November 1968, one week after Nylen returned to the U.S.*

Above. *The Binh Son District Headquarters in Quang Ngai Province, where Lt. Nylen spent the second half of his Vietnam tour.*

Members of the U.S. advisory team and a Regional Forces soldier survey a collection of weapons captured in the November 1968 attack on their headquarters.

One of two Purple Hearts received by Nylen for wounds received in action.

But the new strategy to win was to Vietnamize the war, and one way to do that was through cooperative work with local Popular Forces. These were just ordinary male folk who happened to be wearing military uniforms, a paramilitia, and by and large really crummy troops. The idea was that we should educate them about how the American military went about its business—a totally futile thought—while participating with them on their missions and to be available to call in artillery and medical evacuation equipment.

Even though the work wasn't nearly as tough as that faced by the Marine CAP teams—one teensy squad of Marines working with a platoon of Popular Forces troops—it was frustrating nonetheless. The "Ruff-Puffs" were reluctant to go out into the countryside because we might meet the enemy, and they didn't like that. And when we did come under fire they immediately wanted big guns brought in so they wouldn't have to risk their lives.

One night, for example, we started getting sniper fire from a village adjacent to our position. Nothing sustained, just an occasional round whistling over us but not really coming close. But my South Vietnamese counterpart, the company commander of the Regional Forces, panicked. He requested, then demanded, that I call in artillery, which on the face of it was ridiculous. But after he yammered at

me for half an hour, I finally agreed to call for an artillery flare to light up the sky and see if we could pinpoint anything. The artillery shell fires overhead, goes off, and this brilliantly hot white phosphorous flare drops right smack on a hut rooftop. Instantly it turns the thatched roof into a blaze, and all the people rush out. For the rest of the night we hear their sobbing and moaning. Had it been up to my counterpart, we would have wiped out the village entirely in order to silence one solitary SKS rifle.

I don't think my experience in Vietnam gave me any great insights into the war while I was there. I certainly didn't think geopolitically. When I was thinking most sharply, I thought simply about what was happening with my platoon, my company, and, occasionally, my battalion and my division. I remember having a conversation, though, with a South Vietnamese soldier about what would happen when the Americans left. He smiled at me and said, "The war will be over." And I said, "Well, who will win, who will lose?" He replied, "It doesn't matter. The war will be over. You go, the war is over." It was that simple to him. And I knew that what he said was true without considering what would become of the losers. Still, I didn't think we would win or lose. I just thought the war would last as long as we wanted it to last, as long as we were prepared to be there.

My own part in the war ended sooner than that. In late November the senior adviser told me that my mother had died and that I would be getting an emergency leave to attend her funeral. It was the strangest time of my life. I remember flying back on this huge, nearly empty and windowless transport plane, going through a spiral of emotions of anger, grief, tortured guilt, and ecstasy—all piled on one another. I was thrilled to be leaving Vietnam alive, joyous about seeing my fiancée, guilty about leaving the other members of the advisory team—that guilt that is associated with deserting people you've become very close to—and simultaneously angry and deeply saddened by my mother's death. I suppose I felt partly responsible for that, too, because my mother was diabetic and in frail condition before I left, and I think that the worry and the agonizing over my months overseas probably exacerbated her medical problems somewhat.

Then, when I arrived in Los Angeles, the first people I saw who were my own age gave me a look of such overwhelming contempt I felt as if they had slapped me in the face. They looked at me, standing there in LAX in my jungle fatigues, and began joking with one another about what I looked like with no attempt to disguise their disdain. It was a very ... unhappy moment. Having been separated from my family for half a year, mother dead, having been shot, rocketed, shrapnel in both legs, my hearing damaged—to think that I should be the object of ridicule for my efforts. Jesus.

I never went back to Vietnam. I received a compassionate reassignment for family reasons and completed my term of enlistment in the United States. Later I took advantage of the GI Bill and, with my wife's help, got an M.B.A. at the Wharton School in Philadelphia. By then my doubts about the war had grown, and by the time Nixon ordered the invasion of Cambodia I was strongly opposed to any continuation of it. Good Lord, I thought, *enough*. We could bleed there until the twenty-first century.

Looking back, my feelings about having served in the war are tumultuously ambivalent. I think wars are terrible. Who doesn't? I think about the men in my platoon I saw die—one Indian, one Hispanic, two blacks, and two white kids—and I'm sorry for them. But I'm almost ashamed to say that although I hated most aspects, and was frightened to death during a great deal of it, it was a catharsis for me. I don't know that I'd volunteer to go back again tomorrow if there were a time machine that could transport me back to 1966, 1967, 1968; not knowing what I know now. But it shaped whatever it is that is now my character, in that before I was a confused, insecure, underachieving kid, and afterwards I knew just how precious life was, how easily it could be squandered, and how stupid it would be to throw away something that others fought so desperately to hang on to. ∎

Kathleen Costello Cordova

Nurse, 24th Evacuation Hospital
Long Binh, South Vietnam
1967–1968

"I was a product of the John F. Kennedy era. When he said, 'Ask not what your country can do for you, ask what you can do for your country,' I believed every word he said. So if it wasn't nursing it would have been the Peace Corps. If it wasn't the Peace Corps it would have been VISTA. I would have gotten involved with helping people one way or another during Vietnam. I think it was something I was destined to do."

Kathy Cordova was born in Danbury, Connecticut, and grew up part of a "very close Italian-Irish Catholic family. Strong family ties. To this day, very, very strong family ties." After graduation from high school she entered Bellevue Nursing School in New York City, an "optimistic eighteen-year-old girl with a sense of adventure and an ability to laugh. I was ready for anything."

Today she lives with her husband, Joe, and her daughter, Jennifer, in Newtown, Connecticut, a mile down the road from Fairfield Hills Hospital where she works as a medical review nurse.

I came to Bellevue in the fall of 1963 and graduated three years later. During my second year recruiters came around—air force, navy, and army. My first choice would have been a navy nurse. But the army offered a student nurse program where they paid you every month as if you were a private first class. You didn't have to go to any meetings, you didn't have to wear a uniform, but as soon as you passed your State Boards you had to give back two years on active duty.

I had a friend who suggested it to me in the first place. Neither of us had any plans for after graduation. We really didn't want to stay around the area. It was actually a sense of adventure that led us both into it. Vietnam was something on the back pages of the newspaper, an obscure country. It never entered my mind till much later.

During basic training everyone in my class started talking about going. Maybe this is a poor choice of words, but it was almost the vogue to be going. At first it didn't make much of an impression on me. All I could remember was my mother and father saying they were glad they didn't have sons that they would have to send off to war, so certainly they're not going to have a daughter that's going off to war. But as all my friends were talking about volunteering for Vietnam, it finally began to sink in. My first duty station after basic was Fort Hood in Killeen, Texas. When I got there I looked around and decided I didn't want to stay a year in Killeen, Texas, and I volunteered to go. I can't say there was any strong political feelings on my part. I thought I could do a job over there and off I went.

I can remember it as if it were yesterday, coming off the plane at Bien Hoa after seventeen hours in the air, feeling extremely tired and dirty. I have a problem with my hair when it's humid, so the first thing I thought was that I would come out with a gigantic Afro because my hair was going to frizz. But I didn't have much time to dwell on it because we had barely gotten twenty or thirty feet away when the engines started up and the plane just took off. They didn't refuel. The pilot and stewardesses never got off the plane. It was a matter of maybe ten minutes and off they went. And everybody just kind of standing there and thinking, "Oh my God! What have I gotten myself into?"

The 24th Evacuation Hospital was just what it was called. We would get incoming casualties, stabilize them, send them into the operating room, and then take care of them postoperatively. But most of the time, within a few hours or a few days they were shipped out, either to the United States, to Japan, or back to the field if the wounds were not that serious.

I happened to arrive in country when there was a bit of a lull. After work, you went to the mess hall, you socialized, you played cards, you played football, there were parties at the officers club. It was almost like you were away at a huge summer camp. Whenever they could they would hire bands to play at the officers club, and everybody would dance and have a good time. And around holidays, especially Christmas, they went all out to make things nice for people.

What was hard was when you went back to your quarters at night and you crawled into bed and you turned out the lights. And then you heard the war. There was automatic weapons fire. There were times when shells dropped very, very close to us. There was the outgoing. When I hear thunder it sometimes brings back memories to me because of that boom! boom! boom! Your quarters would shake. If you were working on the ward you could hear the IV bottles clinking together. The constant helicopters—that rocka, rocka, rocka. Some nights you would go out and see tracers in the sky from the gunships. And there was always, always the risk, because over there you never knew who your enemy was. Anybody could walk onto the compound and start shooting at you.

The war was all around you. It was there in your patients. We'd get casualties that the helicopter pilots would tell us had only been shot ten or fifteen minutes earlier. It was a constant assault on your senses. You smelled it, you had your hands in it, you saw it, and you heard it. It was always there. You could never really get away from it.

There was fear—fear that you were going to be shot, fear that the hospital was going to be shelled, that you were going to open your locker in your room someday and find a mine in there. People tried to control that fear, or thought about it when they were alone in their room at night. You suppressed it. You tried not to let other people know you were afraid.

One night the VC blew up an ammunition dump a mile or two from the hospital. There was this enormous explosion. I was thrown right out of bed and found myself on the floor not knowing what was going on. I picked myself up, and I remember staggering out of the room still half-asleep, half-bruised, the shock of it, and just trying to run to find somebody who knew what had happened. And all we saw was this huge mushroom cloud—it looked like it was an atomic bomb. I mean, we figured Johnson had finally done it, the son of a bitch, he had dropped the atom bomb and he had done it while we were all there. I remember being really scared, really frightened. Other than that, the fear never left you but it was always contained. Most of the time you were too busy to think about it.

After the first week or so we started to get heavy casualties, and I think I might have panicked because you want to do everything you can for the patient and spend a lot of ... see, in nursing school they teach you one way. Over there, there wasn't time for the back rubs and niceties and the nurse with her starched white uniform leaning over the patient. All I could do was a bare minimum and not give any more.

I found it very difficult. I liked the patients to be around for a while so you could form a bond. I guess that was part of my training, why I went into nursing in the first place, because I truly wanted to help somebody and have them be around and watch that progression from being seriously ill to getting better and walking out the door with them and sending them home. But in Vietnam you barely had time to get their name before they went into the OR. And when they came out, you were loading them up with pain pills. So you never really had time to sit down and talk to them. You never really felt that you got to know them. Maybe that was best. Maybe that was the best thing, that you couldn't become too involved with them.

You just didn't have time to think about anything else but your job. We were almost always full. It was noisy because there was a lot going on—bottles clanking, respirators going, people milling around. It smelled awful, because no matter how hard you tried with the massive doses of antibiotics, the wounds got infected. You smelled blood, you smelled pus, you smelled infection, you smelled

death. I don't care what anybody says, you can smell death. You can smell fear.

Most of our patients were casualties from high-velocity weapons, mines, shells. They were huge wounds. I think that's what shocked me most of all. Huge wounds. Everything was sucked in with it, so that if you looked at it you weren't sure what you were looking at because there might have been buttons, fatigues, jewelry. I remember one night picking out a stick from somebody's wound. If they had stepped on a mine it just scooped everything out so it looked like you had a rag doll, like the scarecrow in *The Wizard of Oz* when all his stuffing came out.

They'd be brought in with their fatigues on, their helmets, some of them still had their weapons in their hands. A lot of blood. They were dirty, so they looked like hell. They were in pain, perhaps the majority of them were in shock. But if you want to talk about courage. Even when they came out of the OR with no legs, no arms, one arm, one leg, they just carried on and went about what they had to do. Getting better, fitted with a prosthesis, can't wait to go home. I don't know what kind of impression the American people have of the men who fought in Vietnam, but if you want to talk about courage, I saw it every day.

There was constant activity because the patients were fresh out of postop and there's things that have to be done. They have to be turned, they have to be given their pain medication, there was always the next IV bottle to hang, the next dressing to change. And then when you think you've got everybody settled, you start all over again, running, bending, lifting. It was hard. It was hard work because it never ended. You know, it's funny. One of the places we couldn't work at Bellevue was in the emergency room because it was just much too busy to have student nurses milling around. And when we got to Vietnam it was like one big emergency room.

Especially the preop and recovery ward. When you went on shift you never knew what you were going to find. There were afternoons when you'd open the door and there might be 100 to 150 casualties in the room—on the floor, on the beds, in the hallway leading to the OR. The army categorizes patients one through four: One being, patch him up and send him back; two being, they're going to patch him up but let's keep him for a while; three being, they're going to have to be operated on and stay for a while, possibly shipped out to Japan or back home. Four meant, there's nothing we can do. Keep an IV open, give them clean sheets, and just wait for them to die because the wound is so extensive—usually they were head wounds—that we didn't have the time or the equipment or the wherewithal to operate on them. Perhaps they could have been saved back here, I don't know. I don't want to think about it. Over there you just couldn't spend the time. So they were considered four, and we would put them at the back of the ward with a curtain for whatever privacy we could give them, with a clean sheet and an IV.

One day a very, very young man came in, he couldn't have been more than nineteen or twenty, if that. He was a four. He had a bullet wound at the base of his neck that had severed the cervical spine. I remember looking at him. He wasn't bloody. I didn't see a mark on him. I was trying to find out where the hell his wound was when the doctor came over and said put him in the back. I remember looking at the doctor and saying, "What are you talking about, there's nothing on him. Why is he going to die?"

He was fully conscious and alert, and he didn't die for a long time. Nobody ever told him he was going to die. Nobody ever told him they weren't going to do anything for him. I remember sitting with him as much as I could, trying to make conversation. His name was Robert. I don't even know if I knew his last name. His name was Robert, and he had very dark hair and blue eyes. Apparently he came from a big family, if I recall it was the Midwest. He had a girlfriend. He wasn't out of high school but a year or so. He talked about high school and sports, his girlfriend, his parents, his life. He was conscious the whole time. I did what I could for him among all my other duties. I was there when he finally expired.

To this day I'm trying to figure out why he died. Maybe I just didn't want him to. Maybe he was the one. If you're in nursing for thirty years, you'll always remember one patient that struck you, and you'll remember forever and ever and you try to think why. Was it the way they looked, the way they spoke, did they look like somebody you knew, might have known

years ago? They just hit something in you. For me, he will be the one.

It was always so intense. Even when you were supposedly off duty it was intense. It was as if you had to cram so much into so little time. You had to play hard, you had to work hard, you had to talk hard, you had to be hard. And sometimes it was hard to be hard. It's hard to always show up for duty and just function as you would anywhere else.

You find yourself becoming a different person. You went over there as somebody you thought you really knew. You knew who you were, what you wanted in life. And all of a sudden you spend a few months there and your outlook on things starts to change. You start to change.

I found myself drinking a lot. Drinking to relax, drinking to forget, drinking because everybody else was drinking. When people had parties they really let their hair down, they had a good time. It was an outlet, a release. I spent the first two months I was there out in the back crying every time I put somebody in a black body bag. I will never buy black garbage bags. I'll buy white, yellow, green, but do not bring any black plastic bags into my house, I don't care what they're for. I don't want to touch them. I don't want to see them. I put too many people in black bags. I remember putting

Eager for adventure, Cordova joined the Fort Hood Skydiving Club. By February, 1967 she was jumping out of airplanes "just for the fun of it." Four months later another airplane would leave her on the tarmac of Bien Hoa airport, South Vietnam.

Kathy Cordova (left) and one of her classmates on the night of their graduation from Bellevue Nursing School, June 6, 1966.

Above. *Mementos of a war, including: (top left) Vietnam Service Medal, (top right) Vietnam Campaign Medal, and (bottom right) Army Commendation Medal.*

Below. *"You worked so closely with people in Vietnam. You were able to put all the petty things aside and work together for the common cause of the patient." A month after her arrival at the 24th Evac, Cordova (far right), a corpsman, and another nurse pose with an injured Australian soldier.*

these bodies, these pieces of young men into the bags, and the last sound you heard was the sound of the zipper. Then I'd go out in the back and cry. And then I'd come back and do it again, and then I'd go out and cry. After a while you'd stop crying. But you cried for a long time.

You built up a kind of shell around yourself. You have to or you're going to fall apart, you're not going to be able to function. It was day in, day out, so much death, so much destruction, so many shattered lives. You knew it wasn't just the person who was wounded and then goes home. It was the girlfriend, the wife, the mother and father that're going to have to greet their son at the airport with one arm, one leg. I think I started to get hardened to it, but I never let myself get to the point where I had no feelings at all. I didn't want to cry anymore, I wanted to stop running out to the back. But I never wanted to get to the point where I could watch somebody die and not feel *anything* inside.

It was so confusing. You went over there without really feeling anything in particular about the war. You just wanted to go and do a job because you're a nurse. At first I started to feel very patriotic. I found myself saying, "I'm glad I'm here. I'm helping out. We should be here." And then, as the months went on and I put more and more eighteen-year-

old young men in black bags to ship home to their mothers and fathers, I got angry. I began to think, "My God, what are we doing here? This is ridiculous. If we're over here, let's just finish it," not by withdrawing but by bombing them, wiping them off the face of the earth. I know that sounds awful, but just get it over with. Just make them retreat, bomb the hell out of them, do what you have to do.

Some of the people at the hospital went out of their way to try to learn the language or really get to know the Vietnamese, but to be honest, I was never that interested in the country or the people. Maybe I had a certain resentment towards them—a feeling that if it weren't for them all these young men wouldn't be dying or being hurt. I couldn't get past that. I couldn't stop looking at the American casualties and thinking about what they were going through. I knew the people of South Vietnam were going through just as much hell as we were, but they weren't the ones I cared about.

I had never felt the bitterness and anger I began to feel in Vietnam. I'd led a very sheltered life. I went from Mommy and Daddy to nursing school, which protected you, to the service, which protected you. I had never had any reason before to hate anybody or to develop any bitterness for anything. I blamed the government for allowing this to happen. I blamed the military. We had the clout to do something to end the war and we didn't. Why did it go on? Why did they allow so many young men to die?

Coming home was bizarre. The family put a big banner up, "Welcome Home." My mother was glad to see me, my sisters, but nobody knew what to say. I had contracted hepatitis several months earlier, and I looked horrible. I come from an Italian family where all the women should weigh 250 pounds and I was just skin and bones, 95 pounds. My mother kept looking at me like I was about ready to drop dead. I was pale, I was thin, I didn't smile. I was very cold, very distant, very alienated from my family. I didn't know how to act, they didn't know how to act. So the homecoming was certainly not what I expected. I don't know what I expected.

My family tried to smother me and stick food in my mouth. But I didn't need the homemade bread. I didn't need the

homemade pasta to make me feel better. Nothing was going to make me feel better. I was sick inside from what I had seen. They meant well, truly they meant well. But it wasn't what I needed. I wanted to unload. I wanted to go out in the middle of a field and scream and yell and cry or maybe go down to Washington and give every single congressman down there the finger and tell them, "Don't you ever get us involved in anything like this again. How dare you. You didn't see all that death and dying and destruction. You saw figures on a piece of paper. You kept statistics." It always bothered me when I used to hear that casualties were light. How can you even put it in those terms? If one person dies, that one person meant something to somebody.

After a few weeks of leave I was assigned to Fort Devens, Massachusetts. It was a strange feeling after coming from Vietnam. All of a sudden I was working in a white uniform again and white nylons and white shoes in a structured building as opposed to Quonset huts. It was hard to adjust. We took care of casualties from Vietnam, young men who had been injured there, but there was something missing. You worked so closely with people in Vietnam. You were able to put all the petty things aside and work together for the common cause of the patient. The people I worked with at Fort Devens were all into their own little problems. That's what bothered me; I missed the cameraderie.

And I resented the ugly head of the army bureaucracy that suddenly reared up. It seemed so ridiculous to me. Every week they'd have their white glove inspections. I was on a ward with young men who had horrendous infected wounds. It took a long time to do their care, to change their dressings, to debride their wounds and clean them out, and inevitably somebody would come through on an inspection and just cover them up with a sheet as we walked by. That kind of thing didn't set well with me.

I had tremendous guilt feelings. Tremendous confusion. There was so much opposition to the war. You felt guilty that you even went there, so terrible that you were an American over there and here were people protesting against it. You felt guilty that you came home all in one piece when you were shipping a lot of

other people home minus arms or legs or in black bags. I had a lot of anger, but I didn't know what to do about it. There were no support groups yet, it was too early. None of these things had surfaced yet, and they weren't going to surface for a while.

I finally got out of the army in the fall of 1968 and took a job at Danbury Hospital near my home. I purposely picked the night shift to avoid contact with other people. I went to work, I came home, I had a little breakfast, I went to sleep, I got up, had supper with my family, and went to work. When anybody asked me about Vietnam I'd just turn them right off. I always hated it when somebody would say, "Hey, what was it like over there?" I would just snap at them. "What do you think? You really want to hear about it?" As a nursing experience it was invaluable, I'd tell them. The rest of it sucked.

Looking back, I don't know what was wrong with me. Just totally turned off and tuned out. It was a very strange time—for months I walked around like a zombie. I sometimes used to think I escaped totally unharmed from the war. Maybe I didn't.

I still have very mixed feelings. I hate to admit that. You know, I'm thirty-nine years old. I should be at a point in my life where I pretty much have the courage of my convictions. I know what I like and dislike, but I still have so many ambivalent feelings about Vietnam.

The most important effect it's had on me has been a very negative thing. I'm not practicing my profession the way I would have liked to. It's something I've suppressed for many years, but I think I have purposely shied away from the most important thing that led me into nursing in the first place—the human contact. For the last seven years I've had a desk job. I have no contact with patients, and I prefer it that way. In a sense, I've totally withdrawn. I live in a middle-class town in my own sheltered little world with my desk job working for the state.

Shortly after her return to the United States, Cordova receives the Army Commendation Medal for her service in Vietnam.

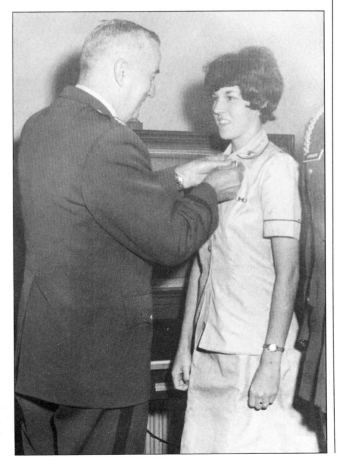

I guess I prefer to remain very low-key about my service in Vietnam. I don't want anybody praising me for it and I don't want anybody criticizing me for it, so it's easier just to remain very low-key. I have a friend who's written a novel about the war and is still very involved with Vietnam veterans. And sometimes he says, "Why don't you come to Washington? Let's go to Washington, let's march—you should be proud, don't be angry, don't feel bad about being over there." I'm not sure. I'm proud I was around to . . . I think I maybe helped a lot of young men get better. I know I did, I know I did. And kept them free of pain or helped them when they needed it. So I'm proud of that. But I still haven't come to terms with being over there. Maybe I'm ashamed, maybe I'm so upset that I was part of something that was so immoral that I can't find a place for the pride.

When you're a trained medical personnel you're supposed to be strong, you're supposed to be caring, you're supposed to be nurturing, you're not supposed to cry. Well, we did need to cry, and we do have wounds just like other veterans. Certainly ours aren't visible. We have all our appendages, and we don't have holes in our bodies or pieces of shrapnel. But that doesn't mean they're not just as real.

You know, I've never seen the Vietnam Memorial. I think I'd like to see it now. Perhaps it's time. Maybe we all have wounds to heal. ∎

Ward Just

Foreign Correspondent for
The Washington Post
1965–1967

"I really had only two ambitions in my life when I was young. I wanted very much to be a private detective—I was sort of under the influence of the Hardy Boys stories. And as soon as I got that out of my head I decided I wanted to be a writer, and I've never wanted to be anything else."

Born in 1935, Ward Just grew up in Waukegan, Illinois, the son and grandson of newspaper publishers. After a series of prep schools and four years at Trinity College in Hartford, Connecticut, he returned to Waukegan to work on the family paper as a reporter. In 1959 Just took a job with Newsweek magazine where he came under the tutelage of then-Washington Bureau Chief Ben Bradlee. After assignments in London and Cyprus, where he covered the bitter struggle between Greek and Turkish Cypriots during 1963 and 1964, he followed Bradlee to The Washington Post.

The author of six novels, as well as books on the Vietnam War and the U.S. Army, since 1970 he has devoted himself exclusively to fiction. Today Just and his wife Sarah divide their time between Andover and Martha's Vineyard in Massachusetts.

I joined the *Post* in April 1965, and for the next seven or eight months I fussed around doing general assignment stuff, feature stories, the kind of stuff that's written as opposed to reported, if you know what I mean. And I began to see that my career was at a weird sort of pause—it just didn't seem to be going anywhere. My marital life was also in disarray. I thought it would be a good idea to just absent myself, and Vietnam seemed about as far away from Washington, D.C., as I could get.

To be honest, I didn't know very much about Vietnam. The war was just sort of a nagging itch in the back of my head. I had some sense that it was important and that it was going to get more important, and I knew because of my Cyprus experience that if there was one thing I was good at it was reporting violence. Why I'm good at it I don't know, because I'm not a violent person myself. Violence is not my cup of tea. I'm certainly not attracted to it either as a solution for anything, or as theater, or for the various other reasons that people are attracted to violence. Maybe what I'm really good at is describing waste, and that's the way I look on violence, as a kind of ultimate waste.

I had the feeling that I was the right person to cover the story. I thought my age was right—too young for World War II or Korea, just marginally too old for Vietnam. I'd had some experience in Europe. Why that mattered to me I don't know, but it did. I'd had some experience covering American politics, which made an understanding of the situation somewhat easier. Coming out of the Midwest I was a little bit abstracted from Kennedy's Harvard, Eastern establishment clique—the Ivy League wasn't part of my background at all—and I thought in some psychic way that was valuable.

I guess I felt that I could approach it from a position of neutrality. I didn't have any hostages to fortune as far as the war was concerned. Neither was I a historian. My interest in history was an amateur's interest only. It was all too easy to become hypnotized by the French experience in Vietnam. The French experience was valuable to know about, it wasn't anything you should tuck away and pretend never happened, but the American experience was a very different experience. The American motivation for Vietnam was a very different motivation. I thought it was useful to enter the situation without a whole lot of preconceived notions, and I didn't have any.

And that was pretty much true for the bunch of us that got out there in '65, '66—Johnny Apple and Jon Randal for the *New York Times*, Dean Brelis at NBC, Bill Touhy for the *Los Angeles Times*. Altogether there were about twelve or fifteen of us. We were all thirty to thirty-five years old. We were all middle-class or upper-middle-class boys, more often than not from the Midwest. All more or less vaguely college educated, all with sort of similar careers abroad. In most cases we were out there on assignment. Some were in flight from unfortunate personal circumstances, but there weren't very many of us who were there for any reason of adventure or easy living. What *was* in the back of everybody's mind was that a good war would do you no harm. There was a lot of competition—some people much more competitive than others—but there was also a real sort of camaraderie. Some of the closest friends I have to this day are guys I came across out there. I've never known anything quite like it.

What was most striking about us as a group, though, was that there wasn't a radical among us, not an ideologue in the carload. When you grew up in the 1950s, ideology wasn't part of your baggage. Looking back on it, it might have been better if we'd been a little bit more ideological. The reporting might have been a little harder, a little tougher. But we were all really very moderate—politically moderate, culturally moderate, however you want to put it. And none of us was doing any grand strategic thinking.

I was out there for a year and a half and I can't remember a single discussion, not one, of why the Americans were in Vietnam. That was simply not the context in which we discussed the war. It never came up. What we were interested in was the fact that the Americans were there. And since they weren't likely to leave, the question became very simple—what was the situation on the ground? We were wholly and totally and 100 percent preoccupied with the world inside the boundaries of South Vietnam. We wanted to know how things were going in I Corps or II Corps, and what was happening with the Vietnamese 25th Division, and

whether Ky or Thieu could hang on, and was Westmoreland a good general or a bad one, and were they using the Special Forces in the proper way.

Some of the "old hands" that were there when I arrived, people like Charlie Mohr or Neil Sheehan or Peter Arnett, were possessed of a skepticism and a pessimism so deep as to be hardly credited. When I was in one of those late-night sessions when guys lean over the table and start shaking their finger in your face and saying this is what you've got to believe, or this is the way things really are, I took it with a grain of salt because I just wanted to see for myself. Of course in time I came to feel exactly as they did, but you had to find out for yourself.

And we just worked all the time. I operated out of Room 101 at the Caravelle Hotel, which served as my office and residence. I'd start work about ten in the

Enjoying a respite from the war, Ward Just shares a smile with a group of children in an orphanage near My Tho.

morning and typically wouldn't finish filing until eleven or twelve at night because of the time change. I spent a lot of time talking to the political people at the embassy, guys like Barry Zorthian at JUSPAO, and to as many Vietnamese as I could.

I had an extremely able interpreter, Vu Thuy Hoang, who, paradoxically, was a government censor. That made him enormously valuable to me because he could tell me what they were taking out of the local papers. And when you know what's being taken out, what's embarrassing them, then you know what they're really interested in. Occasionally he would walk in and say, "I think it would be a good idea if we went to the An Bang Pagoda tonight because I think something's going to be going on." And we'd go and sure enough there'd be a big Buddhist rally. He had ties into that kind of thing, too. So I had certain insights into what the government was feeling and what the opposition was thinking that in a couple of cases maybe put me a step ahead of my colleagues.

Sometimes stories were forced upon you. Particularly during the political crises during early- and mid-1966 it was obvious that what the Buddhists were up to was important and you ought to be there to cover it. Or when a large operation was being kicked off, the unit public information officer would find a way to let you know and you'd head up there to see what was going on. Other times you'd meet someone at dinner and he'd tell you about some district you'd never heard anything about before and you'd think, well shit, that's one province I've never seen and I might as well go down there and see what the situation is.

That's what we used to call it—"the situation." What we really meant was the level of violence. To what degree did the Vietcong hold sway, to what degree did the government hold sway? That's the scale you were measuring everything on. It was valuable to get around to as many places as you could, because the longer you were in the country the more you could use what you'd seen as a measuring stick. You could remember that you'd been in Binh Dinh Province in February, and if you went back in November you could compare what you'd seen the first time with what it was like now. Vietnam was this immense garden of veggies for a

reporter. Whatever furrow you were going down you were going to find something there. When you had an open date you'd look at the map and say, "Where haven't I been this time?"

I'd usually file at least once and often twice a day, but there was no pressure on me from the *Post*. They never once in a year and a half directed me to write a story. I often wouldn't even tell them what I was filing. I just filed stuff, and then the next day they would send me a play cable. They'd say, used your whatever it was, page one, and if they liked it particularly they'd add some nice line and that would be our only contact for weeks at a time. It was well known at the paper that the editor, Russ Wiggins, wasn't all that

The "old hands": David Halberstam (left), Malcolm Browne, and Neil Sheehan.

happy with what I was doing, but I never heard a whisper of it. There was never the slightest pressure from the paper nor any indication that I was doing anything but the most wonderful job they could possibly imagine. I've never had a relationship like that with a boss before, or, I might say, since. It was absolutely ideal.

In fact, life for an American correspondent in Saigon in 1966 could be quite agreeable. There were maybe a half-dozen restaurants in town with decent food and wine that were quite a lot of fun to go to. There were no security problems to speak of. And up until the end of 1966 there weren't all that many Americans either.

When you were in Saigon everybody went to the military briefing—the "Five O'Clock Follies"—and afterwards we'd go to the terrace at the Continental Palace where we'd all drink lemonade. The

Continental terrace was a terrific news exchange. We'd sit there and hash over what the hell was going on, what the situation was, what did this mean and that mean. Somebody just had an interview with Westmoreland and they'd come back and say this is what Westy had to say to me about this, and we'd sort of fit that together with whatever else was happening.

Then we'd decide what we were going to do that night. There would usually be a dinner party somewhere. And there was the famous house at 47 Phan Thanh Gian Street where a bunch of young foreign service officers hung out. Those would be wilder affairs. There'd be young Vietnamese women, a lot of booze, and everybody would stay up until three or four o'clock in the morning.

But mostly we were all working so goddamned hard that it wouldn't be at all unusual to hear of an action in the middle of dinner, pay the bill, get up, and go to it. Or if there was a particularly good story that you were on you'd finish dinner, go back to your office and work on it for another three or four hours, and then go around the corner to Ramuncho's and have a beer. Usually you'd know somebody there so you'd sit down and relate how you'd spent your day, and by then it was time to file and you'd go to bed and start all over again.

Three or four days a week I'd get up early and head off out into the countryside. There was simply a tremendous amount gained by being in the field. You got an understanding of the flow of battle, the morale of U.S. and ARVN troops, the quality of commanders and a little bit about what was on their minds, plus the overall security situation in that particular area. But most important, I think, it was a way of keeping yourself honest, of keeping your mind focused on the fact that it really was a war and a lot of people were dying. Sometimes in Saigon it would recede just a tad, particularly when you were talking to Saigon politicians. Not that you could ever completely forget that there was a war going on, but you wanted to keep it right in your frontal lobes, you wanted that right up front because that was the context for everything.

What I discovered was a war of really enormous tedium. I must have gone out fifteen times on patrols where no shot would be fired in anger. I once went out with one unit for three days. We not only didn't see any enemy, we never found anything—not a hut, not a tire track, nothing. It was just an endless walk in the hot sun. But interspersed in this oceanic boredom was some very serious business indeed. Then the violence was just crazy. Jesus, the air strikes, and they would call in the artillery and all the rest of it, and you suddenly realized you really were in the middle of a war. And it wasn't at all the guerrilla war they were talking about back in Washington. There was nothing guerrilla about it. I mean the Vietcong and the North Vietnamese may have been fighting a partially guerrilla war during the first months I was there, but we certainly were not.

I remember the heat, chewing salt pills endlessly, keeping your canteen filled up. I was in reasonably good shape then, but when you'd get back after a day of walking in the bush not only would your back be soaked through but there would be stains on your uniform, the signs of salt that had leached out of your body. I remember the helicopters flying over, the look of the vast empty spaces once you got back from the coast. The struggle in the highlands where the path was slippery, trying to get a purchase on the slope with a heavy pack on—not nearly as heavy as what the soldiers were carrying but heavy enough. Occasionally, not often, the sense of imminent danger, where you could actually smell it, smell the enemy, the sense of something ominous around the next turn. And at the end of the day taking out your flask, offering the captain a little drink if he'd like one, sitting back sipping the whiskey, talking about what a poor day it had been and what was likely to happen tomorrow.

Then at night, lying on my back in the jungle looking through the canopy. I'd never seen stars as brilliant as those. And the dead vegetation covering the ground. It was the goddamnest thing, it would be glowing, the ground would be glowing so it always seemed to be extremely light in the jungle at night. The men turning in their sleep, muttering, rustling, fantasies going through your head. And there you are in the middle of the jungle with 40 guys, or 140 guys, knowing there were supposed to be men alert on guard and knowing as well as you knew your own name that those bastards were asleep.

When you were covering a major operation you'd usually start at Division to get a sense of where everybody was, then down to Battalion or out overnight with a company, then back to Division. You'd try to square the circle, try to do the small thing but keep the large thing very much in mind so that you could relate the small thing back to it. I'd often go out with an aggressive battalion, usually sticking close to the battalion commander. Other times, depending on what I wanted to do, I'd try to find an interesting-looking company. And occasionally down to the platoon level. Less on the platoon level, though, because it was goddamned dangerous.

Everybody wanted to go out and see

Peter Arnett covered the war for the Associated Press from 1962 to 1975.

the Cav because it was a new concept in infantry tactics, the so-called vertical envelopment, the choppers and all that. And you kept going back to the Cav because they were a very active unit. When General Bill DePuy came in as commander of the 1st Infantry Division the same thing was true of him. In general you'd tend to go back where you knew people. I became very fond of a lot of the guys in the 101st Airborne, particularly at the light colonel level. So by the end of my tour I was spending a lot of time with them. I knew their area of operations, I knew their tactics, and I'd gotten to know a couple of their commanders so well that I was absolutely confident that they were telling me the truth as they knew it about their security situation.

Some of the officers loved to have me around for the publicity they thought it would get them. Some hated it because

they just didn't like the press. Others were literally indifferent. And still others, if they got to know you and like you, wanted you along for somebody to talk to, to tell them what was going on elsewhere in the country. By and large I would say they were more friendly than not because they had orders to be accommodating to correspondents. The grunts, the infantrymen, they were more amused than anything else. Most of them couldn't imagine what you were doing out there, what the hell you wanted. To them you were one more fuckin' officer. I mean it may say "Press," but it's just one more fuckin' officer.

The soldiers were difficult to get close to for one very good reason. There was this enormous cultural gap, not to put too fine a point on it. It didn't take long to realize that this was a poor boy's war. The people who were fighting the war in the bush on the grunt level were not people who had had the benefit of college or even the benefit of a very good high-school education. And in line units you found a larger proportion of blacks than you would have thought normal under the circumstances.

As soldiers, however, I thought they were probably as good as you were likely to find anywhere. They were alert, morale was good, they were well equipped and well led for the most part. And given the confusing nature of the mission, they performed it about as well as possible. I thought the performance of the private soldier was first-rate. Ditto on up to company grade and maybe battalion commander, lieutenant colonel. Beyond that, particularly as one got up into the general officer range and then the two- and three- and four-star generals, you found a lot more rigid thinking, a lot less ability or willingness to look at alternative ways of prosecuting the war.

The senior officers that I encountered were very confident of victory—sometimes recklessly so. I never met one senior field-grade officer, full colonel and up, who would admit to me any serious doubts. Some of them, particularly the ones who had been advisers, who'd been around for a while and were back for their third or fourth tour, they'd sometimes roll their eyeballs as if to say, "This doesn't look like it's going to fly," but never for publication and then not until the middle of '67. A few of them loved to quote the philosopher Hegel that after a time quantity becomes quality. They thought you could put so many men, so many machines, so many weapons of various kinds into the country that after a while the sheer weight of it would begin to tell.

And it was hard to believe in the beginning that it wouldn't. You'd go to Da Nang or Bien Hoa and see the American fighter squadrons. You'd look at all this equipment we had there and you'd wonder how an enemy could possibly withstand it. We had U-2s, we had F-111s, we had B-52s, we had the 7th Fleet out here and the Special Forces down there. It was really hard to believe that all that weight wouldn't make a difference. And it did make a difference in sheer numbers of people killed. But what in the end did that mean with an enemy that was literally prepared to fight to the last man? All you could do with all that firepower was kill people, and that wasn't enough against the Vietnamese. It may have been enough against the Germans in World War II. But it wasn't enough against the Vietnamese. In the last analysis the firepower, the search and destroy operations, the strategy of attrition, it all simply missed the point.

If there was one central problem which sat on all the other problems it was that the South Vietnamese government and the South Vietnamese army and the South Vietnamese people were not prepared to commit themselves, body and soul and heart, to the struggle. They simply were not prepared to engage in the way that they were going to have to engage in order to fight off a very determined and ideologically well-armored enemy inspired by revered leaders like Ho Chi Minh and Vo Nguyen Giap. There was nothing on the South Vietnamese side to counterbalance that. It required a real leader and they didn't have one, or at least none emerged. Certainly they were there somewhere back in the woodwork, but the particular structure of the South Vietnamese army and the South Vietnamese society never allowed them to come to the surface.

I used to go out with ARVN, not with any frequency because frankly they weren't engaged in very many operations when I was there. But one time Johnny Apple and I ran into General Cao Van Vien, the chairman of the Vietnamese General Staff, and we said to him we want to spend three days with the best

unit you've got in your army, absolutely top-drawer. So he laid us on with a battalion of the 15th Infantry Division way in the south in the delta. We went out with these clowns for a day, and it was an absolute parody of a Vietnamese operation. They stole every chicken in sight, they were chasing women, the battalion seemed to have no discipline whatsoever. They moved with such slowness and with such noise that anybody within a mile would know they were coming. And then, goddammit, at the end of the day they found a suspicious-looking house—and don't ask me what looked suspicious about it, they'd taken no fire, there was no evidence that the house was anything but a house—and goddamned if they didn't call in an air strike. It was an inventory of every complaint the Americans had about the South Vietnamese army for ten years, right there in this one unit which the chairman of the South Vietnamese General Staff had laid on as the best unit they had in the country.

Of course by that time we had virtually taken the war away from them. Americans were directing the war, running the war, supplying the war, devising the strategy and tactics of the war. Everywhere you looked there was this great American sea spreading over the country, and the tide was rising all the time. Ho Chi Minh called the Saigon government a puppet government and it really was in many ways, despite the elections and the constitution and all that. I'm sure that after a while a lot of Vietnamese just threw up their hands and said, "If they're going to do it anyway let them do it, and meanwhile we'll just try to figure out how we can survive."

And as the American commitment became greater and greater, the more the Vietnamese suspected that it was a mile wide and an inch deep. In a way, they turned out to be right. It seemed to me that Americans really didn't have the correct mentality for the situation. We didn't have anybody who spoke the language, who understood the myths of the society, the attitudes of the people. Of course, when I say that we didn't have the correct mentality I'm implying that if we had the correct mentality somehow the war might have been won. But I don't believe that with any kind of mentality the war could have been won. I don't think it was winnable. At all. Under any circumstance.

The trouble was that American officials in Vietnam, civilian and military, were so fixated on reporting progress that it blinded them. Some of it was the pressure they felt from their superiors. An infantry officer learned goddamned quickly that he'd better find progress or he was going to be the oldest captain in the army. But for the civilians, the embassy people, the CIA, the AID, it was more subtle than we've got to report good news, much more subtle. A lot of people in the American government really believed in the Vietnam effort, and if you believe in something it gives you a certain cast of mind.

I used to have arguments all the time with Dan Ellsberg who was attached to the Lansdale group.* Ellsberg maintained that American officials in Vietnam were lying. He said you will go out there and they will talk to you and they will be lying. But the longer I stayed out there the more I decided that they were not lying. From time to time, yes, somebody would tell you a lie, so what else is new. And the "Five O'Clock Follies," the military briefings, were absolute bullshit. On the other hand, the political stuff you'd get from some of the people in the embassy was often first-rate. I thought that within the limits of their employment they were being as candid as they could. In '66 and '67 there wasn't that terrible fracture between the civilian officials and the journalists there had been in '63 or would come later after Tet. Relations were relatively harmonious. The main problem was not officials telling you a lie, it was officials misapprehending. And not because they were knaves or fools but because that was their job—they were being paid to force progress. To them something goes forward one inch and it looks like a mile. To a journalist coming in it looks pretty much like what it is—an inch.

That's not to say that the journalists were always right, because we weren't. Most American correspondents had bloody little understanding of classic infantry tactics or military organization. I learned all that stuff but it took me a

* A team of Defense Department analysts headed by General Edward Lansdale that investigated pacification programs and preparations for the 1966 election to the South Vietnamese constituent assembly. In 1970 Daniel Ellsberg would become famous as the man who leaked the Defense Department's secret history of the war—"The Pentagon Papers"—to *The New York Times*.

while, and I would have been much better equipped as a reporter if I had had some understanding in the first place. I don't think we did a good job of covering the GI's war. Reporting civilian casualties was not done as aggressively as it should have been. We had relatively little success in getting inside the Saigon government and figuring out what Thieu and Ky really had in mind, nor were we able to find some way to talk to the VC in the South and get some reading on what they saw as a solution to the war other than total victory.

Nonetheless, I think the journalists tended to be more accurate about the overall situation than either the military or civilian officials and for two very good reasons. First, they had no stake in either pessimism or optimism. Most reporters were indifferent, and I think indifference gave a rather clearer vision than commitment. And second, a careful, attentive journalist was the only American in the country who could look at things all the way around. You could look at the American military, you could look at the GVN military, you could look at the American civilian effort, you could look at what was going on politically. As a result, with all these impressions coming in, you could form a general judgment about the state of the war in South Vietnam.

No one else could do that. Westmoreland certainly couldn't do that. He didn't get into the roots of it far enough. The ambassador couldn't do it because he had no firsthand understanding of the military and security situation. There was something about one set of ears, and one set of eyeballs, and one brain collecting all this stuff, somebody with a memory, somebody who knew the local people and the situation, that simply got you farther down the road to understanding what the hell was going on.

What has to be stressed, however, was the difficulty of knowing anything in South Vietnam, and this applied to the journalists as well as the officials. We were always, all of us, grabbing at shadows. The war was so confusing, the definition of success or progress was always in doubt. You've got a very shadowy enemy with a mysterious infrastructure and you're trying to gauge your security situation on the basis of reading your own people as opposed to really serious interrogations of the enemy. That's hard. It was hard for

the officials, it was hard for the journalists. It wasn't as if you had a series of numbers that you could add up and get the correct answer. It was these vague will-o'-the-wisps that you were trying to pull out of the air. Sometimes it seemed as though the very best you could do was get a little bit of the drift of things. It was really a hall of mirrors out there.

The complexity of the story was daunting, but I looked on it as a terrific challenge. I thought you could write your way out of it. I thought you could write about the war in all of its manifold and manifest ambiguities, that you could put together a piece in such a way that a reader would finish it and say, "Hey, Jesus, it really is cloud cuckoo land," which in many ways it was. We talk very seriously about the war and criticize each other for this and that, but the fact of the matter is that the atmosphere there really was cuckoo most of the time because of the difficulty of finding anything you could believe.

Still, if you were there long enough you began to have a certain amount of confidence in your own judgment. If you lived in it the way say Apple or Touhy or Dean Brelis or I did, or guys like Charlie Mohr and Peter Arnett, if you were really in the belly of the whale as far as we were, you had some sense that at least the piece of it that you were reporting was accurate. You realized that nobody had 360-degree vision, but the part of it that you'd chosen to write about, you were getting that right.

Although spending time in the field had its attraction for a journalist, it also had its dangers. Accompanying a reconnaissance patrol in the mountains near Dak To, Just was wounded by a grenade during an ambush in which several men were killed. A fragment of that grenade was removed from his hand in the summer of 1985, nineteen years later.

When you get that kind of feeling it's like riding a wave. It was exhilarating. When I came back to the States for a month of home leave in the middle of 1966, I watched television for one full week, switching back and forth from the battle coverage on ABC to NBC to CBS. And to me television, as good as it was, didn't make it half so horrible as it was in fact. In the first place, the blood didn't look like blood. And you couldn't smell anything, and there wasn't that tremendous atmosphere of violence. I thought you could really write it better than it was depicted in pictures. So whenever I got in a situation like that I just had to write the hell out of it.

The one thing I was after was that when the Joint Chiefs of Staff were down there in the war room and moved a pin on a map somewhere they would by God understand, as well as I could do it, what that meant for the private soldier. I wanted to show them the results, the bodies. The person who was always in the back of my mind was Robert McNamara, as though I were saying, "Okay, Mr. Secretary, this is what it is. You want to go up and take this village or take that hill, this is what happens to the people who do it." And it made me happy to know that when I wrote a piece it would show up right on the front page of the paper where the people you wanted to see it would read it.

Professionally it was very gratifying. But by the end of my tour I had come to see the war as a momentous error, a majestic tragedy for everybody involved, not the least the South Vietnamese. After Tet it almost became irrelevant to me who won. The tragedy was so great, the bodies had piled up so high, that it almost didn't seem to matter who came out ahead. Whether the hero fell on his own sword or had a sword thrust into him, it didn't seem to make much difference. The hero in this case was a country and the country was dead. It didn't matter who had the nominal supervision of the corpse.

The war was a tremendous turning point in my life. After a short return visit to Vietnam in the fall of 1967, I came back and immediately began to cover the 1968 presidential election campaign. It was just impossible. My interest in politics had once been so high, now I couldn't take any of it seriously. It all seemed to me such a trivial exercise as opposed to what I'd been seeing, which I thought was of really supreme and profound importance and, from my point of view, something truly worth doing. I finished out the campaign and then worked as an editorial writer for a year and a half before leaving the newspaper business. But I wasn't worth a damn as a reporter after I left Vietnam because no story could measure up to that one.

I think it made us all quite perverse. Far from politicizing me, it gave me a kind of distrust of the political process that I'd never had before. It made me an extreme skeptic of the ability of government to do anything well, and it brought me to the notion that Americans just shouldn't mess around with other people's lives. It also produced in me a pessimism, a fatalism about human nature that's been very hard to root out.

I've spent a lot of books, a lot of print trying to explain the war to myself, but it remains very complicated. It's like a thread that goes through my whole mind, my whole memory, so that when I pull at one thing something else jiggers off at the other edge. You know that picture that Salvador Dali painted, *The Persistence of Memory*, with the dripping watches? Well, Vietnam is kind of like a dripping watch ticking away. I have a hunch that the war hasn't released the last of its surprises, an odd feeling that there's a shoe yet to fall somewhere. God knows what it is. It won't be a happy one, I can tell you that. ∎

"The thing everybody told me was that you've got to get out of Saigon. It had become a kind of cliche, but maybe that was because it was true. I knew I would get out into the countryside right away and spend as much time out there as I could. Which is what I did."

Gordon Fowler

Corporal, United States Marine Corps
Combat Correspondent, I Corps
January 1967–January 1968

Gordon Fowler is the son of well-known Texas journalist Wick Fowler. In 1965 Gordon had a child, worked at a TV station during the day, played rock 'n' roll at night, and was successfully ignoring events in South Vietnam. When he divorced, however, within a week his draft status changed from 3A to 1A and he was ordered to report for induction. Gordon survived vicious combat and three wounds while covering a number of Marine Corps operations. He returned to Texas and with his mother and sister built a multi-million dollar business packaging and selling "Wick Fowler's Two Alarm Chili." Fowler also has a growing reputation as a painter. Many of his canvases deal with Vietnam themes because, he has found, "If you can't talk about the war, painting offers a safe environment to express your feelings." He is married to Austin-based rhythm and blues singer Marcia Ball.

After infantry training I got orders to Camp LeJeune, North Carolina. We were supposed to cover the 2d Marine Division, but all they had us doing was mopping the office, pulling a lot of guard, and writing hometown news releases—real shitty duty. Meanwhile, guys kept getting orders for Vietnam. By that time, my curiosity was up. I'd interviewed a lot of guys who'd been in Vietnam. I wanted to go cover the war. I wanted to be Hemingway. Also, my father was a newspaper and a war correspondent in World War II attached to the 36th Division, the old Texas National Guard outfit, and was kind of a war hero when he got home. An acquaintance of mine who had just got married had orders to Vietnam. Since we were the same rank, same time in grade, everything, I asked to take his place. They didn't really give a damn as long as somebody filled the post, so they changed the orders and sent me instead.

Our office at Da Nang was just below the command bunker for the 1st Marine Division. We had our own hut down at the bottom of the hill, an area where the lifers didn't like to go because of the mosquitoes and the mud. But Division was so chickenshit and lifers so bad that you'd rather take your chances in the field than take your chances at Division. We had to fight a two-front war. In the bush we fought the NVA and in the rear we fought the lifers. I always believed in the old cavalry adage that you feed the horses, then you feed the men, then you feed the officers. These guys had it backwards. So I wangled orders to Chu Lai. I thought it would be better because it was a smaller operation. That and I was getting restless and wanted to get on with it. I was really gung ho to get out and see what the war was all about, both as a journalist and as a Marine. I just wanted to get out and mix it up. I didn't know any better.

Chu Lai was just really hot and boring, miserable conditions—110 degrees, humid. You'd stay in a hot tent on the side of a bare hill with no shade and just have to sit there all day waiting for something to happen. And if you sat there long enough a lifer would come along and put you to work filling sandbags. The Marine Corps had taken a whole bunch of staff, gunnery and first sergeants, and made them temporary officers. So you saw a lot of gray-haired second lieutenants. Some of those guys were pretty good but a lot of them were just terrible. They had us cleaning up the area and running personal errands for them. Their greatest contribution to the Marine Corps was getting drunk at the officers club.

I was getting real bored and real restless, so after a couple of weeks in Chu Lai I decided to get things off dead center. I walked over to the command bunker one day and asked the operations officer, "What's going on today?" He said not much but there was a recon going out in about two hours. He pointed them out so I went over and explained what I did and the CO said, "Do you want to go with us?" They taped my dog tags, made up my face, issued me an M14 that could fire automatic, loaded me down with something in the neighborhood of eighty or ninety pounds of gear—extra ammo, claymore mines, chow—and then a soft hat which they all wore. I said, "Well, I don't want to be a drag on this thing." And the captain said, "Actually, we could use the firepower." I knew right then that I might have screwed up. The patrols were not too secret and the gooks knew when you were leaving. It was only a seventeen-man patrol, and there wasn't much support once you were out there. I'd stepped in it, but I couldn't back out then.

We landed on the side of a big hill and fanned out and very quietly made our way to the top and sat up there all afternoon. Sure enough, about three o'clock there was movement down below us in the paddies. Just like in the movies this column started moving out of the tree line single file. Three were carrying weapons, the rest of them were carrying supplies. Most of them had on the conical hats and black pjs, but a couple of them had on khaki. It was like living in a fantasy world sitting up on this hill watching this go on. Our AO started calling in artillery, and we just lay there and hammered the hell out of them with 155s. We called in a couple of air strikes too. We didn't sweep the area because they decided that we'd been spotted, so right after the air strikes we made our way down to this LZ and a CH-46 came in and picked us up. We went back and the guys started playing touch football. I couldn't believe it. We went out and there's the enemy and we called in artillery and killed a bunch of them and then we left and nobody got hurt and now we're all playing football. This is unreal.

Top. *Gordon Fowler interviews an officer of the 1st Marine Division in Da Nang, November 1967.*

Above. *Elements of the 5th Marines on patrol during Operation Swift in the Que Son Valley, September 1967.*

I was feeling pretty salty because I had been out with recon and I'd been out with the 7th Marines. I had gotten a taste of combat, but I really hadn't been scared bad enough to realize what was really happening. A certain amount of naiveté goes a long way over there. Then one day in early June I walked into the S-5's (civic action) office and he said, "They're looking for you at operations. They're going out in about thirty minutes." So I grabbed a pack and a pistol and a couple of canteens and a helmet and jogged down to the end of Hill 55. What had happened was the 5th Marines had

walked into a shit storm out in the Que Son Valley about 25 miles southwest of Tam Ky. They had a division on them and they were getting cut up. The Que Son Valley was a terrible area. It was bad for the French, it was bad for the Marines, and it was bad for the army later on. It was a big NVA stronghold with lots of tunnels, a valley with high mountains all the way around it, and a lot of places for ambush sites.

I was going with Delta 1/7, and it was just getting dark when I caught up with them waiting for the chopper. It didn't look good. When you look around at a company of Marines and they're not talking and laughing and cutting up and they're real quiet, you know you got problems. Everybody knew we were walking into it. We were supposed to go out and somehow or other in the middle of the night relieve the pressure on the 5th Marines. So we loaded up on CH-46s and took off. I based myself with headquarters' platoon because that way you know what is happening, you are right by the radios and the corpsmen and everything that is going on and you can hear about it right away.

Anyway, I jumped on the chopper and we got out there and we unloaded in a hot LZ and all I had was a .45, which was my mistake. But we cleaned them out and then formed a column and started walking. We could see down into the valley, which was completely lit up. It looked like daytime. There were flare ships up, gunships shooting, air strikes were going in. The whole horizon was glowing. It looked like something out of the apocalypse. It was like watching a huge Fourth of July show until you realized you were walking into it. We were going to go over there where all this was happening, right then.

We went in single file spread out about ten or twelve meters apart, one company of Marines walking into this inferno. We walked about two hours—it must have been getting on towards eleven, twelve o'clock at night—and got to this big graveyard with all these pagodas around the graves on this little hill. Sure enough, we weren't there more than twenty seconds and the NVA started mortaring us. I had been in some mortar attacks but this was incredible. We were just absolutely bracketed. They didn't have to fire a round to see where they were hitting, they already had the coordinates worked out. They were just waiting for us to get there. I would guess six 60s opened up on us. You could hear the tubes thumping out there. They weren't very far out, I mean these guys must have been firing straight up. The first barrage killed four guys within a two-yard radius of me, all of them command post guys. I wrapped myself around one of those round graves. They're about six or eight feet across and humped up, and I just wrapped myself around the edge of it to get some protection.

This was the first real bad action I'd been in. Everybody was getting hit and hurt and killed, people were screaming. They were raking us by then with machine guns from our left. I didn't have an entrenching tool, didn't have a rifle, and was just laying there wondering what the hell to do. We were still too bunched up, but you couldn't get up and move. You didn't want to raise a finger. Being mortared is the worst thing in the world because those things come straight down,

and if it comes on top of you it doesn't matter if you're in a hole or not.

Then it sort of quieted down. There was a ten- or twenty-second lull and I raised up to look around for a better place to be. The minute I raised up, this black Marine jumped right beside me to move and a 60 landed right at his feet. He was between me and the 60, less than ten feet away. All I remember is his silhouette against the explosion. It blew him over on top of me and I caught a bunch of shrapnel in my shoulders, back, and neck. Knocked me silly and blew my helmet off and killed the black Marine. So I had him on top of me, and I knew I was hurt and things were getting worse.

I was in shock for awhile. I said to a guy beside me, "Hey, am I dead or what?" One of the things that still haunts me is remembering lying out there with the mortars coming in and small-arms fire and machine guns raking our position, and I'm thinking we're supposed to be the most powerful country on earth

Marines carry wounded buddies to a waiting helicopter during a "medevac" operation in 1967.

and this shouldn't happen to Americans. I'm sure it's always been this way in every other war that we've ever fought. We're still out there slugging it out twenty meters away from a bunch of other guys.

The Marine discipline must really pay off though because after the initial shock was over people started to do their jobs. Squads were moving out in fire team rushes trying to knock out the machine guns and dig in out on the perimeter. The corpsmen were working like mad, and the officers were getting people into work parties and they were getting the wounded out of the way. It went on until about four o'clock in the morning. They probed us off and on and the mortars kept coming in, but evidently our taking pressure off the 5th Marines had worked to some degree because the whole area started quieting down a bit.

By nine o'clock I realized I was going back, but there were a lot of people hurt worse than me. I remember the captain said, "Let's get these KIAs out of here, it's bad for morale." I helped load the bodies; it was damned sure bad for my morale. It was the first time I had walked in with a lot of guys and a bunch of them died.

After we got all the dead and serious wounded out, there were nine of us walking wounded left, and they put me in charge of them because I was in better shape than the rest. They put us in an old H–34 which got up to about treetop level, lost power, and smashed back into the ground, the next thing to a crash. It threw everybody into a big pile and hurt everybody all over again. Finally we got into the air. They didn't know where to take us, I guess, so they landed us at Tam Ky. When we got to the LZ there were body bags stretched out for about a hundred feet. There were a lot of flies and by that time the bodies were starting to smell. I was starting to stiffen up and get sore and I was exhausted mentally and physically. It was just one of the worst days of my life.

Finally, I went over and found somebody that proved to be in charge and I said, "I've got nine wounded here, what do I do with them?" He said, "Well, we can't take care of you here, we're full up. Let me see if I can get you into Chu Lai." So we waited two hours in the sun with these dead guys and they finally got us a chopper, a CH–46 this time which was better, and took us to Chu Lai. They're full

The telegram informing Gordon Fowler's mother of the first time he was wounded, June 1967.

up too, but it takes about an hour to realize they can't take care of us. After awhile some colonel comes out and says, "Take them to Da Nang." So we pile back on this 46 that takes us all the way to Da Nang from Chu Lai. By this time it's late afternoon and I'm really starting to hurt and the guys with fractures still hadn't any morphine.

They landed us at an air force hospital down by the runway. This place looks like something out of one of the hospital shows, whitewashed and it's real tidy and orderly and the doctors look like they're all stateside. Everything is manicured and they had grass and sidewalks. These two doctors came out and this nurse and I'm standing there with ... I'm talking about some really ragged-ass guys. By this time most of them didn't have shirts; some of them didn't have pants because they'd had their pants cut off because of shrapnel wounds. Nobody wore underwear because it was hot. This spotless air force officer came over and I told him who I was and that I had all these wounded guys and we needed some help. And he said, "Well, I hate to say this, but I don't have the facilities to take care of you. We treat malaria and dysentery and appendicitis. We're not equipped for this." Now I'm standing there with this detachment of wounded guys thinking this is pretty ridiculous. Finally, they had a little conference over on the side and decided it would be okay if they gave us some morphine, especially the guys with the fractures. About thirty minutes later they finally sent a truck over from the 1st Medical Battalion, which was just at the other end of the runway.

We got there and they knew what to do with us. They cut your remaining clothes off, x-ray you, and put you on a table. I was sitting there waiting to be treated and this navy doctor said, "Fowler, I want you to sit there and look straight ahead. I do not want you to move." I said, "Yes, sir," and then he operated on me for quite a while. He probably cut on me for forty-five minutes. He gave me a local but it hurt like hell, it was excruciating. A little while later he came around and said, "I want you to look at your x ray." I looked at this picture of my neck area and it showed this razor blade looking thing about the size of a thumbnail leaning up against my jugular vein. I guess if I'd jerked my head one way or

the other, I would have just bled to death. I don't remember much after that. It all caught up to me and I pretty well conked out. When I woke up they had to pull me off of a lieutenant commander chaplain. He had come by and evidently I was having a nightmare. He bent over to see what was the matter and I latched onto him. I was still out there, I guess.

It took the guys from my section all night and most of the next day to find out where I was. They had guys looking for me everywhere and finally found me just right down the hill from where we bivouacked. I'm a guitar player and I play blues and country, always did. And I had this old Yamaha that I carried around all over the war. Anyway, they came down the next day and brought my guitar to me in the hospital. The guys from the 7th Marines came by too, just piling me up with whiskey and cigarettes. They're pretty good to you when you get wounded.

But from that summer of '67 on, the war was never the same again. We were now clashing with the big NVA units, and we knew that we weren't playing games and we weren't Hemingway and we weren't going to get a Pulitzer Prize or anything. We were out there and we were going to be Marine Corps, and the best thing we could try to do for ourselves would be to stay alive the rest of the time we were there. I realized then that it really was war and that people really were dying. ∎

Famous for his recipe even then, Fowler delighted in hosting "chili parties" for the men in his unit.

Long Way from Home

Like other soldiers in other wars, Americans who went to Vietnam often wanted to communicate their experiences to others. Here are but a few examples of the torrent of poems produced by those who served in the war.

I Wanna Go To Viet-Nam

"I Wanna Go To Viet-Nam
I Wanna Kill A Viet-Cong

With A Knife Or With A Gun
Either Way Will Be Good Fun

Stomp'Em, Beat'Em, Kick'Em In The Ass
Hide Their Bodies In The Grass

Airborne, Ranger, C.I.B.
Nobody's Gonna Fuck With Me

But If I Die In The Combat Zone
Box Me Up And Ship Me Home

Fold My Arms Across My Chest
Tell My Folks I Done My Best

Place A Bible In My Hand
For My Trip To The Promised Land"

—Army Marching Cadence

Flight

Good morning,
we hope you have enjoyed
Flight 327
on the proud bird
with the golden tail,
and hope you will be
flying again with us soon

It is 10:35 am in Da Nang
and the current temperature
is one hundred and eight degrees

—from *Meat Dreams*
by Robert Borden

Greetings

Each morning at six,
radios started with
"Goooooooooooooood morning,
Vietnam!"

a cheery, insane greeting
to a day
some would not live through,

a curious blend
of comedy and horror,
like a fighter bomber
with a smile painted on it

—from *Meat Dreams*
by Robert Borden

And so

and so
en masse
the marines have landed
bringing with them
a high state of nervousness
and inexperience
and my little city
is not itself anymore
whenever american military people
come into any land
the people smile and cheer
the americans are touched by their sincerity
the people's hands go out to the american
and their eyes light up like neon bulbs
spelling out

welcome suckers
  ★ ★ ★
it certainly makes a person feel proud
to stand back and look at america this way
to see our ambassadors of the
    democratic way of life
build the vietnamese economy
and raise their aggressive spirit
so they will be better equipped to fight
that poor viet cong guerrilla
that stands on the same pier
with his palms up to the same americans
it is hard to tell palms apart
americans are certainly democratic

—Dick Shea

The Next Step

The next step you take
may lead you into an ambush.

The next step you take
may trigger a tripwire.

The next step you take
may detonate a mine.

The next step you take
may tear your leg off at the hip.

The next step you take
may split your belly open.

The next step you take
may send a sniper's bullet through your brain.

The next step you take.
The next step you take.

The next step.
The next step.

The next step.

—W. D. Ehrhart

Reptiles of Southeast Asia

Reptiles of Southeast Asia

There are two kinds of snakes in Vietnam
Mr. One Step
And Mr. Two Step
Named for how far you go after being bitten

—Larry Rottman

Night Patrol

Another night coats the nose and ears:
smells of fish and paddy water,
smoke from cooking fires and stale urine
drift uneasily, cloaked in silence;
the marketplace deserted, shuttered
houses, empty paths, all cloaked in silence;
shadows bristle.

Our gravel-crunching boots tear great
holes in the darkness, make us wince
with every step. A mangy dog
pits the stomach; rifles level,
nervous fingers hit the safety catch.

—W. D. Ehrhart

Front Street

His distrust of trees came in the war
he said, every night watching
looking them over before bedding down.
Birds deceived by searchlights
perked up, sang songs
in dust covered branches.

Couldn't walk in the open
or under trees
because of snipers, and
even now refuses the sidewalk
that busy elms have made
into a tunnel on Front Street,
refuses except when walking
his four year old daughter
to the far corner and back,
returning always with a blot
of wetness on his pants
and the squallings of a child—
her hand held too tight too tight daddy

—Frank Higgins

Early Years
1961-1968

They called themselves "grunts," this new generation of American soldiers, a term that derived from the sound they made hauling their packs under the unrelenting tropical sun of Southeast Asia. Inspired by a president's idealistic rhetoric, they came to Vietnam to win what they assumed would be a quick war for freedom. What they found was a strange world of jungles and paddy fields, primitive villages and uncertain allies, determined foes, and sudden, savage, often random violence. Back home, the war's administrators remained confident of their mission, the public largely supportive of the U.S. commitment. But for the young men who actually fought the war there emerged a different recognition. Begun with such enthusiasm, the struggle for the "hearts and minds" of the Vietnamese people had by 1968 become a grim, slow war of attrition whose end was nowhere in sight.

At first, American troops served as noncombatants and advisers. South Vietnamese marines ferried into battle by U.S. Marine helicopters disembark in the Mekong Delta, August 1962.

Opposite. The beginning of American combat involvement. Marines of the 9th Expeditionary Brigade splash ashore at Da Nang's Red Beach Two, March 8, 1965.

Above. Marines share C-rations during Operation Prairie, a mission to engage and destroy NVA units invading Quang Tri Province, October 1966.

Operation Prairie. Above. Members of the 1st Marine Division carry their wounded during a firefight near the southern edge of the DMZ. Opposite. Two members of the 3d Marine Division fire on NVA defenders of battle-ravaged Hill 484.

Following pages. A camouflaged A-1E Skyraider drops a phosphorous bomb on a South Vietnamese village, 1966.

The battle of Dak To was a shock to many of those predicting an imminent American victory. Beginning in late November 1967, it took U.S. paratroopers twenty-two days to dislodge the four NVA regiments surrounding the town at the northern tip of II Corps. Here the paratroopers regroup during a lull in the fighting.

Above. Paratroopers leap from their plane during Operation Junction City on March 3, 1967. The airborne assault in Tay Ninh Province was the first U.S. combat jump of the war.

Opposite. VC suspects are herded into a U.S. Marine helicopter during Operation Deckhouse V, 1966.

The siege of the U.S. combat base at Khe Sanh, coupled with the Tet offensive of January 1968, dealt a telling blow to the optimism that had earlier characterized the American war effort. Here a Marine scrambles to remove burning debris from ammunition pallets as enemy rounds pound the base at Khe Sanh.

Reassessments

The Tet offensive launched by the Communists in January 1968 brought into question the conduct of the war and America's goals in Indochina. It also helped end Democratic control of the White House. Lyndon Johnson declined to run for re-election and Richard Nixon became president with hints of a secret plan to end the war. Some signs suggested the war's last days were in sight: The bombing of North Vietnam ceased, troop withdrawals were announced, and negotiations with Hanoi began. However, the North Vietnamese Army took over the war from the shattered Vietcong and U.S. casualties mounted even faster than before. The protracted combat, escalating costs, and stalled talks sparked protest among groups that had once favored American intervention. With battlefield victory no longer an objective, turmoil spread to the military as many soldiers began to question their mission. No one wanted to be the last to die in a war Americans no longer supported.

U.S. Marines wait as an airstrike destroys enemy positions in Hue during the Tet offensive, February 1968.

Norman L. Russell

*Infantryman
Charlie Company, 4th Battalion
9th Infantry, 25th Infantry Division
November 1968–November 1969*

Norman Russell was born on August 9, 1948, in Montague, Massachusetts, the youngest of eight children. When he was twelve years old his family moved to Indian Rocks Beach, Florida, a small town outside Tampa-Saint Petersburg. After graduating from high school in June 1966, he moved back to Massachusetts, "floated around for about a year," and eventually landed a job as a reporter for the Greenfield Recorder. Drafted into the army in the spring of 1968, he served with the 25th Infantry Division from November 1968 to November 1969. He now lives in South Ashfield, Massachusetts, with his wife and three children. A free-lance writer, he hopes soon to publish a full-length account of his Vietnam experience under the title, The Year the Mets Won the Pennant.

I was only about nine months old when he died, so I never knew the guy at all. I just knew this sort of mythic legend, this persona—my Father—almost like a deity or something because he was never spoken of. But that's the way it is when you commit suicide in a small New England village. There was an air of shame attached to it, at least back then.

I got the story in bits and pieces over the years from my older brothers and sisters. I found out that my father had volunteered for the army after World War II broke out, even though he had six kids at the time and could have exempted himself, and that he served as an infantryman in Europe. Supposedly he was a truck driver with Patton for a while until he took shrapnel wounds to the head. Then they shipped him back to England and eventually reassigned him to an antiaircraft battery.

After the war he had these terrible headaches from the head wound, and he was haunted by the memory of an incident in England when his battery shot down an American transport plane that failed to identify itself. He also lost his job. Before the war he worked as a lead engraver, but lead became scarce during the war and the company he worked for went out of business. When he came back he ended up getting a job as a printer at

the *Recorder*, but it wasn't the same kind of highly skilled labor. Apparently that really bothered him, and he became very depressed. Between the combination of things, he finally just decided to pack it in, I guess. Another KIA—three years after.

But even though no one talked about him, or maybe because no one talked about him, I was intensely curious about him. The unspoken things are always the most powerful things, right? And I think perhaps on some unconscious level that probably influenced my decision to go to Vietnam, since the one way I could know him a little bit was to share a common experience like going to war.

Consciously I didn't feel right about the idea. I didn't like violence, and I was opposed to the concept of war. I was the kind of kid who went out of his way to avoid fistfights in school. So when my draft notice arrived in the spring of 1968 I thought seriously about ducking out of it—going to Canada, whatever. But in the end I decided I couldn't. I knew that if I didn't go someone else would take my place. And I didn't want to feel the rest of my life that I had avoided a difficult and dangerous task at someone else's expense. It just went against my basic feelings of human responsibility, my sense of duty.

I suppose for some people who fled to Canada or went to jail it was a courageous act. But for a large number of those who avoided the war, I've come to realize, it was purely a matter of self-interest. They didn't want to take a chance on getting hurt. They were the same as anyone who allows an injustice to occur and doesn't stand up to speak about it because he might lose his job or because his neighbors might disapprove. I still don't respect that kind of civic behavior. On the other hand, we were all just kids at the time, and you can't expect too much out of a bunch of kids.

I spent the summer of 1968 doing my basic training at Fort Benning, Georgia. We weren't assigned an MOS until the very end. I think it was early August. I remember standing there and getting this piece of paper that said "11-Bravo." So I asked, "What's that mean?" and somebody said, "Infantry." I felt like I'd just received a death sentence. They immediately piled us on buses and drove us eighty miles across the border to Fort McClellan, Alabama, for advanced individual training. Didn't give us a chance to run. Probably just as well.

After AIT they gave us a month's leave. I took a bus down to Florida to visit my mother for a few days. While I was there I went to an antiwar demonstration with a couple of friends from high school. This was in late October '68, at the height of the presidential election campaign. Spiro Agnew had come down to pump up the Old Faithfuls. In the middle of his speech some guy burned his draft card and the fire marshals came and dragged him out, leaving four of us holding these antiwar signs. Spiro went wild—youth of America gone to hell, that sort of thing. Afterwards, an old man jumped me, knocked me down. Here I was, a week from the war, GI-shaved head and all, and he's shouting "Coward! Traitor!" over and over until I finally managed to get the hell out of there.

Then I flew up to Massachusetts to visit my old friends, the ones I'd known since boyhood. I remember it was a very sad time. I remember saying good-bye to people, and I was firmly convinced that I'd never come back. It wasn't some melodramatic thing; I just really thought that I'd never live through it.

Next thing I knew I was in San Francisco, waiting for the plane that would take me to the war. The night before we shipped out they offered us a one-evening pass, on the stipulation that we went in uniform. I'd never been to San Francisco before, the mecca of our generation at the time, so I was really interested in doing that. I put on my dress uniform, went out, and started walking around the streets. Immediately I attracted a crowd and got trapped on a street corner by a bunch of long-haired hippies. And one guy came up, pressed his face in mine, and started screaming, "That's it, man, Kill! Kill! Blood! Kill!"

So in a couple of weeks I went from being a coward and a traitor to a killer. But that's the way America was in 1968. It was just extreme reactions, one side or the other.

I left for Vietnam in November 1968. Landed at Tan Son Nhut, then on to Long Binh for processing, and finally up to Cu Chi to join the 25th Infantry Division—"Tropic Lightning." At Cu Chi we were broken down into our individual units, and I got assigned to Charlie Company, 4th Battalion, 9th Infantry.

I'll never forget those first few days. There I was, obviously a New Guy—you could always tell the New Guys because their uniforms were clean and their boots shiny and they still hadn't adjusted to the heat—and these short-timers would come by and ask where I was going. So I'd tell them, "Charlie Company, 4th of the 9th." And they would call their friends over, point to me, and laugh: "Hey, man, this guy's going to 'Suicide Charlie.' Kiss your ass good-bye, mother, 'cause you're dead."

It turned out that "Suicide Charlie" had just been annihilated again—third time in the last year—so there was about fifty of us scheduled to go in as replacements. As I was going through the line to receive my orders, one of the clerks noticed that I'd been a newspaper reporter. Well, as always in the army, people who could type were in short supply, so this guy called me out of the line and asked if I'd like to be a clerk. And of course I immediately said yes because at that point I would have done almost anything to get that 11-B off my name. The clerk told me to wait while he made the necessary arrangements. But when he came back a half-hour later he said, "Sorry, we got orders this morning. Anybody assigned to Charlie Company has to go to Charlie Company. We can't take anybody out." Apparently there were guys going AWOL to Saigon rather than serve with the company. So instead of becoming a clerk I became a rifleman.

But that's the way Vietnam was. So much depended on chance, on specific time and place, on where you were and when you were there. I remember running into a few guys from AIT when I got back to Tan Son Nhut to fly home, and they were laughing and joking about the year they'd spent in the delta. You'd have thought they'd been on a picnic or something. And I was a nervous wreck, because it hadn't been that way for me at all. Not at all.

I spent most of my year in Tay Ninh Province, right along the Cambodian border. Our job, basically, was to interdict the southernmost entrance of the Ho Chi Minh Trail. By and large we fought a regular conventional war, big pitched battles against regular NVA soldiers—207th and 208th Regiments of the 9th NVA Division, if I remember correctly. The "crack," as we called them. They had

William Russell, Norm Russell's father, shortly before he joined the war in Europe in 1943.

On leave after completing AIT (advanced individual training), Private Russell poses in uniform outside his mother's home in Indian Rocks Beach, Florida, in late October 1968.

haircuts, clean uniforms, and were well equipped. And they'd come in a couple of thousand strong and try to wipe us out. One company, a hundred guys.

The first battle I was involved in took place just before Christmas. They'd taken us by helicopter to this spot right on the border and had us build a network of trench lines and underground bunkers that was virtually invisible from ground level. Called it Mole City. Supposedly they were experimenting with a new concept of infantry defense. Make it more difficult for the enemy to fix our position. But the North Vietnamese knew where we were. And one night, not long after we arrived, they hit us.

It began with a barrage of mortar and rocket fire, hundreds of rounds exploding all around us. As soon as that lifted we ran to take our positions, and then they opened up with the small arms—500, maybe 1,000 guys creeping in, and they all open up with their AKs at once.

It's the spookiest sound in the world. You see, an AK47 sounds different than an M16. An AK47 is primarily an assault weapon, and it's meant to create this sound to terrify the people you're shooting at. And it does. It has a bullet that makes this high-pitched whine. It's almost as if the air is screaming, as if the air was made out of flesh itself and it's being torn to pieces. I always equated that with the sound of the Devil. I mean, if the Devil spoke, that's how his voice would sound.

We were greatly outnumbered— twenty to one our own people later told us—and it didn't take long before they were on top of us. They overran the 3d Platoon bunker line entirely and wiped it out. Only two guys in the 3d Platoon survived. The rest were KIA. "Suicide Charlie" being "Suicide Charlie" one more time.

Then, finally, we started to get some artillery support. Up to that point, our CO later explained to us, they didn't realize back in Tay Ninh that we were getting hit as hard as we were, that in fact we'd already been overrun. So they decided they had no choice but to call in artillery on the base camp itself. They ordered everybody to get into a bunker. They told us they were going to VT it—vertically time it—so that the shells would explode before they hit the ground. The idea was that the enemy would be running around exposed and we would be protected.

You have to remember that this was my first battle. I had never experienced anything remotely like this in my life. I had never even shot at anyone before. And I said to one of the other guys huddled in this horseshoe-shaped bunker, "This is it, man, we're gone." But luckily we didn't take a direct hit, and the vertical timing pretty much worked. A few guys were killed by the splash from the exploding shells, and one mortar position took a direct hit that killed all eight guys in the squad. But we were never sure whether they got it from our artillery or from the NVA's opening barrage.

Altogether we lost forty or fifty guys that night. Even though we never again suffered that many losses in a single battle, the next six months we were pretty much in constant combat. Even during the day we were usually under some form of attack—mortars, rockets, snipers. But the big attacks, the full-scale ground assaults, always took place at night.

So every day, as nightfall approached, you started getting nervous. And when darkness finally came, you waited . . . and waited. You could never really sleep. You could never relax. And when you combine that constant vigilance with that underlying sense of terror, that's where the true stress of combat comes in.

When most people think about war, they tend to think of courage and fear as opposites. But I don't think that's true, or at least it wasn't in my experience. I don't think I ever experienced fear, because in combat I was always very calm. But terror, that was something else. It was always with you, and it could be summed up in one sentence, "Are they coming again tonight?" All that waiting. It ate at you and ate at you until it was almost a relief when you got attacked. Because then you had an enemy you could actually deal with. It was the invisible enemy that was the worst. The enemy inside your mind.

Just staying alert is the toughest part. The tension's so great all the time that people get slack after awhile if nothing happens. And that's what you have to watch out for more than anything else, because that's when you're most vulnerable. You need to develop a sixth sense in combat, where you're aware of your environment in some nonrational, almost nonempirical, way. You become psychically connected to the plants and the trees and

the hills, sensitive to the slightest change in the total environment. It's as though you go back into an almost prehistorical state of mind where the world becomes reenchanted and has spirits and ghosts and feelings.

I wasn't particularly religious, but I wanted to be on the good side of all of this. I figure anything that was aligned with the forces of good against the forces of evil I wanted to have some connection with, preferably a physical one. So I used to have all these beads and amulets, and anytime I'd come across anything of spiritual significance I'd add it to my repertoire. Soldier's cross, rosary beads, you name it. Eventually they became old and worn, or some of them would break. And whenever that happened, whenever anything out of the ordinary happened, I'd become very concerned. I'd be sure that if I went on a sweep I'd get shot or something horrible would happen.

It's similar, I think, to when a batter gets on a hot streak in baseball. Because a combat soldier, like a hitter, has to do something that requires instantaneous reflexive response. And you can't really make sense out of it. It's so quick that it's almost an unconscious function. So you get very superstitious and won't change your underwear, or shave your beard, or you'll eat the same thing night after night until you go 0-for-4 or lose a game—or get shot. Same kind of thing. Whatever's working, you just want to stay with it. I wore the same pair of boots my entire year.

One of the many ironies of the war, of course, was that all of this terror and bloodshed took place in a physically beautiful country. In the borderland area where we operated, there were no houses to speak of, no factories, no pollution, no incidental light whatsoever. So sometimes we would lie out at night and count the falling stars by . . . the hundreds it seemed. And then they'd start doing B-52 runs along the trail a few miles away and bring us back to the war. I'd be bouncing up and down on my air mattress, and the earth would quiver, and I'd always wonder about those poor bastards underneath it. I just don't know how they stood up to it.

I had all the admiration in the world for the North Vietnamese soldiers. I think they just must have been incredibly resilient men. I doubt that I could have attacked an American base camp. They used to dig their graves ahead of time, and then they'd wear these tourniquets around their necks so they could be dragged away if they got hit. Imagine digging your own grave and putting on a tourniquet before you went into battle. Against us, with all that firepower.

Like the time they hit us at Frontier City. This was another base camp along the Cambodian border in the middle of a real no man's land. The terrain looked sort of like the American Southwest—flat, arid, lifeless. There might have been more vegetation at the height of the rainy season. But this was in May of '69, and it was still very dry.

So one night the word came down that we were totally surrounded by a reinforced regiment, and they were closing in. But the command didn't want them to know that we knew they were there. So the CO ordered us "to act like nothing unusual is going on. Turn on your radios." And all at once everybody tuned in Radio Vietnam or whatever it was called, and the song "Harry the Hairy Ape" by Ray Stevens began blaring all over the camp. This is like midnight, right? And in the meantime we're all getting ready for a major ground assault by a couple thousand NVA regulars, and rumors are going around that the enemy has tanks.

But unlike Mole City, this time they were ready to give us all the back-up we needed. First they sent in a "Shadow" gunship, which is a specially equipped C-119 that has incredible firepower. The earlier versions were known as "Puff the Magic Dragon" or "Spookies." The "Shadow" was an improvement. But we knew that as soon as the gunship left they were going to hit us, because that's what they always did. They'd wait until it passed and then rush the wire.

What the North Vietnamese didn't know was that this time the American command had decided to send in a second "Shadow" behind the first. Just gave them time to really expose themselves, then brought in this flying arsenal that started chopping them to pieces. Then they called in the artillery and strike aircraft to work them over some more. And just across the border, meanwhile—maybe five miles away—the North Vietnamese open up with their antiaircraft guns, the only time during my tour that I actually saw them use it. Between the flares, the jet strikes, and the ack-ack, it looked just like something out of World War II.

The NVA just got decimated that night. The next morning we found forty or fifty bodies around our perimeter alone. And we knew that they had probably carried most of the bodies away. And we didn't suffer any significant casualties whatsoever. A few guys wounded, but not a single KIA. So the battle of Frontier City turned out to be a spectacular victory for the American command. Made the front page of *Stars and Stripes*. Everything went right, like pitching a perfect game, though in the end it didn't amount to a damned thing. Just killed a whole bunch of people.

Anyway, a few days later the division PIO man, the public information officer, choppers in and says, "Russell, we know you were a newspaper reporter before you got drafted. How'd you like to work for the division newspaper?" Well, it didn't take me long to grab my gear and get on the helicopter back to Tay Ninh. And one of the first things they had me do was a story on the battle I'd just been in—the battle of Frontier City. So I wrote it up, and they loved it and printed it in the division newspaper.

Aerial view of Fire Support Base Sedgwick, better known to the troops of the 25th Infantry as Mole City, near the Cambodian border in Tay Ninh Province.

But I was bothered by it. I can't fully explain why. I guess I just couldn't deal with the separation between the reality of combat and the reinterpretation of it through the written word. The distinction just tormented me. And I started feeling this terrible guilt about leaving the other guys, because in a combat unit there's a depth of emotional commitment that develops after a while that is hard to experience anywhere else in life—except maybe in a marriage. So, finally, after working as a writer about a week, I decided "this is bullshit" and packed up and went back to Frontier City. I wouldn't say it was a matter of courage, or if it was, it was the same kind of courage that gets you to jump off the high ledge at the swimming hole because everyone else is doing it.

I can't really remember much that happened after that. I know that we went on a lot of sweeps, and set up some ambushes, and saw a lot of action. But it all blends together in my memory. After six months in the field I'd entered a different realm, a kind of timeless place, where I was no longer consciously aware of myself or my surroundings.

It's like what James Jones—the writer who's written a lot about World War II—says in one of his books about "the evolution of the soldier." He talks about this process that begins with basic training and continues through the experience of combat and reaches a point where you accept the fact that you're already dead. That's when you've fully evolved as a soldier, because otherwise you could never do the things you're called upon to do. I mean, if your main concern is simply to stay alive, so many of the things you have to do in combat seem illogical or irrational—like charging an enemy position or just firing back instead of ducking your head and hiding. But—and this is the paradox—it's only by taking those risks, by exposing yourself to death, that you increase your chances for staying alive. So psychologically you come to a point where you realize on some level that you're better off assuming the fact of your own death.

Jones was writing about soldiers in World War II. But when you're talking about the psychological effects of combat, I don't think there's any real distinction between World War II veterans and Vietnam veterans, or combat veterans of any other war for that matter. They all fell prey to the same things. Like my father committing suicide and all the guys who drank themselves to death. So many of them died young. The stress never really went away.

The other side of it is when you come back, you have to learn to become alive again. For me it was a tremendous struggle. For a long time I couldn't feel. I was just numb, like I was locked in this emotional vise. At first I wanted to talk about my experience, but there weren't a lot of people who wanted to listen. It wasn't "cool" to talk about Vietnam in the early seventies, not even among Vietnam veterans. Part of it was the individual rotations. Since I got out of the army, I've never met a single guy I was in the war with, not a single one, whereas many of the guys in World War II went over together and came back together on the same ship. They had a chance to integrate the experience in some ways. But part of it was because society rejected our experience at the time, so there was a tendency among veterans to reject the experience as well and avoid associating with one another.

After a few years I went to see a psychiatrist, but by then everything was so heavily repressed that I never even mentioned the fact that I'd been in the war. And he never asked.

But no matter how much I tried to keep a lid on it, I was always aware that just beneath the surface there was this rage, this tremendous, almost uncontrollable volatility that I somehow had to absorb. It's a common problem for combat veterans which is tied up, I think, with their fear of their own violence. They're aware in a way most people aren't of their capacity to engage in violent acts because they've done it. Whether they enjoyed it or not is beside the point. The fact is that you know you're capable of picking up a gun and trying to kill someone, and you're never sure—at least not for many years—if you might do the same thing again.

Part of it, I suppose, is just a matter of being entrusted with too much power at too young an age. If you've ever walked along with an M16 on full automatic and a couple of bandoliers of ammunition strapped around your body and some grenades hanging from your belt, you understand what I mean. Here we were, nineteen or twenty years old, entrusted with all this brute physical power. Then all of a sudden it's taken away, and the lessons you've learned about how to use that power become invalid. I remember how naked I felt after I turned in my rifle before coming home, like leaving behind something that had almost physically become part of me. For a long time I was always aware of its absence.

It wasn't until the birth of my first son in 1979 that I really began to come to grips with the war. I felt such powerful emotions at that moment that it just seemed to blast through everything and give me a renewed commitment to living. That's what it took, something of such raw biological power that it forced me to feel again, to have a full range of emotional abilities. But even so it was a great struggle after that. I still had to learn how to deal with the rage, to realize that it could even work for me if I was able to release it bit by bit and channel it into my work.

I had already started to write again, after not being able to write anything for more than seven years. That helped a lot. I also went to the VA for counseling. I'd been to the VA once before, in 1977, I think, but they told me they couldn't do anything for me. Diagnosed my condition as "inability to adjust to adult life," which was a non-service-related problem.

But I went back anyway in late '79 for the sake of my family. Even though I cared deeply about my wife and son, I was having problems with my family life. And I wanted to work them out. This time I met with a terrific psychologist, a very empathetic man who actually seemed concerned about helping me out. He told me about this new PTSD classification—post-traumatic stress disorder—and put me in for it. Together we documented my case.

I found a lot of irony in that, because for all those years the VA wouldn't admit that people who had been through intense combat might actually have some particular responses to the experience that weren't the same as others might feel. So we were ignored, or told we were suffering from "inability to adjust to adult life," until they began running out of clientele with all the World War II guys dying off. And since their regulations stipulate that they're only responsible for service-related problems that are diagnosed within one year after you get out, they developed this new "delayed stress" classification. But of course there was nothing "delayed" about it. I'd been living with that stress for ten years.

Still, I'm glad that the VA, and the American people, have begun to recognize the problems of Vietnam veterans. In my own way I've worked hard for it—with my writing, by giving lectures, by working with disabled veterans. But I resent, in fact I absolutely detest, this idea that we are all social "victims." It's very denigrating. It robs a person of his sense of dignity because it denies his sense of responsibility for his own actions. Our nation called us to service and we did our duty, and we ought to be honored for that if only because that's the kind of value you want to emphasize in a culture. We don't want any rewards, even though there are a lot of us who could use some financial help. All we really want, as Aretha Franklin said, is a little R–E–S–P–E–C–T.

It would be tragic if the current "Rambo" mentality, this view of war as some kind of epic and glorious thing, were to be the final legacy of Vietnam. Because war is a nasty, brutal business, as anyone who's been through it knows. And it's up to veterans, especially combat veterans, to remind people of that. But it's also important for the veterans themselves to recognize that there are some positive aspects to their experience, that it wasn't a totally negative thing they went through. It let me learn at a very young age, for instance, that there are things in life more important than mere material possessions and my own sense of ego. It was a profoundly humbling experience in a way, and I think a little humility is good for people. And it also gave me a deeper appreciation of human life, a sense that somewhere buried in that miasma of suffering and death and despair there is always hope. I suppose there's some wisdom in that, the kind of wisdom that makes me a better father. And I'm thankful for that. ∎

Members of the Wolf Hounds (1st Battalion, 27th Infantry, 25th Infantry Division), mortar platoon provide fire support for an infantry operation at Mole City in May 1969.

James Morgan

Lieutenant, U.S. Navy
Patrol Commander and Operations Officer
River Division 593, Rung Sat Special Zone
September 1968–September 1969

Jim Morgan was born in New Orleans, Louisiana, during World War II, the son of a naval officer. He graduated from Villanova University in 1966 and as an NROTC participant took a commission in the U.S. Navy. After a tour on destroyers, Morgan volunteered for duty in Vietnam and was assigned to river patrol boats in the area just south of Saigon. After his return to civilian life, Morgan graduated from Catholic University Law School. He is now an attorney with the Department of the Navy and a reserve lieutenant commander in the Judge Advocate General's Corps in Washington, D.C.

My first tour in Vietnam, when I was on a destroyer, I had seen both Swift boats and river patrol boats, PBRs. When we were off the mouth of the Long Tau River, they would come out for supplies and trade their ball ammunition for belts of machine-gun ammunition that alternated tracers, incendiaries, and armor-piercing rounds which gave them more firepower. I realized that's where the action in the navy was and thought I would miss out on something if I had the chance and didn't serve in the river force.

I volunteered because the PBRs sounded like a great change from the confines of destroyer life. You would be a junior officer with your own command: two thirty-two-foot fiber glass patrol boats with little pleasure-craft radars and two FM radios. Also, the PBRs were pretty freewheeling. We saw the crews pull alongside in shorts and shower shoes, while on the destroyer we officers periodically had to dress to the nines for formal dinners.

We flew over in late '68 on a bright green Braniff 707 with stewardesses wearing Pucci-designed cocktail pajamas. I remember as we got to the Philippines the stewardess said, "No need to change your watches anymore, we're in the same time zone as Saigon." She was real cheerful, but of course she wasn't getting off the plane in Vietnam. And it hit me like a ton of bricks that I only had days to live. On the final two-hour leg of the flight, I passed up my "all-American hot dog snack." No appetite at all. When we landed at Tan Son Nhut it was unbelievable. You'd think it would be an attitude that, "we're all in this together," but everybody was shorter than you were when you got to Vietnam for the first time, and they weren't shy about letting you know. There were guys giving us the raspberry and showing us how many days they had left and how many we had left. It just wasn't what you expected.

I still had my case of nerves, which didn't help when we ran into a bunch of guys from PBR school in the States who had arrived two days ahead of us. The rumor mill was working overtime and all we heard was, so-and-so's been killed already, so-and-so's been maimed and sent back to a stateside hospital.

But then we went around to one of the MACV BOQs for dinner, and while we were having a couple of drinks the news came on Armed Forces Vietnam television. There was Bobbi the weather girl. She was a good-looking blonde who worked for the State Department, and when she'd predict rain the stage crew would throw a bucket of water on her and of course she predicted rain every day. She'd start in the north of the country reading the weather and finally got down to your "in country R & R center in Vung Tau." The absurdity of all this in a war zone suddenly struck, I had a good laugh, and that was the end of my nerves.

The base I went to was only about fourteen miles south of Saigon. It was part of a little town whose main street ended at the river where our docks were. Its importance was that it was right at the junction of the Long Tau River, the shipping channel between Saigon and the South China Sea, and the Soi Rap, which was the main link between Saigon and the delta. Our job was to keep the shipping channel open with our PBRs and a small fleet of mine sweepers. Later we did three and a half months just north of the delta along with five other river divisions to slow down Communist infiltration along the Vam Co rivers near the Cambodian border and another three months north of Saigon near Cu Chi.

The area south of Saigon was the Rung Sat Special Zone, a navy area of responsibility between III and IV Corps because it was almost roadless. Normally there would be four river divisions deployed in the Rung Sat at any one time. Each division would usually have fifty to fifty-five men, four or five of them officers and the rest enlisted. There'd be ten boats with each boat assigned a crew of four commanded by a first- or second-class petty officer. The boats patrolled in pairs, and each patrol would have a junior commissioned officer or a chief petty officer as patrol officer.

Patrols were twelve hours long starting either at 6:00 A.M. or 6:00 P.M. You'd have two day patrols, two night patrols, and a day off before starting the cycle again. But the day off wasn't a vacation because you came back from a night patrol on the river, cleaned up the boat, had breakfast, and then tried to sleep in the 105-degree heat. You might get up in the afternoon, have a few beers, take liberty in the little town outside our base, and then go to sleep so you could get up at 4:30 for briefings, breakfast and patrol at 6:00 A.M.

The PBRs had twin GM diesel engines driving Jacuzzi water jet pumps that sucked water in through the bottom of the boat, compressed it, and shot it out the rear—no propellors, no rudders. They had twin .50 calibers in an open turret forward, an M60 light machine gun, and a hand-cranked 40MM grenade launcher midships. It was a point of pride to get the last round of the thirty-six-grenade belt in the air before the first had hit so you'd get a continuous burst on top of somebody's head. Finally, in the aft part of the boat was a single .50-caliber machine gun. Occasionally we'd also carry a 60MM mortar for shooting illumination, but you couldn't get any accuracy with it from a moving boat. We also carried two M79 grenade launchers and four M16s, so we were pretty well prepared.

If you were patrolling on the Long Tau, you reported the merchant ships as they came up or down the river and recorded their position. Then they'd mark it down at the base TOC, tactical operations center, as having passed your patrol area. Now the VC had a rocketeer school in the Rung Sat, and the story we had was that they'd train these guys how to shoot their rockets and for the final exam would send them over to fire at a merchant ship. So this poor VC kid takes a shot at the bridge of one of these cargo ships, the captain calls in the attack, and all of a sudden the VC has seventy-two grenades coming down on his head from two PBRs and six barrels of .50s firing at him, which is a real disincentive to shoot any more rockets.

The Long Tau River was not nice to look at. It had been defoliated, the banks were all mud, and there was no greenery around. We checked out a lot of big fishing junks that would come up from the South China Sea to Saigon to sell their catch. You'd find shark fins drying on the roof, and the big fish would be iced down below. The machine guns and rockets would be under that if there were any. Another thing we looked for was big wads of cash. If we found half a million or 750,000 piasters we wanted to know why, the suspicion being it was to buy supplies or provide payrolls for the VC.

We'd sometimes check as many as 250 to 300 sampans during the morning rush hour. People usually weren't afraid of us. There was always a lot of joking and kidding, and in the afternoons, we'd sometimes be offered whiskey or dried fish chips. But we would always keep one boat for cover, standing off to keep an eye on people, and we never let the sampans come up on both sides of us at once.

A Navy PBR Mark II patrols the Mekong Delta, 1968. PBR crews worked to keep open the shipping canals that were Saigon's vital link to the delta and the South China Sea.

Jim Morgan in the cockpit of a Navy river patrol boat in the Rung Sat Special Zone.

After a week or so on the river, I had finished my five orientation patrols and was finally planning and leading operations of my own. After about a month, I put in for a special operation on a piece of the river that we normally didn't have control of, north of our regular patrol area. We wanted to make our presence known and try to keep the VC off balance. Because it was a strictly prohibited area, any other boats we found up there would be fair game.

I had located a little canal and intended to put a boat on either side of it, just blend in with the undergrowth for the night, and hope that some VC would come down the canal to cross the river. As we approached the ambush site, I cut the engines and let the boats drift with the incoming tide under the cover of darkness. Suddenly an illumination round went off right over our heads. My first move was to call the base TOC and tell them to pass the word to all the local units to stop using flares in case it was our people, since there was always a lot of artillery fired into the area. Almost as I finished the message, a high-explosive round landed between me and the cover boat, which was astern about 100 yards. We hit the throttles, spun around, and started south at full speed. Just as we cranked the boats up, the port bank of the canal just erupted with automatic weapons fire, and another high-explosive round hit just ahead of us catching the boat in a shower of fragments.

Later I was struck by what thoughts and impressions stay with you from your first firefight. All of our guns started to return fire, and as I looked aft I could distinctly see our new gunner's mate on the back .50, a picture of concentration, aiming at the beach, firing low, and squeezing off four- and five-round bursts so as not to burn up the barrels, just like they taught him in school. My second reaction was to think, "Oh shit, I don't have my helmet on. If I get hit in the head, the boss isn't going to have any sympathy for me at all." The firing seemed like it lasted forever, but I'm sure it was less than three minutes.

About the time the shooting slackened, the TOC called back and advised that we cease fire, that we were shooting it out with a battalion of Thai troops with American advisers who had set up a river ambush without clearing the operation with U.S. headquarters before they went in there. I was later told the adviser called the TOC very angry and said, "You killed one of my men and wounded another." The TOC, another lieutenant (jg) like me replied, "It would have been a lot worse if I could have got my helicopters there on time." A strong reaction force was on the way, and they could have suffered even more for their carelessness. I'm sure sorry we killed a guy, but we never blamed ourselves and I still don't.

In mid-January on the Vam Co Dong River, we lost the guy who was closest to me, my first boat engineer. The guy already had a Purple Heart and a Silver Star. When his patrol started taking fire, he jumped to his gun and took one round in the chest. Nobody else in the boat was hit. His boat captain, an older first-class gunner's mate who was extremely close to him, radioed back, "He's gone." That knocked everybody out for a day or two. Then less than two weeks later I was hit.

It was evening and a thin cover of smoke from burning rice stalks, in preparation for the next planting, had drifted over the river and had caught the rays of the setting sun. I was headed up the river into this tranquil sunset starting an evening patrol when suddenly there was a big boom and the cockpit was full of smoke. I felt pressure on both legs and heard a burst of machine-gun fire over our own return fire. I knew I had been hit, but I didn't want to look at my legs to see what was going on down there. I thought we were hit below the water line and that the forward gunner was wounded, because the rocket would have had to come in right through his legs.

What I didn't know was that we'd been hit in each bow—had taken two rockets simultaneously. The one that wounded me had not detonated in the boat. It hit an aluminum fuse panel, which shattered and filled my legs with shrapnel, and then glanced off the engine cover, went straight up into the sky, and went off. The cover boat reported that. The other went through the starboard bow, on through the boat, and exploded in the river. When I turned to tell the driver to steer away from the direction of the fire, he already had the wheel turned full over. The forward gunner was unscathed, the rockets went on each side of him. I got back and the pants I'd been wearing were well ventilated, probably a hundred holes, but it looked about ten times worse than it was. I wound up getting only about ten stitches. The corpsman offered me a shot of brandy, which for some reason I turned down. There are those on the crew who never forgave me for that. I got my legs wrapped up and a ten-day vacation from patrolling. Fortunately my shrapnel was aluminum and didn't go very deep; the last piece popped out about seven months later.

Danger in the river division wasn't constant, however. In the Rung Sat many of the rivers were wide, and even on night patrol the big ones were usually sort of pleasant. You'd go weeks without getting into a shooting scrape. But the danger was just frequent enough that it was always in your mind that things could turn brown in a hurry.

Operation Giant Slingshot down on the Vam Co Dong River west of Saigon near the Cambodian border was much more intense. There was a lot of foliage on the banks, and one patrol officer got into four firefights in one day. That's where we began to see the cumulative effects of prolonged strain.

It was in the narrower rivers and canals where the banks were closer that you usually would tighten up, get a little more nervous both day and night. There's a big difference between going through a river that's a kilometer wide and going through a canal that's fifty meters wide, where the VC can hit you with a grenade from either bank.

People were affected in a variety of ways. One first-class petty officer who made it through his entire year's worth of patrols had to start going to sickbay for tranquilizer shots once he was pulled off the river. He performed perfectly when he was supposed to but then needed help when it was all over. One of our best boat captains, as solid as a rock and already awarded a Silver Star, came apart during a night ambush. He started calling on the radio every couple of seconds, "Did you see that? What was that? Let's get out of here." The next morning, after we got back to the LST that we used as a base, he went down to one side of the ship and started putting shots over the bows of sampans with his .45 pistol and calling them alongside, screaming at them. He had just lost control and was a case for the corpsman. We had to send him home early. These were fellows for whom the pressure had built up over a long time. In one case we had a lieutenant (jg) who didn't last his first day. When I picked him up in Saigon he said he just couldn't face going on patrol. We sent him back to the squadron with a little note pinned to his uniform, so to speak, and they sent him down to flotilla where he was put on staff and liked it so much he extended his tour in Vietnam.

During my year we had only five people that we had to take off the river and assign to other duties because they couldn't patrol anymore. This really wasn't a lot when you consider that we

Hanging Tree Canal off the Long Tau River, fourteen miles south of Saigon in the Rung Sat Special Zone, Fall 1969. Canal patrols were particularly hazardous, as the enemy could attack from the cover of either bank.

A monitor boat, equipped with a flame thrower and 20MM cannon, plies a canal in the Rung Sat Special Zone on a defoliation mission, Spring 1969.

driving because the boat captain had been wounded, but he received a direct hit in the head from an anti-tank rocket. In the first few seconds of that ambush all but two people on the two crews were wounded. An injured boat engineer held a compress to the throat of another seaman while the boat was maneuvered out of the kill zone. He saved the seaman's life and the boat. We heard the fight on the radios at the TOC, and everybody went down to the docks to meet the boats when they came in. One of our boat-swain's mates jumped into the cockpit to get the chief's body, and I remember he recoiled out of the boat almost crying and in total reflex. He had an arm thrown up as if to shield himself. The chief had been a hard charger, very popular with the men, and all of a sudden this was what was left of him. His brain, intact, was on the gunnel of the boat.

Normally if you had a firefight, even if there were light wounds, everybody laughed it off and, if it was your first time, they snipped the loop on the black berets that we wore. It was a lot of fun, and the guy whose loop was snipped bought the beer. But after a death everybody sort of went his own way. It brought home to everybody that this was a serious business. There was little reminiscing except to reassure each other that the guy never knew what hit him. People took comfort in the fact that everybody went immediately and didn't suffer. If you took antitank fire, which was usually the case with us, you went out fast. It wasn't like the infantry where you might be wounded and pinned down for a long time, and we knew we were lucky in that respect.

As far as my own mental state, it usually depended on what area we were in and what had been happening. If it was a bad area and we had been getting jumped with some regularity, I was very happy the nights I didn't have to go out, and I would be edgy and down on days when I had a night patrol coming up. I can also remember a lot of fear when I was called on to patrol aboard the ASPBs, the assault support patrol boats, which were about the same length as our PBRs but with a deeper draft and made of steel instead of fiber glass and more heavily armed. It was like being surrounded by shrapnel because an anti-tank rocket-propelled grenade, an RPG, needed resistance to explode the war-

started with fifty-four to fifty-five guys and every month rotated about one-twelfth of them. Interestingly enough, though, the guys that kept patrolling didn't seem to begrudge those who came off. The feeling seemed to be that everyone had a limit, and some guys reached it sooner than others. As for shipping these people out, we had good support from the flotilla command. There was little resistance if we wanted to unload somebody. Anyway, it would have been impossible to nursemaid anyone at the division level. We were just too small to carry those who couldn't perform. We had to get them out of there so we could get a replacement.

But more typical of our seamen was the case of one young sailor whose boat had been hit and who had been singed all over when the fuel tanks caught fire. Back on the LST that night, he looked at me and said, "Mr. Morgan. . . ." And I knew he was going to ask to come off the river, but then he thought about it a second and said, "Oh, never mind." That was the only thing I ever heard from him. He just canned it, continued to patrol for another six months, and everything he did was fine. That's the sort of reaction we normally had, people continuing to operate in spite of everything.

We lost our first man about two months after I got there—the chief who had taken me out on my second indoctrination patrol. He was ferrying Vietnamese troops into a thickly forested area, and his two boats ran into tremendous rocket and machine-gun fire. The chief jumped from his boat to his cover boat to take over the head, and usually it just went through fiber glass without detonating. Not so an ASPB; I could picture a big explosion with lots of flying steel and casualties.

For me the stress peaked a couple of times. Once was shortly after I was wounded and had to go upriver past the spot where I was hit. My stomach turned over as we approached the ambush point, but after that it was over. The second time was after a rocket exploded behind a crewman on one of our boats, and he took the full force of the explosion. Two other officers put him in the body bag and that had to be the worst. I had to go down and clean up and wash parts of him off the map case. The smell stayed with me, and I didn't eat for three days.

I came off the river, stopped patrolling, a couple of weeks before I was to leave Vietnam. That was always a big deal, the idea being to shelter you from getting killed or hurt there at the very last. But leaving produced very mixed feelings, joy initially but also sadness because I was going to miss the guys. We were really a small, tight unit and, too, you felt like you were leaving the job unfinished. By the same token, I didn't want to expose myself for a minute more than I absolutely had to because it would have been a total waste to die over there or to get some sort of permanent damage.

I had a strong conviction at that point that we were just marking time. We weren't really accomplishing anything and weren't really intending to accomplish anything. Although individual servicemen and units were doing great things, politically it would never amount to anything. I went over there fairly gung ho. Peace talks had started before I went, and most of us were afraid they were going to declare peace before we got a chance to see what the action was like. But by my fifth day in Vietnam I had seen the Regional Forces down on the riverbanks hailing sampans over and putting shots over their bows to halt them to take off food and firewood. What kind of nonsense is this where you're supposed to be looking for VC tax collectors and turning the other way when the government people are doing exactly the same thing? Then when they put shots over our bows as well, just to be wise asses, it was the end to the belief that we were trying to accomplish something of lasting good over there. Eventually it became a case of doing a good job because you were proud of being an American.

Leaving Vietnam was a strange experience. It was not normally celebrated, guys just slipped away. You'd be on your way to patrol, and the other guy would be on his way home. You'd get a letter a little bit after that. The classic was the guy who went back, got the clap from his girl, and then she broke up with him. With no girl, no job, and no prospects, Vietnam started looking pretty good.

When the plane took off from Saigon, there was no big cheer. There were probably 180 of us, and we just sat back and breathed a sigh of relief. Nor was it any big deal when we got to the States. I can't remember any real euphoria because there was still this strong sense of identification with the guys who were still back there. I think more of me was still in Vietnam than in the United States. I don't remember any protesters annoying servicemen. I think the typical reaction from a combat guy would have been just to walk right past these characters. I flew on to Philadelphia from San Francisco, got off the plane, my parents were there with a couple of cold beers in the car, and we came home. I think their philosophy was let him say as much or as little as he wants, although my father immediately commented on my Purple Heart since I had been telling them how boring Vietnam was. I had a million stories, but I wasn't ready to tell them right then. Even now things only come out piecemeal, a bit at a time.

I think the Vietnam Memorial is terrific. I was down there the night before the official opening on Veterans Day of 1982. I had not seen it until that time, and I really wasn't prepared. It was late, but even so there was a crowd and volunteers to help you find names on the wall. I started to ask for the names of the guys from my river division and absolutely choked up. I couldn't get the first name out, it just stuck in my throat. I just croaked.

Every once in a while I swing by and look up 34W29, my engine man who was killed in January. It's not going to change and it's not going to bring him back. But I know it's going to be there, someone I was with in Vietnam who's gone. Every time you go there it's sort of a reunion even if you don't meet anybody else, just being there with the names. ∎

Morgan displays a Russian-made sighting device recovered from a sampan following a firefight on the Mo Nhat River in October 1968 in which fifteen enemy soldiers were killed.

Geoffrey M. Boehm

*Helicopter Pilot
Company C, 227th Aviation Battalion
(Assault Helicopter)
1st Cavalry Division
(Airmobile)
August 1969–September 1970*

In his second year at Nassau Community College on Long Island, New York, where "sports were more important than grades for me," Geoff Boehm's average dropped below a C, and within two weeks he got his draft notice. He enlisted in the army warrant officer helicopter pilot program and in August 1969 joined the 227th Aviation Battalion of the 1st Cavalry Division (Airmobile) at Phuoc Vinh, fifty-six kilometers north of Saigon. There his mission as a "slick" pilot in the UH-1 "Huey" aircraft ranged from inserting combat troops into hostile areas under fire to ferrying large caches of weapons out of Cambodia when U.S. forces entered that country in 1970. After his discharge in 1971, Boehm went back to school for a degree in management and later became executive director of the Air Pollution Control Commission of the City of Boston. He is active in veterans' affairs and also flies helicopters for the Massachusetts Army National Guard.

About eight of us high-school buddies got our draft notices at the same time in 1968. We were all on the same bus going down to get our physicals, and we were talking about what was going to happen. We talked about different ways we had heard you could flunk the physical. But we didn't try any of them. One guy got rejected, and we were happy for him and kind of disappointed that it wasn't us, but it was a new experience and I was kind of excited about it. We were not necessarily prowar and definitely not very liberal. We all felt hey, if your country needs you, then it's your duty to do it. That's the way I was brought up. Of course I was scared and didn't want to go to war, but I wasn't going to run away from it.

I went to talk to a recruiter and discuss options. One of the things they needed was helicopter pilots. I thought, I've never flown before, but I'd love to fly. I sure didn't want to be humping through a jungle; I'd rather be flying over it. The recruiter didn't bullshit me. He said it's no joy ride. You get shot down; the casualty rate's pretty high for helicopter pilots. But I took it anyway. I liked to be a star, a hero, or something like that, whatever I go after . . . like on a baseball team I was the pitcher, the focal point. I liked the little glorification I got from whatever I did. So I figured I wouldn't be just the average guy. I'd be a helicopter pilot.

I went to Fort Polk, Louisiana, for basic training in July 1968. It was especially hard for the handful of us that were going on to warrant officer helicopter school. The drill sergeants pushed us even harder. In fact, I was one of the "prime trainees." I beat the champions from all the other platoons in the bayonet drills. And here I was, a helicopter pilot candidate. I thought, if a guy ever got that close that I would have to use a bayonet, wait a minute.

At primary helicopter school at Fort Wolters, Texas, there were a lot of basic courses in helicopters and a lot of harassment and discipline. It was like basic all over again but ten times worse. It was a weeding-out process. They would see the really weak ones and jump on their case and out of the program they went because of the pressures later of flying a quarter-million dollars' worth of aircraft.

Eventually we moved into learning about basic flying techniques: what to do, how to move the controls. There were films and classroom demonstrations. We'd sit in the TH-55 trainer on the ground and eventually go up with an instructor and get hands-on experience. That was another big breaking point for dropouts: seeing if a guy had any coordination. You needed a lot of coordination; everything has to work together, eyes, hands, and feet. It was amazing that more people were not killed during training. I mean, you had all these new pilots out there, there were literally hundreds of aircraft flying and hovering around, none of us really knowing how to fly.

There were over 200 in my flight class when we graduated from Wolters in March 1969. At this point the need for helicopter pilots was at its maximum, and a lot of guys that did pass flight school should not have passed, because they just didn't have the proficiency and knowledge to handle the aircraft. Letting them fly was dangerous, but the army needed bodies. They had quotas to keep up with. Many of the pilots were just kids. I was twenty years old, and I was one of the older ones. For most of them it was like having your first driver's license, only you didn't have a car, you had a helicopter.

The top 10 percent of my class got its choice of whether they wanted to fly Cobra gunships, Chinooks, or Hueys. Everybody wanted to fly the new Cobra gunship. I was in the bottom of the top 10 percent, so when it came down to my choice, Cobra ships were all taken. They said you could take Chinooks, but I said no, I would like to take the Hueys simply because it was more exciting to fly a Huey than a cargo helicopter.

For the next few months we were taught the basics of the Huey at Fort Hunter/Stewart in Georgia. We also learned about combat flying. We'd go out in the woods and simulate combat flying, combat assaults and extractions, night flying, everything. They had firing ranges for door gunners, so you got used to the sound of the guns in the helicopter. We got some really good training at that point, because all our instructor pilots were combat vets, and they could tell you what was actually going on over there. We even used to talk to the pilots over at the club and listen to war stories. They would tell us about getting shot down, about going into a hot LZ and bullets going through the aircraft. A couple of guys showed us their bullet wounds and Purple Hearts and things like that. These guys impressed me. They were war heroes. I wanted to come back and be just like them.

After I graduated from Hunter/Stewart in July 1969, I had thirty days before I was to report to go to Vietnam. It was summertime, so I went to the beach a lot, partied a lot. Less than a week before I reported I went to the Woodstock festival. There I was, with my short hair, singing along with Country Joe and the Fish: "One, two, three, what are we fighting for? Don't ask me, I don't give a damn, the next stop is Vietnam." That's exactly where I was going.

By the end of August I was in Saigon, waiting for my final assignment. My original orders from Hunter/Stewart said "1st Aviation Brigade, Can Tho," which was in the delta, in IV Corps. I was glad I wasn't going to the 1st Cav. From talking to the flight instructors, you knew that if you were a helicopter pilot with the 1st Cav your chances of surviving were even less, because they were where the action was all the time. That was a little too hot, even for our anxious selves. I had told my mother, "Don't worry, I'm going down to Can Tho, in the delta. There's nothing going on down there, it's nice and quiet." But when they posted the orders on the bulletin board, lo and behold, there it was: "Boehm, 1st Cav."

I was assigned to Charlie Company of the 227th Aviation Battalion, based at Phuoc Vinh. At first they had more copilots than they had helicopters. I got kind of obstinate and got into a little trouble for complaining that I hadn't gotten to fly yet. On numerous occasions I went out and flew door gunner for other pilots to get out of the base camp, to see what it was like out there in the real war. Then my company commander found out that his copilots were flying as door gunners, so we couldn't do that anymore.

But after two weeks we started flying regularly. At first I flew a lot of courier and supply missions. They wanted to get you oriented to the area first. Then you started flying with an experienced pilot in actual combat assaults.

I had a good friend named Tom Brown serving with me while we were still copilots. We had been together all through basic and flight school, and now we were both at Phuoc Vinh. One day in October

Tom wanted to fly with a pilot that I was assigned to, so we traded assignments that day. Tom and a helicopter pilot named Varney were resupplying a company when their helicopter hit a tree limb and crashed and burned. Everyone on the aircraft died.

When I came back and found that Tom had been killed, I just couldn't deal with it. We were still learning, we were excited, and we weren't really sure of the dangers over there until this happened to me. That's all we talked about lots and lots of times before we had even gotten over there: When your number's up, your number's up. You're trying to rationalize why, but there's no rationale to that. Tom had just gotten married, he had a baby on the way. We had just switched missions. Why had God wanted him dead and not me?

I didn't want to fly anymore. It was difficult walking by Tom's room and seeing everything packed up. Everything was gone, just a vacant room there. I had to go see the chaplain for the next couple of days to get my mind turned around.

Tom's death was the cause of the major change in my attitude and my flying. Suddenly I just turned around and said, all right, I'm ready to fly. I just wanted to go out there and get revenge for Tom's death. I believe it made me a better pilot, because I was a little more daring. But I was good at it. I wasn't going beyond my capabilities. I was able to fly into hot LZs,

Before he got a chance to fly Hueys, Geoff Boehm flew several missions as a door gunner "to see what it was like out there in the real war."

flying with no problem, and handle everything. I was recommended for aircraft commander, the pilot responsible for the whole aircraft. I made aircraft commander very quickly, ahead of everyone else. It would have taken me longer, I think, if Tom had not died.

After that I just wanted to do a bang-up job, and I guess I was a bit egotistical, too. If you weren't flying gunships or medevacs, there was another mission that had the glory because you were getting actual combat and fire exchanges all the time. That was the Night Hawk.

Night Hawk was a volunteer mission, a lot more exciting and a lot more dangerous than the others. It was a regular Huey set up for night operations, with a minigun that fired about 6,000 rounds a minute, a .50-caliber machine gun on the other door, and a xeon light and starlight scope. You would go out into a free fire zone with a Cobra gunship above you with no lights on. You would have all your lights on, flying at treetop level at sixty knots, trying to draw fire. The idea was to let the enemy take a few pot shots at you, then open up on them.

We came under fire quite often because the Vietcong and NVA liked to attack at night. But if nobody fired at you, it would start to get boring. Sometimes you'd actually want someone to fire. Lots of times we'd open up and fire anyway, and hope that someone would return fire. We'd fly the rivers, looking for sampans, because anything that moved at night was fair game. We shot a lot of sampans out of the water.

One particular time on the Night Hawk, an element of the 11th Armored Cav was getting overrun. They had artillery and mortar support from other units, they had air force tac air on station, and they called in Spooky to help out. They needed real close support, and that's when I went in. I just hovered over the APCs and let my door gunner and my crew chief on the minigun just start working out. The grunt lieutenant came on the radio and said, "You're doing outstanding. I've got nothing but dead gooks on the wire. Keep going, keep going."

Bullets were flying all over the place. Plexiglas was popping out of the chopper. The door gunner got hit with a .50-caliber round and eventually lost his leg, but nobody else got wounded and we were able to fly back. The helicopter looked like a piece of Swiss cheese, but, knock on wood, it never hit anything that was going to bring us down. I was put in for the Distinguished Flying Cross for that mission.

By December I was flying almost every day of the week. A typical mission day would start with getting woken up with a flashlight in your face at about four in the morning, getting dressed, going down to the mess hall for some rotten eggs and coffee, and then going out to the flight line to preflight your helicopter. After that you would check in at the TOC to get your mission sheet and get briefed on where you were going.

The missions would be varied. Something like, first you're going out to Song Be to pick up supplies to resupply some companies. At 1100 hours you're going to Quan Loi to meet up with four other helicopters to form a flight to do several combat assaults. Then back to your original unit at Song Be to do more resupplies or whatever they want you to do. Hook up again at 1400 hours for more combat assaults, taking troops from a firebase to drop them in the jungle somewhere,

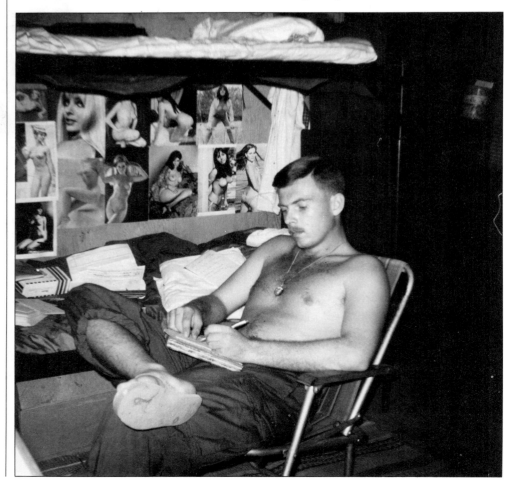

Relaxing in his hooch in Phuoc Vinh, Boehm writes a letter home.

sometimes under fire. Maybe a few hours later you'd do an extraction, which was just the reverse. And then perhaps in the middle of that you'd hear a call for a medevac, and if you were in the area you'd go do the medevac. Some days you were home at 8:00 P.M. but most days not until ten at night.

There were other types of missions. I used to spray Agent Orange around firebases. We didn't take any special precautions; it was just another mission. On "psyops" I flew with a Vietnamese who would drop leaflets or talk over a loudspeaker, telling enemy soldiers to *chieu hoi* and warning the people not to help the Vietcong. Another job was a "sniffer" mission, where we flew over free fire zones with electronic equipment that detected body heat. Once the needle on the instrument went off the board, and we thought we had discovered a whole enemy battalion down there. So we opened fire and called in Cobra gunships and artillery, and a platoon was inserted later. It turned out that we had killed about a hundred monkeys. On the other side of the coin, I even spent several days in December flying troops from the field down to the Bob Hope Christmas show at Cu Chi.

We also did a lot of reconnaissance of enemy bases in Cambodia in the spring of 1970. We were told to radio where we took fire from, but we could not return the fire. Then one day at a briefing they told the pilots: We're going into Cambodia.

We were constantly moving in Cambodia. I flew combat assaults, medevacs, logistics, and a lot of resupply missions. We shipped out a lot of enemy caches and blew up the ones that were too damn big to take out. The amount of arms and supplies over there was just amazing. And a lot of it was American. I got a Remington 9MM pistol, brand new, packed in grease. There were huge hospital complexes, concrete buildings, and even swimming pools that the enemy used. It was phenomenal.

I was on a resupply mission to a unit in contact in Cambodia when I got shot down. We went in on one pass and just threw the ammo out, close enough to the ground unit, and the enemy got it. So we loaded again, came back out, and tried to find the exact location of the men. The commander was talking me into him on the radio, and the whole time I was tak-

ing fire like crazy. The door gunners were working out and all hell was breaking loose. We found them, dropped the ammo, and started taking off, but a couple of rounds hit some lines in the engine. The pressure gauge went to zero and the temperature was climbing out of sight, so I knew that the engine was going to quit and I didn't have long to go.

I got up to about 500 feet and started making an approach into an open field when the engine quit. I had radioed for help when we were hit, so we were only on the ground for about ten minutes before we were picked up. But it seemed

Top. *Boehm (right) and his copilot with Cambodian children, June 1970.*

Above. *In a picture taken by Boehm during the U.S. invasion of Cambodia in May 1970, one company of the 1st Air Cav replaces another that had spent a few weeks in the field.*

like an eternity. Boy, was I scared then. We heard stories about people, especially pilots, who were later found tortured to death, because the enemy really hated helicopter pilots and helicopters. That went through pilots' minds all the time; we often talked about whether we would actually commit suicide before getting captured. I was convinced I'd be able to do it, but I fortunately never had the opportunity to test my will power. I got shot down three times during my whole tour, but each time I was picked up. My aircraft took many rounds all the time, but I didn't get hit at all. One of the medals I definitely did not want to get was the Purple Heart.

When I finally got to Saigon to ship out in early September, I started seeing classmates from flight school, because our tours ended at the same time. We all found out who had been killed or wounded and who was making it back. A little more than half my class didn't make it back. I thought about what the recruiter had said to me about the dangers of flying when I enlisted. I knew that I had definitely seen and been *in* a war—and it was real. And the danger was real until our "Freedom Bird" left the airspace of Vietnam. But I guess I survived because I took on the challenge of the war, the enemy, and the helicopter and said, "I'm going to win this battle." And I guess I was a very good pilot, because I'm here today.

Of course, I would still like to have flown the Cobra gunship, but I wouldn't have really seen a lot of the action that I was involved in, especially in the medevacs—helping people out like that. That was gratifying. At the dedications of the Memorial in Washington, guys I didn't even know saw me in my flight suit and were coming up to me and saying, "You were a helicopter pilot? Well, thanks for getting me home." That made me feel good. I was proud to be a slick pilot. ∎

Richard W. Grefrath

Clerk Typist
101st Airborne Division
November 1968–February 1970

Richard Grefrath grew up as "a typical baby boomer" in Paramus, New Jersey, outside New York City. He attended public schools, played little league baseball, and became an Eagle Scout. In 1964 he enrolled at Carnegie Institute of Technology (now Carnegie-Mellon University) in Pittsburgh and two years later transferred to New York University because, "I found out I was more interested in art and literature than in math and engineering."

After serving in Vietnam with the 101st Airborne Division from November 1968 to February 1970, he earned a master's degree in library science at the University of Maryland. He now lives "a quiet family life" with his wife and two sons in Reno, Nevada, and works as a librarian at the University of Nevada.

I didn't really become seriously interested in the war until my senior year in college. I had been aware of it before that, of course. From the time I entered Carnegie Institute of Technology in the fall of 1964 the draft had always been hanging over my head, and I remember that in the spring of 1966 I had had to pass the Selective Service College Qualification Test to keep my 2–S deferment. I got very tense about that. I even went out and bought a paperback on *How to Score High on Your Selective Service Draft Deferment Test*. I also recall that after I transferred to NYU in the fall of 1966, I participated in a few local antiwar demonstrations. I had already come to the conclusion that the war was a no-win situation, and that being the case it just didn't seem right to sacrifice so many American lives for nothing.

Still, it wasn't until 1968, just after the Tet offensive, that the war came to the forefront of my mind. I had just received a fellowship to do graduate work in English at Temple University when President Johnson announced that he was abolishing all graduate student deferments. So suddenly the possibility that I might be drafted became something almost certain, and imminent. And sure enough, a week after I graduated I got my 1–A reclassification.

Since I was opposed to the war, I had already thought about alternatives. I considered going to Canada or Sweden or someplace else but ruled that out because I didn't want to dishonor my family. I didn't want them to think of me as a source of shame. I had also looked into the Peace Corps, thinking that it might not be all that pleasant, but at least it would be safer than going to Vietnam. But then I discovered that the Peace Corps didn't get you out of the service, it only postponed it. So that didn't leave me with too many options.

I realized that I could cut a better deal for myself if I enlisted, but that meant giving up three years instead of two. And I figured that since I was a college graduate, I could probably get a desk job even if I were drafted. The one thing I didn't want to do, though, was just sit around and wait indefinitely for my "Greetings" to arrive. So ultimately I decided to "volunteer" for the draft. I'd heard somewhere that you could do that. I called the draft board in Hackensack, New Jersey, and asked about it, and they said, "Oh, yes, all you have to do is sign a paper saying 'Take me,' and we take you," which is what I did.

I remember that when I told some friends in New York that I'd volunteered for the draft, their reaction was, "Oh, well, the war's almost over, right? The peace negotiations have begun" and so forth. But I was really apprehensive. I expected the worst. In fact, the day that I reported for induction at the Armed Forces Entrance Examining Station in Newark in mid-July, I was sure of two things: that I was going to Vietnam and that I'd be killed. Fortunately I was only half-right.

By evening of that first day we were at Fort Dix, ready to begin basic training. I didn't get off to a very good start. Right away I got real sick from the shots they give you. I had a fever, felt real weak, ached all over. But I refused to go on sick call, figuring that if I started to complain, they'd immediately send me off to Vietnam. My whole attitude, in fact, was to make as few waves as possible. Don't be noticed. It was bad enough I had an unusual name. I can't begin to count the number of times I had to do pushups because the instructor shouted out "Griffith," or "Gersetz," or some even more unrecognizable version of my last name, and I would chime in, "Do you mean, 'Grefrath,' sir?" and he would shout, "Gifford, Gritzwitz, what's the fuckin' difference—gimme fifteen."

Physically the training was very difficult for me, the kind of thing where you just don't think you can do it. I never thought, for instance, that I'd ever be able to run five miles. But then I did it. And it was also kind of terrifying, because every time you went to a lecture, whether it was on hand grenades or on chemical warfare or whatever, the instructor—some half-shaven Vietnam veteran buck sergeant—would invariably start out by saying, "When you get to Vietnam, you are going to find that. . . ." That sure got my attention. I listened real careful.

The big thing I was afraid of, of course, and I think everyone else was too, was to be assigned MOS 11-B: Infantry. And they fed that fear by repeatedly saying, "Those of you assigned to 11-B will need to know this." And I would listen closely, and I'd think to myself, "The fact that I like Shakespeare and Romantic poetry won't mean anything when I'm 11-B."

So even though I ultimately was assigned to cook school, which is a terrible job usually reserved for the dregs of the army, I was delighted. Anything but the infantry. I wanted no part of combat.

Cook school lasted two months. About halfway through it, a notice went up on the bulletin board ordering ten of the guys in our training company, including me, to report for "RVN Orientation." Of course, none of us knew what "RVN" meant, so we asked some sergeant and he told us, "That's Republic of Vietnam." Then we asked him, "Does that mean the guys on the list are going to Vietnam?" And he said, "Oh no, that just means that the guys on the list are going to Vietnam *training*. It doesn't automatically mean you're going to Vietnam." But if that's so, I asked myself, how come only ten of the eighty guys in our training company are on the list? So from that point on I was convinced that I was going. I went back to the barracks and chain-smoked a lot of cigarettes and got sick. A month later I got my orders for Vietnam.

We flew out of San Francisco just after Thanksgiving 1968 and stopped briefly in Hawaii and Guam before eventually landing at Bien Hoa Air Base north of Saigon. From Bien Hoa we went to the 90th Replacement Battalion at Long Binh. It was there that I saw my first Vietnamese, a wrinkled old woman standing in the mess hall. And she looked so strange. Even having grown up in the New York area, having seen lots of different people from different cultures, did not really prepare me for it. I suddenly realized that I hadn't just entered a war zone, I had entered an entirely different world.

At Long Binh they gave us our fatigues and supplies and then our orders for individual units. You got a computer print-out that indicated your unit assignment, and mine said "101 AG-Admin." I had no idea what they meant. But when the guy next to me, who had "1 AG-Admin" got assigned to the 1st Infantry Division, I quickly figured it out. And my immediate reaction was, "Oh, shit, this is just *not* going to work out." I had heard a lot about the 101st Airborne in basic training. In fact, a couple of our drill sergeants were from the 101st, the ones with no front teeth, tattoos on their arms, and scars all over their bodies. These were the "Screaming Eagles." So I was just devastated . . . and terrified. It was bad enough to be in Viet-

"These were the 'Screaming Eagles' . . . the 'Marines of the Army.'"

"Every day was summertime." Specialist 4 Richard Grefrath relaxes outside his hooch at Bien Hoa, 1969.

nam, but to be in the "Marines of the army...." And all I could think of was how they kept telling us back in the States that if we screwed up as cooks we'd be sent out on patrol.

Then two miracles happened. Miracle number one was that I was assigned to the Administration Company of the 101st. And the Admin Company was located at Bien Hoa, while the rest of the 101st was up north, where it was much less secure. Miracle number two came just after I arrived at the Admin Company and was about to begin my duties as the company cook. I saw all these guys sitting at desks behind typewriters and thought, "It's ridiculous that I should be a cook. I'm a college graduate. I can type." So I sat down in the orderly room and asked this youngish guy with a southern accent if they had any openings for clerks. And he said, "Goddamn, you mean you're a college grad and they made you a cook? Hey Sarge," he called over to the first sergeant, "what about Thorsen? Thorsen's leaving and we don't have a replacement and I've got a guy here who can type." And within fifteen minutes I had become Thorsen's replacement. I felt relieved. I was a clerk typist in the rear, a long way from the front lines.

I spent the first eleven months of my tour at Bien Hoa, working seven to seven, seven days a week. My most vivid memory of that period is one of overwhelming boredom. In my letters I often compared it to being in prison. Bien Hoa was a big sprawling base, but you couldn't go anywhere. You had to stay right where you were. You had a very small area where you could walk around, like an oversized cell. You'd walk to the mess hall, to the office where you worked, to your hooch where you slept, and maybe to the theater or the bar or the PX. That's about it. And what made the sense of confinement worse was that every day we could see the "Freedom Birds," these robin's-egg-blue Braniff airplanes, taking off from the airfield with another load of GIs headed back to The World.

The sheer boredom really got to some people. One of my jobs was to type up various orders for the Administration Company, things like "Promotion to . . ." or "Request for Extension" or whatever. And every two weeks or so I would get one marked, "Request for Helicopter Door Gunner Duty." A very dangerous job,

right? But still you'd get these guys in the rear, clerks like me, who would volunteer to be helicopter door gunners because they were so bored, "sick of standing inspection and all the other bullshit," they'd tell me. And the army, of course, was willing to take them because door gunners were so often killed or wounded that they were always in short supply.

From time to time, of course, the war would intrude on us when we came under rocket or mortar attack. And when that happened we would scramble out of our hooches or the movie theater or wherever we happened to be and get in our bunkers or dive into the nearest ditch. While I was there a few guys were wounded, so we knew we weren't invulnerable. But we also knew that it was a big base and the chances of getting hit were small. Nothing like the danger that the combat troops faced out in the bush.

After I'd been in country about nine months, I came up for R & R. There were several options. A lot of guys went to Australia because they preferred "round-eyed" girls. But I just wanted to have fun. So I chose Bangkok because I heard that was where you could have the most fun. And it was wonderful from the beginning.

The way they had it set up was terrific. We flew out of Tan Son Nhut by commercial jet, and as soon as we landed they put us on a bus and gave us a half-hour briefing. The bus is rolling and an NCO is standing in front telling us, "We all know you guys are gonna get involved with women, so here's what you have to remember. The best thing to do is avoid streetwalkers. Don't just pick up anyone off the street. Go to the bars because the girls in the bars are A-1 licensed and have medical inspection."

Then we arrived at the official R & R center, a place called "Tommy's" Tourist Agency. As soon as you get inside, a girl comes around, kneels down and puts her hand on your knee, and asks you if you want a beer. So everybody starts slugging down Thai beer, which is like the strength of wine. And the girls are asking if you want to sign up for some tours. And guys are signing up for all kinds of tours all over Thailand even though you didn't have to.

Next you had to figure out where you were going to stay. And this too was all arranged and systematic. There was a table with boxes, and in the boxes you

had six or eight choices of "authorized" R & R hotels. So you picked up a card—mine was the Rich Hotel—went down to pick up your luggage, and then got on another bus that took you directly to your hotel. Within two hours you had gotten off the plane and were in your room.

I'd only been in my room for about a minute and was about to change my clothes when I heard a knock at the door. I opened it, and there's this little kid standing there, no more than eight years old, and he's raising his fingers up to his lips saying, "You smoke pot? You want girl?" And I said, "No, thank you," on both counts, and he just moved on to the next room.

After I changed I went out with a buddy of mine to find some girls. We had hired a cab driver for the week—can't remember how much it cost but it was real cheap—and he took us around. Our first stop was a massage parlor. I'll never forget that because it reminded me of the American Museum of Natural History in New York—you know, where they have the animal displays behind windows. It was just like that except there were girls and they were arranged on a stairway sort of lounging around, like a harem. And they all wore little poker chips with numbers painted on them. If you saw one you liked, you just chose a number. We did that and got a massage and then decided to move on. I guess we didn't like them as much as we'd hoped.

We went to several bars before we made up our minds. I found my girl at a place called the Hollywood Bar. We were dancing and drinking and there she was across the room. She was very pretty. So I turned to my cab driver-guide and requested whatever number she was, and he made the arrangements.

I kept the same girl for the entire week, or five days, or whatever it was. And by the time it was over I had fallen in love. Part of it, I think, was that by that time I had gotten very much into the Orient. Had I been in combat I'm sure my attitude would have been different. But as it was, Asia had become really romantic for me—the whole different world, the different people, different customs and religions. And Lek—that was her name—became the focal point for all of that. She was just incredible.

I was so entranced by her, in fact, that I went back to Bangkok two more times. I managed to get a week's leave in early October '69, and as soon as I returned from that I immediately put in for a three-month extension so I could get another R & R. I took that the first week of December. In the meantime we wrote letters back and forth and talked about getting married and going to the States after I got out of the army. I even bought a Thai dictionary, and eventually I started writing these long letters in Thai, asking all kinds of serious emotional questions—detailed questions like, "If you were to come back to the U.S., how would you feel about this and that?" and "What do you think of this kind of relationship?"—things that were, I'm sure, just beyond the capabilities of this girl. And she'd write back these short, cheerful letters answering none of the questions I'd raised. But, of course, when you're in Vietnam for a while you really lose perspective on what it's actually like back in The World and, well ... it was just hard. At the time, though, I really thought that I would come back and marry her. Only later did I realize it just wasn't going to work out.

After I extended my tour they sent me up north to Phu Bai, which was much closer to where the 101st was actually operating and because of that a whole lot scarier. It was also much smaller than Bien Hoa and less comfortable. In Bien Hoa, I used to say, every day was summertime. It was the Florida of Vietnam. But Phu Bai was like Seattle. It rained a lot and got cold at night. I spent most of my time processing guys in and out of the country, and when I wasn't working I went to the library—this long, air-conditioned trailer lined with books—and read about Bangkok. And thought about my girl there.

The only significant thing that happened when I was at Phu Bai took place in early February. A nearby artillery base—Firebase Rifle—was overrun one night and a couple of guys were killed. And immediately I got scared, thinking that maybe we might be overrun too. I wanted to get out of there as soon as possible. My three-month extension had already qualified me for a "five-month early out," so I went ahead and took that. A lot of guys did that. If you were scheduled to return to the United States with five months or less than your listed term of duty, which in my case was two years, they would let you out of the army early. I

Grefrath and his boss, Staff Sergeant Mac Douglas, at their desks in the Bien Hoa orderly room in late December 1968.

computed it to the exact day and left after serving in the army a year and seven months.

When I left Cam Ranh Bay for the United States in February 1970, I had mixed feelings. I was very happy to be out of the war and looking forward to seeing my family again. But the Orient was still in my blood, and I thought I'd soon be returning. Not to Vietnam, of course, but to Bangkok. But I never did.

Instead I traveled around Europe for a few months and came back in the late summer to begin graduate school in English at Temple. Just picked up my life where I'd left off. Got an apartment in downtown Philadelphia, grew my hair long again, and immersed myself in the academic world—you know, books, writing, intellectual discussion.

I enjoyed thinking back on my experiences in Southeast Asia, but I didn't talk about it much. Of course, a lot of people didn't want to hear about it, and I knew that. I still followed the war in the news but not as closely as I did when I was there. And my basic views about it had never changed. I still thought it was a no-win situation and a pointless waste of American lives. I only knew one guy personally who was killed over there, a guy from cook school named Orville Hill. But I often think of him and his family and the other families who lost spouses or sons and are still living with that. Like the woman in Buffalo I read about who lost

Grefrath and his Thai girlfriend, Lek Tim Puongpoi, dance at the Hollywood Bar in Bangkok in September 1969.

her son in Vietnam and still wears black and goes to church every day because, she says, "Since he is gone there is only darkness." The political passions of the time have cooled and lots of people now agree, for different reasons, that the war was a mistake. But it was a mistake that cost the lives of a lot of good people.

Still, I don't regret having served in Vietnam. For me it was an education, ranking right up there with college and graduate school. It was an important part of my life. And I still enjoy thinking back on it. I belong to several Vietnam veterans organizations, and in the course of my library work I review a lot of books on Vietnam.

You know, I read a lot now about the resentment that some combat veterans felt and still feel toward those of us in the rear, the REMFs—the Rear Echelon Mother Fuckers. And I can understand that. I particularly remember one night when about ten or fifteen guys from the 1st Air Cav came barreling into a bar where we were drinking, straight from the real war. Their fatigues were falling apart, their boots were so dirty they were yellow, half of them didn't have shirts, and the other half hadn't shaved. And there we were, our shoes shined by hired servants, looking like we'd just walked off the quadrangle at West Point. They immediately took over the place. Sent the Vietnamese bartender away screaming and then started tossing bottles of beer out from behind the bar. They didn't have anything to say to us. They just kept to themselves.

So even then I was aware of the distance between us. But I think it's unfortunate. It's unfortunate because I have nothing but respect for the guys who went out into combat and risked their lives and saw their buddies shot and blown up by booby traps. I know darn well that I was just a desk-bound clerk, and I don't pretend to have been anything other than that. But I still think that we should emphasize the things that we shared rather than the things that made us different. We all served in Vietnam. We are all Vietnam veterans. ∎

Michael Benge

Agriculturalist
Agency for International Development
Central Highlands, 1962–1968
Prisoner of War, 1968–1973

Mike Benge was born in 1935 and grew up on a ranch in Oregon. He dropped out of Oregon State University to join the Marines in 1955. During his hitch, Benge served in Japan and developed a fascination for the Orient. He returned to university and completed a degree in agricultural engineering. In 1961 he took a job with the International Voluntary Services and was sent to Vietnam where, in 1965, he was hired by AID and by 1968 was its second highest ranking official in Darlac Province. He was fluent in both Vietnamese and Rhade, a montagnard dialect. Today Benge is in Washington, D.C., still an AID official. He is married and has a daughter.

At the end of January 1968 a bunch of us had gathered at my house in Ban Me Thuot to celebrate Tet. Sometime after 1:00 A.M. on Tuesday the thirtieth, I went out on the balcony of my house to toast the New Year with Dr. Gerald Hickey, the anthropologist. We had received warnings of a big Communist attack scheduled for Tet, but I thought it was part of the Communist disinformation program since we got the same warning every year. During Tet there are more rounds fired off at the moon, something about a troll trying to eat it, than during the entire preceding year. And with firecrackers going off all over town it was an ideal time for the NVA to infiltrate because, hell, they could have the whole town captured before anybody knew it wasn't part of the Tet celebration. The popping, pop, pop, pop, pop, pop, that began going off we thought was just more firecrackers. Gerry and I toasted each other and I said, "Well they missed another good chance to take over." Just as the words were out of my mouth an 82MM mortar round landed in my front yard and Gerry said, "Oh shit, it's real."

I had montagnard guards at my house, so I quickly set them up in a defense perimeter. Then I got all my noncombatants, those who had never been in a firefight or didn't know which end of a gun the bullets came out of, under a central stairwell which was surrounded by heavy walls. We got a smattering of firing off and on, so I kept everybody inside and was up most of the night walking the perimeter. The other Americans in Ban Me Thuot were scattered out in a number of compounds around the town. There were CIA, military intelligence, police advisers, an air force R & R billet, army helicopter units, plus all sorts of civilians with various organizations, including a group of missionaries out on the edge of town.

On the first morning of the attack, however, the Communists left the missionaries alone while they struck at the nearby province headquarters and blew up an ammunition dump. Our telephone to the province headquarters started working again after first light, so I called to find out what had happened to the American civilians. Unfortunately nobody there knew, nor could I find the American army officer responsible for the evacuation of U.S. noncombatants. Since no one else was looking out for the civilians, I decided

I'd better round them up. I strapped on a shoulder holster with a .38 revolver and drove off.

I picked up one of our doctors and dropped him off to tend the wounded at the province hospital and went from there to the local orphanage and girls school to see if anyone had been wounded. Then I set out to get the two Americans farthest out: a refugee adviser and a logistics adviser who I ordered to pack up and get their asses out. On the way back I stopped at the province headquarters and talked to the province chief. He was worried about his family, which was in a house near the missionary compound. Since I had to check on two IVS kids down in one of the villages, I told him I would look in on his wife and ten children. I found them scared but okay, radioed the information back, and headed down the hill toward the village. I was just about there when I saw a bunch of guys crossing the road in light sage khaki uniforms, a different color than ARVN, and wearing different kinds of hats. I said, "Oh shit, they don't look like they're ours." So I backed up the hill and drove into the missionary compound.

The missionaries knew NVA and VC groups were all around, but at this point they had not been attacked. When they saw me coming they started waving at me to get out. I stopped and started to turn around when thirteen NVA regulars raised up out of the ditches at the sides of the road and pointed their SKs and AKs and B40 rocket launcher at me. I felt like I was in a horrendous dream where people just suddenly appear. I had five rounds in the pistol under my arm, but I divided five into thirteen and decided, it just doesn't work, baby, there's no way out of this.

The leader of the group looked like a Vietnamese Hitler with his hair hanging down in his eyes and a little mustache. Later I found out he was head of a psychological warfare team, which was lucky for me because the propaganda types followed the official line that prisoners were to be taken alive and given humane treatment. The regular Communist troops made it more of an operational procedure to kill prisoners than to take them. They took away my gun and marched me to their headquarters, which was located in a nearby graveyard. One of their officers interrogated me a little,

but I told him I didn't know anything, I was just an agricultural adviser. However, a couple of things made them suspicious of my story. I was wearing a cadre hat, a green beret with a silver tiger pin on it, and black jammies. I also kept my old Marine Corps dog tags on my key chain. I looked military to them and that may have been another reason why I didn't get killed, because military prisoners had political value while civilian prisoners were seen strictly as encumbrances.

They marched me away from the battlefield several kilometers to the Ban Me Thuot leprosarium. Upon arrival I encountered a surreal scene. They had captured about two dozen young montagnard troops, some as young as fourteen years, and had them lined up before a group of lepers the Communists had organized into a kangaroo court. The VC cadres were acting as prompters for this jury. The prompters would first offer the accusations, such as crimes against the people for serving in the army, and then suggest the punishment, in this case execution. Under this psychological pressure the lepers, many of them mentally unstable to begin with, began chanting, "Kill them, kill them." Saying it was the will of the people, the NVA then shot every one of the montagnards, just blew them away. It was very, very, very macabre, like something out of an insane movie.

I guess they let me see this to prove they were serious, because my question-

Flanked by a montagnard villager and a member of a student medical assistance team, Mike Benge surveys damage after a catastrophic flood in Phu Bon Province, September 1964. Benge served as an interpreter during relief efforts.

Children stand by a well drilled by Benge and a montagnard team for the International Voluntary Services at Dr. Pat Smith's montagnard hospital, Kontum, March 1964.

ing was taken over by an NVA intelligence officer and became more intense. He wanted to know where the province chief was, where the ARVN division commander was, the names of the American advisers and their addresses, and a great deal more information. When I repeated that I was an American civilian and just an agricultural adviser, the officer very deliberately took out a 9MM Russian or Chinese automatic pistol and put it up to my head and asked me again. I told him I didn't know anything. Then he cleverly let me see a shell go into the chamber of the gun, put it back to my head, and asked me again. I said I knew nothing. He cocked it, the sound was as loud as a bomb going off, and put the pistol against my temple again. I decided I had to talk. If their intelligence was as good as what we claimed, they knew everything anyway. Luckily they had recently rotated most of the Americans and had new advisers in. So I began giving him the names of everybody who left. I learned something that helped me over and over: it didn't matter what you told them, just give any answer to relieve the pressure of the moment. After my interrogation they got me on the march again, and we circled around to a mountain camp overlooking Ban Me Thuot. There they had built two bamboo cages and chained me in one of them.

When the NVA had hit the city, they came up the road past the compound where the thirteen Americans from The Christian and Missionary Alliance group lived. Two days later the Communists occupied the compound and dynamited the missionaries' houses. The survivors hid in a garbage pit and watched while the NVA occupied the church and used it as their headquarters. The missionaries bargained with the North Vietnamese to evacuate a severely injured woman, but when they emerged from the shelter, three were gunned down [including Ed and Ruth Thompson—see page 152], and three others were killed by grenades thrown into the bunker. Two who remained unwounded were led away.

A couple of days later they brought the pair—Hank Blood, who had been translating the Bible into Mnong, a montagnard dialect, and Betty Olsen, a nurse who specialized in treating lepers—into camp and chained us together. There were also a number of RF/PF troops and

a few South Vietnamese officers imprisoned there who were constantly being pressured to write statements and make radio broadcasts. As an object lesson, the VC who were now in charge of our captivity periodically took out those who wouldn't cooperate and killed them. One ARVN captain came to me and said, "How will my wife and kids survive if I don't cooperate with them?" And I said, "You're right. What can you do? I don't condemn you for that." They also recaptured a couple of young soldiers who had escaped and held another summary trial and firing squad as an example. The VC ran the prison camp, but it was evident that the NVA were in charge for there was a continuous flow of NVA officers coming through checking on us and questioning us. They had Hank identified as a CIA operative and were still somewhat confused about my status. We were there for about a month.

We discovered that the Communists were so bureaucratic that once Americans were in the system our guards would get in trouble if we were killed. The only way they could justify your death was if you hotly defied them or if you tried to escape, except later it became obvious the Communists could just ignore you until you died of neglect. They knew that we were of no value to them as political prisoners, and they began telling us so. We just ate rice that should be given to the troops. As a result we received almost no food during February and March, our first two months in captivity. We managed to keep going on a diet of manioc, but we were slowly starving to death.

I was in good shape when captured, thirty-two years old, 155 pounds of muscle, and used to living off the local market. I had, in my years in South Vietnam, generally eaten with the montagnards so if they killed a pig for sacrifice, I ate the raw pork. I also ate grasshoppers, rats, lizards, and locusts just as they did, and we used ants scalded in hot water as a dressing on greens. It was like putting vinegar on your salad. I had been raised on a ranch, too, and was used to scavenging wild berries and roots and whatever else I could find. I was probably as good a candidate as a survivalist as anyone around. But the missionaries weren't. They didn't exercise much and looked pale and drawn even before they were captured. Their diets didn't consist

of much; they ate hardly any locally grown food or produce because they were afraid of catching diseases and relied instead on a lot of canned goods.

During the first months of captivity I had been talking to a provincial montagnard who had been conscripted by the VC and was one of our guards. I had been working on him, saying he would be awarded with $10,000 and a piece of land if he would take off with me. But when it looked like he was about convinced, I had a moral problem about leaving Betty and Hank, because I was sure they would die on their own. While I was deciding what to do they started moving us again, first to the southwest and then they hooked back due east and stopped in the Chu Rulach area, a longtime VC stronghold called Happy Valley. The camp was near a stream that produced clouds of mosquitoes and we stayed there for several weeks, caged most of the time. The main job being done there was the indoctrination and reeducation of montagnards who were forced to farm for the NVA and VC, so after awhile the VC became a little more lax with us and let us out sometimes. The food was still mainly manioc, and we were given small amounts of salt and tobacco. I traded most of the salt and tobacco to the montagnards for whatever greens they could get us, although I started smoking some because it killed the hunger pains. By this time, in addition to the first stages of malnutrition, we were suffering from a parasitic skin disease and dengue fever, but for me the worst was to come.

After all that worrying about how the missionaries would survive, I came down with cerebral malaria, at that time in Vietnam about 80 percent fatal. I became feverish, had diarrhea, loss of appetite, and then loss of vision. I would "white out." I'd get a rushing sound in my ears, everything would just turn white, and I might wake up three days or a week later completely exhausted. For somewhere around a month I was delirious most of the time and blind. The only thing that kept me alive was the nurse, Betty Olsen. Whenever the guards would let her, she washed my face, cleaned me up as best she could, forced me to drink, and spoon-fed me. She would rouse me enough to where I could kind of dreamlike realize what she was trying to do, and then I'd just blank out again. When I began coming around after about five weeks, we were living in a cave underneath a cliff in another part of Darlac Province. I had walked there, but I can't remember much of it except stumbling along supporting myself with a bamboo staff. I had lost 30 pounds, probably down to under 120, and was as weak as a kitten.

In July they moved us again. The monsoons had started, and it was as wet and slippery as hell. By now they weren't much worried about us running off because we were all three pretty much a mess. Their attitude was one of benign neglect. They wouldn't kill us, but if we died of natural causes it was good because we had no practical value and bureaucratically they could get away with it. At the new camp they gave us a couple of sheets of plastic to keep the rain off, but there was no way that all three of us could keep dry at the same time. Hank was particularly run-down both mentally and physically. With the constant soaking he soon developed severe chest pains, and we knew he had pneumonia. The Communists had raided the provincial medical warehouse in Ban Me Thuot during the Tet attack, so we knew they had supplies at the nearby field hospital. Betty and I begged them to give medicine to Hank, but they refused. It took him a little more than three days to die—sometime in mid-July. We buried him in a shallow grave in Darlac Province and moved on. Now we had been prisoners for six months.

Soon after we were put in the charge of some harder-core VC. They took me around to show to the troops and would say, "Here's one of the invincible Americans. He's so used to riding in limousines and airplanes he can no longer walk." A couple of times I turned around and in Vietnamese said, "These guys are lying like hell. I only get half a bowl of rice a day to eat, I've had goddamn malaria with no medicine, and I doubt if you could do any better." Then they'd jerk the rope and hustle me away. I don't think I was very good propaganda material.

By this time I was also covered with ulcers from infected leech bites. We had marched through an area where the ground was just covered with leeches, and they dropped from the trees down your neck and crawled into your genital regions. They were huge and there was no way to avoid them. Hundreds of them got on Betty and me. I was bleeding all over and even now, nearly twenty years later, I've got scars all over my body from those bites.

For Betty, the leeches were just about the last straw, she was getting pretty damn weak, and in addition to the leeches we had lice all over us. The VC wouldn't let us boil our clothes and blankets to kill the vermin. To annoy us they just let the lice eat away. By October we had walked from Darlac Province to Tay Ninh, then hooked back north. As we crossed Quang Duc Province and then circled toward the Cambodian border, they began taking Betty on a different trail than me during the day. I learned when they brought us together again at night that they often dragged her along or kicked her when she dropped from exhaustion. When I started to protest she tried to stop me saying they would kill me if I complained. I replied, "Look, we're dying anyway, what the hell's the difference?" So I argued with the guards and declared that Betty was just not able to go on. For once they listened, and after a couple more days they let Betty and me rest at a camp near a river where they had a couple of regiments stationed.

I was down to about 100 pounds, and I guess one thing that helped me survive this period was acting as moral support for her, because it kept my mind off how bad I was. I told a doctor from a medical unit there that unless Betty got some halfway decent food she wasn't going to be able to make it any farther. So after a

At a celebration in his honor, Benge drinks ceremonial wine with montagnard villagers in Buon Kô Sir, Darlac Province, 1966.

Captive journey. This map depicts Benge's route while a prisoner. It shows the sites of (1) Hank Blood's and (2) Betty Olsen's deaths.

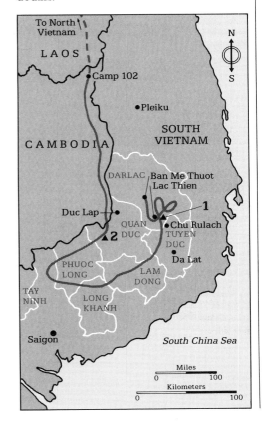

good deal more cajoling, the guards finally said they would give us a good meal. Betty and I dug up some young bamboo sprouts, and they gave us some mung beans and rice and corn and boiled the bamboo for us. We were so ravenously hungry that we began wolfing it down. It registered in my mind that the bamboo shoots were extremely bitter, but we just kept eating.

Jesus Christ, right after we got through we were struck by extreme stomach cramps and then projectile diarrhea and vomiting. I could bend over and hit a tree. I later concluded they had decided to kill us, because with bamboo you have to boil it twice and each time pour off the fluid to lower its high acid content. They had only boiled it once, or it was poisonous. This way they could say we died of natural causes. All Betty and I could do was go back to our area and move our hammocks to a place nearer to a little ravine. Betty had it so badly it just tore her to pieces. She became so weak she couldn't get out of her hammock. The guards did nothing but let her lay there in her own defecation. They wouldn't let me take her down or wash her or bring her water. They did loan me a knife so I could cut a hole in the bottom of her hammock and let the defecation drain out. It was the best I could do. She just completely dehydrated and died within three days in late September. This was the low point, psychologically my worst time.

But I soon made up my mind; fuck you people, I'm going to live in spite of it all. Being a bit stronger than Betty I survived the diarrhea and they moved me again, this time into Cambodia because, I later found out, there were now orders to take all prisoners to North Vietnam. Fortunately it was the hatching season for some little green frogs, and they were everywhere. Whenever I could I'd reach down and pop one into my mouth whole and swallow it before the guards saw me. If they did, I would be kicked or get a rifle butt on the head. Also, I discovered something similar to a pistachio nut, and once again if the guards were in a good mood I would gather them as we walked along the trail and throw them in the coals of the fire to roast at nighttime.

I had another trick. I occasionally convinced the guards to let me take baths when we crossed a stream because I remembered reading a book about the fa-

mous frontiersman Hugh Glass, who had to crawl 200 miles for help after being mauled by a bear. One thing that kept him alive was allowing maggots to breed in his wounds to eat the decaying flesh. Then he would lay down in the rivers he passed, and the fish would eat out the maggots and the rest of the dead tissue. I layed down whenever they would let me bathe, and sure enough the fish would nibble away at my ulcers. Once in a while I was fast enough to catch one of the fish and would immediately eat it raw.

I knew the minute we crossed into Cambodia in October because in Vietnam we were constantly hiding from the airplanes and helicopters, but as soon as we got over the border, the Communists walked out in the open and we passed large groups of soldiers coming south on the trail. Also there were rest stops every four hours along the trail manned by regulars and flying the NVA flag. I was turned over to the NVA at this point, but I was so weak I could hardly walk. I propelled myself along with that bamboo cane I'd picked up when I was first struck with malaria. When I came to anything more than eight or ten inches high in the road, I would have to go over to a tree, lean against it, lower myself to the ground, and lift one leg at a time over the obstacle with my arms. Then, with my arms and shoulders, I would pull myself back up and continue along the trail. When we came to stairs cut in the mountainsides, I would have to crawl up them on my hands and knees. If they didn't think I was traveling fast enough, they would knock me down to the ground or hit me with a rifle.

Once, however, a North Vietnamese aspirant, an officer candidate, saw me being knocked down and complained that mistreating me was against Uncle Ho's teachings. He walked north with me for about three days to see I wasn't beaten anymore until, he said, any farther north and he would get into trouble.

After the aspirant left, the brutal treatment began all over again, and I was just about on my last legs. I had eaten a few fish that I caught with my hands, and a few land crabs, and the little green frogs, as well as any nuts or bugs I could find. But I could hardly walk, my morale was gone, and I was about ready to give up. Finally, down to about ninety pounds, I was in such bad shape the guards

shoved me off into this one camp that had a medic—a barefoot doctor. He looked me over and said, "This guy's almost dead." He gave the prison chasers hell, told them I had beriberi and aggravated malaria, and then proceeded to pump me full of vitamin shots. He told me, "If you can just hold on for three more days you'll be there, at the prison camp"—and then he kind of laughed and used the propaganda line they fed the prisoners to describe it—the land of milk and honey, just as if they'd translated it from the Bible.

Once again I made up my mind that I was going to hold on for three more days. I pulled myself along on the cane, saying in my mind, "Just put one foot forward of the other, just three more steps, I'm almost there." Then I'd say, "It's a piece of cake." That went through my mind all of the time. I remember very little about it except I was totally exhausted and often delirious, but I just kept that chant going all day long for the next three days. Finally I reached the top of one high mountain, and I was there. After ten months of walking, no shit, somebody said, "Welcome to the land of milk and honey."

An American Special Forces lieutenant that saw me come into camp that November day later told me he estimated that I was sixty to sixty-five years old. I was still wearing the green beret but I was hobbling, barely able to walk, the hair on my body had fallen out, and what was left on my head had turned pure white. On my arrival at Camp 102, as it was designated, a North Vietnamese Army doctor was called up from the main hospital. He went through a very elaborate performance and declared I was completely dehydrated and he was going to give me an intravenous feeding. He brought out a bottle with a piece of inner tube over the top and some plastic spaghetti tubing coming out the bottom that was filled with a sugar and water solution. He had a needle but couldn't get it in any of my veins until I finally showed him one on the back of my arm. Embarrassingly for him, after the elaborate hookup there was no act two. The vein wouldn't take anything and the audience began to wander off. Finally, the doctor sent the guard for a bowl, and he took the needle out of my arm and poured the solution into the bowl and gave it to me and said, drink it. I looked at it and thought, so this is the great medical treatment they've been promising me. Welcome to the land of milk and honey.

It was, however, the end of the worst period, nutritionally, of Benge's captivity. During his year's stay in the camp in Cambodia, his food improved marginally, he received periodic treatment of his malaria, and was able to rest and regain some strength. After about three months he began "to feel like myself again," and on Christmas Day 1968 he was put in with other American prisoners. In November 1969 he was moved into Laos and then on to North Vietnam, where his final stay was in the infamous "Hanoi Hilton." He was repatriated with the military prisoners on March 12, 1973, after more than five years of imprisonment, twenty-seven of those months in solitary confinement.

I still believe in what we were doing in Vietnam. I went back in September 1973 and worked for the minister for ethnic minorities, at his invitation, helping to work out a foster parents program for Amerasian kids of montagnard descent, developing a livestock improvement program, trying to get veterans benefits for montagnards who had been in the Special Forces, and doing some political work with the montagnards. I later moved to the Philippines but continued to fly back to Vietnam when I had a vacation until it fell to the Communists.

I have absolutely no misgivings about the U.S. being in Vietnam, and looking back, I'd do it all over again. We were doing the right thing, although we weren't doing as good a job as we could have. We never carried out the reforms that we needed to. The people who were in authority knew damn well that if the Communists took over they were dead meat. We had them virtually by the balls and could have forced them to make more political, social, and economic reforms. Why didn't we? Most of the time we didn't know what needed to be done. We went over there ignorant. In the whole bureaucratic structure we never got it so that the little people could rise up into any command or authority position. We never built nationalism at the grass-roots level in South Vietnam.

It's not recognized really that there were American civilian prisoners of war. When you talk about POWs, everyone thinks that's only military. So I think you can draw a parallel, an analogy, between that and our whole presence in Vietnam. The military effort over-

shadowed everything that we did. But when I talked with the political commissars in North Vietnam, they actually felt more threatened by us, that we civilians were actually harming their cause more than the military.

To me personally I think the most appalling aspect of my whole experience is that when I got home from prison and was debriefed for the record, the tapes were never transcribed. Nobody really gave a damn about the lessons learned. Nobody really gave a damn what I found out about communism. Nobody really gave a damn about anything. ∎

Top. *April 20, 1973. One month after his release, Benge appears at a State Department press conference as the first POW to speak openly about his experiences in captivity.*

Above. *A D'Jarai woman presents an award of appreciation to Benge in Phu Bon Province after his return to Vietnam in November 1973.*

Robert L. Reynolds

Company Commander
199th Light Infantry Brigade
October 1967–October 1968
Staff Officer
199th/1st Cavalry Division (Airmobile)
February 1970–July 1971

Robert Reynolds grew up in Cleveland, Ohio. He began his military career when he joined the ROTC program during his freshman year at Bowling Green State University. Commissioned as a second lieutenant upon his graduation in 1964, he later served two tours in Vietnam as a staff and field officer. After leaving the army in 1972, he held a number of corporate sales and marketing positions before deciding to devote himself full-time to the task of aiding fellow Vietnam veterans. Formerly the Vietnam era veterans coordinator for the Massachusetts Office of Affirmative Action, he now works as the director of the Veterans Education Training Program at the University of Massachusetts's Boston campus. He also volunteers eleven hours of his free time each week to counseling homeless Vietnam veterans in Boston's South End.

The stories my father used to tell me about the motivation for the family migrating north in the 1930s had a lot to do with wanting vertical mobility and realizing they weren't going to find it in Pulaski, Tennessee. They had a little land of their own, but for all practical purposes they were sharecroppers. So they saw moving to Cleveland—a big, heavily industrialized city with a lot of good-paying jobs—as a step up, an opportunity to make much more money than a rural black could ever dream of having.

My father was working at St. Luke's Hospital when I was born. He was whatever they call folks who mop floors. But shortly after that he got a job working on the city streetcar line, which was really a rather prestigious job for blacks at that time. Then, during World War II, he became one of the first eight or ten blacks to join the Cleveland Police Department. A few years after that he became one of the city's first black detectives.

I grew up going to Cleveland public schools and received a very good education, in part because I was selected to participate in a special "enrichment" program and in part because of the support I got from my parents. Even though my mother and father separated before I was five, they both took an active interest in my education. My father in particular was very protective. He had very strong ideas about what my limits were, and one of his major concerns was that I not make some girl pregnant and screw up the rest of my life. After I graduated from college he didn't much care what the hell I did, but he was determined that I should go to college. And I did. During my senior year in high school I applied for admission to Bowling Green State University and was accepted.

In the fall of 1960 I drove up to Bowling Green with my father for freshman orientation. And one of the presentations we went to was for army ROTC. A captain spoke to us, and after he finished my father asked me, "Well, what do you think?" I said, "I think I want to join that." And he said, "I don't think you should join that." For the next two or three days we repeated that same conversation, back and forth. But in the end I joined anyway.

One of the major reasons I wanted to enter the military was because of the example of my uncle, my father's younger brother. He had enlisted in the army at the age of sixteen, fought with one of the more celebrated black units in Europe during the Second World War, and was very highly decorated. After the war he had stayed on in the army and later fought in Korea. By the time I entered college he had been in the service nearly twenty years and had attained the rank of E-8, which is just about as high as you can go in the enlisted ranks. Even though he and my father didn't get along too well, throughout my childhood my uncle was always a hero to me. I also saw a lot of myself in him. Like me, he could be very aggressive and confrontational, whereas my father was much more even-tempered and a mediator. The two brothers were very competitive with each other, and I suppose they competed as role models for me as well.

But in addition to my uncle's influence, I remember reading a book by Stendhal, *The Red and the Black*, that had a strong impact on me. Stendhal wrote about how young men sought to redeem themselves socially by going off to war, because whether they came back or not society made heroes of them. As a young black man, the idea of validating myself so that no one could ever question or challenge my rights as an American very much appealed to me.

My plan at the time was to go through ROTC, get my commission, fulfill my two years' obligation, and then get out. But I soon found out that accomplishing even those simple goals would not be easy. Because while quite a few blacks had gone through ROTC at Bowling Green, as far as I've been able to determine no black had ever before been commissioned as an officer. Often the candidates were screened out by biological tests that were supposedly immune to social influences, such as too much albumen in the blood. But I had my doubts. The general environment at B.G. was too racist for me to believe that it was strictly coincidental. Not openly or actively racist; it was more subtle than that. For example, blacks on athletic scholarship who were believed to be dating white girls would have their scholarships mysteriously taken away.

During my senior year I ran into a similar sort of situation when I applied for the position of commander of the ROTC's Special Forces Detachment, which was a new program modeled on what the Green Berets were already doing in Vietnam. I was a cadet captain at the time and very much wanted the position. But there was another guy, a white guy, who was equal in rank and he wanted it too. Even though we had participated in equal fashion the previous year, our major gave it to the white guy. He didn't offer any reason for his decision, so there was no way to challenge it. Then, very shortly after, the white guy decided to drop out, so in the end the major had no choice but to give me the position.

By that time, the fall of 1963, Vietnam was already beginning to appear pretty regularly in the news. But the way I perceived the situation was that it was small, not likely to grow, and that our role there was strictly advisory. I knew that there would probably be an opportunity to volunteer for Vietnam if I received the proper training. But that wasn't the reason I got involved in the Special Forces Detachment. I think it just appealed to my sense of adventure, something that involved a certain amount of risk taking. I was always looking for ways to extend myself, to take on new challenges and responsibilities and meet them.

Upon graduating from college in the spring of 1964, I received my commission as a second lieutenant as well as orders to report to Fort Benning, Georgia, the following November for the infantry officers' basic course. I remember that as I was preparing to leave I was frightened to death because I'd never been to the South before. When I was a child my father would never allow me to visit his own hometown because he thought there was a great potential for danger to me there. And the negative feelings I had about the South had been reinforced by the media coverage of the civil rights struggle. But as it turned out I didn't have any problems there, except for getting in a car wreck that put me in the hospital for a few months.

After completing the officers' basic course, I went to Fort Polk, Louisiana, to take up my first active duty assignment as a training officer of a basic training company. This was in June 1965, shortly after the first American troops had arrived in Vietnam and just before President Johnson made the decision to commit large numbers of U.S. ground forces. I wasn't totally aware of those decisions at the time, since I was living on an army installation and pretty insulated from what was going on politically. But as time went on I saw the effects of those decisions. As more and more people came into the pipeline, Fort Polk almost doubled in size to accommodate the swell. Parts of the facility that had been closed down and boarded up were reopened and refurbished, and new roads, new housing, new theaters, and a new PX were built.

My own job at Fort Polk turned out to be much less satisfactory than I had hoped. My commanding officer and I just didn't see eye to eye. In many ways it was a classic confrontation between a white man and a black man, the black seeing himself as equal in every way to the white and the white not willing to give up his assumption of superiority. He was, in fact, my superior in strictly military terms since he was my commander and I was his executive officer. But we were similar in age, had similar educational backgrounds, even had identical cars. And in terms of rank he was only three months ahead of me. He took full advantage of that, though, and made sure that anything that was routine, anything that was boring, anything that was undesirable would be done by me.

So after a while I went to my battalion commander and told him that I wanted a transfer to another unit as soon as possible, because if I stayed where I was the CO and I were going to have a fight and that would not be good for either of us. His initial response was to tell me to stay where I was, but not long after that I did manage to get a transfer. It wasn't the battalion commander's doing. A major in charge of a new "special training" program at the Fort Polk Academy was looking for a training officer. He had heard about me and arranged my transfer.

It turned out to be one of the most satisfying jobs of my professional career. I was put in charge of a program designed to help young men lacking in certain basic skills to meet the army's minimal academic and physical standards and allow them to complete basic training. This was part of Secretary McNamara's "Project 100,000." The idea was to give these guys, many of whom were poor or underprivileged, some marketable skills so that when they got out of the army they could contribute to the economy and general welfare of the country. A surprising number of them, for example, couldn't even read; others had never learned how to

Robert Reynolds's father, Charles L. Reynolds, in Cleveland, Ohio, in the late 1930s.

Reynolds's uncle, James L. Reynolds, and his paternal grandmother, Lela Bassham, shortly after his uncle's return from World War II.

throw a ball. So it was a real challenge. But it was also very exciting. I was given a great deal of autonomy to design the program, implement it, and manage it as I saw fit. And I enjoyed that. I always found myself doing more than I thought I could do, so at the end of the day I felt not only tired but very satisfied with what I had accomplished.

I'm aware of the criticism of "Project 100,000," that it was a way to justify bringing large numbers of poor blacks and Hispanics into the military while upper-class whites avoided it. But I also know that for many of these guys the army offered the only way of getting out of their circumstances and the only hope of ever getting a real job. For many young men of color seventy-five dollars a month, in addition to food, clothing, and shelter, was a lot of money. And it's still that way. We don't have a formal draft, but we have a draft of economic necessity. What's harder to justify is why such a high proportion of blacks and Hispanics, once they got to Vietnam, ended up in combat units and why whites were more likely to be rotated to the rear.

As enlisted men, of course, these men didn't have many options. But as an officer, I did. In fact, that's one of the reasons I decided to go into ROTC. I figured that I would eventually be drafted anyway, so it was a way to gain more control over my circumstances. I didn't have to go to Vietnam. I chose to go, primarily because of my experiences at Fort Polk Academy with the special training program. I suppose my thinking at the time was that I would continue to be given new challenges and responsibilities, that I would continue to be promoted—it was there that I was promoted to first lieutenant—that it would make a good career. So in 1967 I made the decision to extend my tour of duty indefinitely, knowing that meant I would wind up going to Vietnam.

Once I began to appreciate the gravity of the action I had taken, I was absolutely frightened out of my wits. So I decided that I'd better do everything I could to prepare myself for the war. I went to Ranger school and jungle school and sought the advice of people who'd been in Vietnam or fought in other wars. I also spent some time with the 3d Training Bri-

Company commanders of the 199th Light Infantry Brigade flank their battalion commander (center) at a III Corps firebase in February 1968.

gade, which was Fort Polk's Vietnam-oriented training group, so I could be more in touch with the technology of conducting operations over there.

My first tour in Vietnam ran from October '68 to October '69. I remember that one of the first things that struck me when I arrived at Long Binh was how calm it was. Clearly there was a war going on because you would hear the bombing runs and the artillery firing, but in general the American effort had evolved into a very orderly, bureaucratic kind of process. The installation at Long Binh, for example, was like a small American city. The buildings were temporary and that sort of thing, but you had all of the amenities and virtually all the commodities you could find in the United States. But I suppose that's what I should have expected. Because the military is a business. And working for the military is not all that different from working for any other business, except that your job is to wage war and you get the opportunity to die.

At the beginning of my first tour I was the commander of a headquarters company of the 199th Light Infantry Brigade, which meant for all practical purposes I was a noncombatant. I was a logistician who arranged and provided services to other units. Although I'd already been promoted to captain, I knew that as an infantry officer any further career advancement depended upon my getting command of a rifle company and going out in the field. Part of getting my report card punched. So I went to my battalion commander and explained that I had come to Vietnam to command a rifle company, and he promised me that as soon as the commander of B Company rotated out, I would be given B Company.

But shortly after that our battalion commander got promoted, and we got a new battalion commander. So I went to him and told him about the promise I'd received, and he said OK, and then a couple of months later when B Company opened up he turned around and gave it to another guy who'd just arrived in country. I was real pissed. It was like ROTC all over again. So I confronted this guy and said, "I don't want to make this a racial incident, but I wondered why you did it. It certainly doesn't escape me that he's white and I'm black and that I'm the only black officer you have." He told me that that was the decision he'd made, that he

had no regrets about that decision, and I would get a company eventually, but not this time. But that didn't give me any satisfaction because there seemed little possibility of another company in the battalion opening up any time soon, and I was approaching the midway point in my tour. If it didn't happen then, it wasn't going to happen.

I decided to go to the deputy brigade commander, Colonel Davison, and tell him my story. Frederic E. Davison was at that time the highest-ranking black officer in the U.S. Army and would soon become the third black general officer in American history. He thanked me for coming to him, said that he was happy I wanted a rifle company, and told me he would see to it, if possible, that I got one. My battalion commander really chewed me out for having gone over his head, but within about three weeks I got a company. Not B Company, but A Company.

I spent the next six months, roughly the second half of my tour, as a combat commander in the field. I don't think I was a typical commander because I was far more protective of the people who worked for me than some other commanders. My major focus was not so much waging the war as surviving the war, which was very different from the kind of cowboy company commanders who didn't care what they did or how many casualties they took as long as they were charging and killing the enemy. I knew that that kind of behavior was fre-

Frederic E. Davison, deputy commanding officer of the 199th Light Infantry Brigade, with General Creighton Abrams, COMUSMACV, on the occasion of Davison's promotion to the rank of brigadier general in September 1968.

quently rewarded with very big medals. I knew it was a war of attrition, and the name of the game was body count. But my own personal philosophy was to do whatever was necessary to fulfill my mission in a way that minimized the danger to myself and my men.

During my entire time in the field I operated from the point of view that I was going to do them before they did me. If we were walking into an area where we suspected a reinforced enemy unit, I prepared the area first with all of the destructive technology at my disposal—air strikes, artillery, gunships. If I thought there was something in the tree line, I decimated the tree line. We're talking about pretty brutal stuff. But my attitude was, you can always buy some more bombs and shells, but you can't buy someone a new arm or leg. And you can't tell a dead man you're sorry.

In most circumstances, though, the way I preferred to operate was to beat the enemy at their own game. I liked to send out far-ranging small patrols and have them do concentric circles around an area, looking for obvious signs of an enemy presence—places being dug, remnants of mortar fire, throwaway packages of B40 rockets. Then, using that intelligence, we would close in in force or set up ambushes. We pulled off some really spectacular ambushes while I was there. To me that way of operating made a lot more sense than sending 300 gum-chewing, cigarette-smoking nineteen- and twenty-year-olds thrashing through the jungle or moving along predictable paths in single file. That's just asking to be ambushed or booby trapped.

I suppose my concern for my troops and my way of operating in the field is the major reason a strong bond developed between me and my unit. In any case, I had very few problems that required me to exercise my disciplinary authority. Early on, I had a radio telephone operator, a young kid from the South, who gave me some problems. This guy had a habit of making racist remarks in my presence—innuendos, comments about southern black women, that sort of thing. For a long time I put up with that until one day he flatly refused to carry out an order from me. "I'm a white man," he said, "and I don't take orders from niggers." At that point I realized that my responsibilities as company commander re-

quired me to take action. So I talked with the guy and told him that if he couldn't work for me, I could arrange for him to do something else until he decided he wanted his old job back. So for several weeks, no matter which platoon was out in the field, he walked point. But eventually he did come back and ask to work for me again. I agreed, and after that we no longer had any problems.

Aside from that, I don't recall any other racial incidents. In part that may be because as company commander I had little contact with the day-to-day problems of the enlisted men. I dealt primarily with my platoon leaders and NCOs. But I think it was also because the men in a combat unit are so interdependent that racial tensions rarely surface in the field. They're more likely to manifest themselves in the rear.

Still, you have to understand that the extreme polarization between black and white troops in Vietnam was just beginning to develop during my first tour. The turning point was the assassination of Martin Luther King, Jr., in April 1968. Because when that happened, I think every black person in Vietnam said to himself, "Well, there's a war going on at home, so what am I doing here? What is my role here? Am I fighting a white man's war?" I know I myself began asking those questions, even though at that point I didn't fully appreciate how radicalized many blacks had become back in the United States. I had been in the military so long I had been insulated from many of the changes that had taken place. I had never even heard of an "afro," for instance, until some white guy pointed one out to me in *Time* magazine.

I was in the field during the summer of 1968 when I heard about the riots in Hough, the area of Cleveland where I had lived with my father during my high-school years. Then I found out that a black nationalist whom my father had arrested had threatened my father's life and that my father had bought an M1 carbine and moved into the third floor of his house. And I felt very confused because I really didn't understand what was happening or why it was happening. My father had always seemed to me to be, if anything, a sort of activist. Regardless of the fact that he was a policeman, his ideals were very problack, pro getting our share of the pie. So I couldn't under-

stand how anyone could view my father as anything other than a strong black man. Even when my father told me the story and showed me his rifle after I returned from my first tour, it still didn't fully sink in. I was too caught up in the excitement of my homecoming, too happy to be with my family and friends, to really understand. In fact, it wasn't until I went back years later that I saw the extent to which lots of areas around Hough had been burned out by the rioting.

Shortly after my return I got married, went on a honeymoon, and then moved down to Fort Benning, Georgia, to take the Infantry Officers' Advanced Course, which is a kind of middle management course for career officers. My aspirations at that time were still pretty traditional, even all-American. Having gone through the experience of the war and come out in pretty good psychological shape, I wanted to settle down with my wife, buy a house, have a kid and a dog, and be happy, like I was before all this shit started. But even before the course was over I got orders to return to Vietnam. And I had no choice but to go, because in accepting the infantry officers' career choice I had incurred an additional year's obligation. From the army's point of view, it was just a matter of maintaining the personnel flow to the critical military occupational specialties still needed in Vietnam. That was the name of the game. You need those warm bodies as replacements over there for the guys who die or rotate.

My second tour began in February 1970 and ended in July 1971. When I arrived I went back to the 199th, and the commanding general immediately offered me a rifle company. And my response was, "Sir, I've done that before. I know what that experience is about and I want to do something different." Besides, it was clear to me that the United States was no longer invested in the war—the stand-down or withdrawal process was well under way—so I thought it would be foolish for me to go out and risk my life again for no reason.

So I got a job as a briefer, hand-delivering time-vital operational information between the commanding general of the 199th and the III Corps commander. Then, when the 199th stood down, I got the same job with the 1st Cavalry Division. And it was a very desirable job because I was living in comfortable circumstances at the Long Binh post. I had a nice room in the bachelor officers quarters near the handball courts, I had a jeep and a lot of free time, that sort of thing. I also had an opportunity, given the nature of my work, to get a macrocosmic view of the war. I knew what all of the American units were doing in the field, where the problems were, where we were having success. During my first tour, like most people who went to Vietnam, I never really had any sense of the big picture.

Then, after I'd been doing that for a while, the major who had hired me was replaced by this lieutenant colonel who used to say things to me like, "You know, you're a really talented guy. You're much too talented for this job you're doing. You ought to have another job that stretches you a little more." And I would say to him, "I like this job a lot. I'd like to stay in this job until I go home." But in the end this son of a bitch wound up putting me in the worst job anyone could possibly have in Vietnam at that time, and that was to be second in command of a replacement detachment at Bien Hoa, processing people out of the country. It was a meat factory. You got guys in, gave them a place to sleep, fed them for a couple of days, tried to keep them from killing each other, and then made sure they got on the plane.

It was very demoralizing. Not only was the job itself thankless, but there was a total lack of professionalism. Since everyone knew we were pulling out and there was no chance they'd be coming back, nobody cared about anything. Nobody saluted. Blacks and whites were completely polarized. These guys had nothing to do but get drunk and get into fights. Every night there was some situation where we either had MPs doing crowd control or I was doing crowd control. It was very unpleasant and at times very dangerous.

I had a few other jobs after that, but they were all similar in that they involved trying to maintain what ability we had to carry on the mission in a highly reduced sort of posture. So by the time I got back from my second tour I was really disillusioned. I'd even begun to question whether I wanted to continue with a military career.

Even so, I wasn't really prepared for what happened six months after I got back. I was an instructor of military justice, race relations, at Fort Gordon, Georgia, at the time—this was January, maybe February 1972. I had just bought a house, I had a stepchild in the school system, and I was beginning to settle in when I received notification that I would be released from active duty after ninety days as part of the "reduction in force." My first reaction was to freak. I told my wife not to spend any more money. Then I got angry. I felt betrayed. But finally I just accepted it because, as I said before, the army is a business. And business is business. When you no longer have 500,000 men engaged in a war and can't maintain those kinds of numbers in the services overall, you have to get rid of some of them. You have to have a reduction in force. Just an orderly personnel routine.

I don't know if I can separate my Vietnam experience from the rest of my military experience because they really go hand in hand. Looking back, it's difficult to say what I got out of that experience because so much of it was assimilated as part of my self-image, as part of what I am. In the army I repeatedly had to deal with white men, usually conservative white men, who could not get beyond the superficial fact of my color and evaluate me as a person, as Bob Reynolds the individual rather than Bob Reynolds the black man. I suppose that experience made me more defensive, but it also made me more confident.

Having served as an officer in the United States Army, having put in two tours in Vietnam, I no longer feel any need to validate myself. Because I know, as Martin Luther King used to say, that "I am somebody." I also know that this is my country, and I deserve a piece of it. It's mine, and it has been mine as long as my family has been here. And no matter what anyone else thinks of me, no matter how many times I am challenged to prove myself again, that will never change. ■

Captain Reynolds plots artillery fire during a search-and-cordon mission in 1968.

Steven Sharoff

*Graduate Student
Kent State University
March 1969–June 1971*

Steven Sharoff spent his childhood and adolescence in the Catskill Mountain resort town of Monticello, New York, where his father served as chief of police for more than thirty years. After graduating from high school in 1961, he spent three years at Orange County Community College and then transferred to Plattsburgh State University, where he earned a B.A. degree majoring in history. Rejected by the military for chronic hypertension in 1967 and again in 1968, he spent a year and a half traveling around the country, working at odd jobs, before enrolling in the graduate program in history at Kent State University in Ohio in the spring of 1969. Currently a faculty member of the University of Maryland's European Division, he teaches history, including a course on the Vietnam War, to American servicemen stationed abroad.

You can't really understand what happened at Kent State in the spring of 1970 unless you understand what happened the year before. Because the events that took place in April 1969 tremendously politicized and radicalized a lot of people like me, people who had never been actively involved in the student protest movement.

Not that I hadn't strongly opposed the war in Vietnam before then. I had. But my opposition had been as much personal as political. I had lost one very close friend over there, a roommate from Orange County Community College named Jack Wolpe who had gone off and joined the Marines in 1965. I was very upset and bitter about that. I was also very angry about what the war was doing to the country. It seemed like everyone had gone crazy—the King assassination, the Bobby Kennedy assassination, the Democratic National Convention in '68. I remember how infuriated I was watching the Chicago cops beat the shit out of people and shouting at my father, "See that! See that! What's wrong with this country? Is there any reason for that?" And as a professional police officer he agreed there wasn't.

But politically I'd have to say I was still relatively naive. At Plattsburgh I'd had a terrific professor, an American diplomatic historian named David Glaser, who had challenged me to reexamine some of the fundamental beliefs I'd grown up with—the assumption that America was the shining beacon of freedom and democracy in the world, that we never did anything wrong, and so forth. David's basic thesis was that since World War II the United States had tried to make the world over in its image and, in order to do that, had supported regimes that were dictatorial and repressive. And of course he related that thesis to what was going on in Vietnam. So I had begun to have doubts. Still, it wasn't until I began graduate school at Kent State, something I did with David's strong encouragement, that those doubts crystallized into action.

When I arrived at Kent in March of 1969, the first thing that struck me—aside from the huge size of the place—was how politically active the campus was. There were SDSers, the Young Socialist Alliance, the Black United Students, even the Young Americans for Freedom—all these groups I'd heard about but never really come in contact with as an undergraduate. So right away I started going to all sorts of rallies and meetings just to find out what was going on. I would just sit in the back and listen. Radical groups, liberal groups, conservative groups—it didn't matter. I found all of it fascinating.

That's why, one day in early April, I decided to go along when the SDS announced that it was going to protest the university's "complicity" in the Vietnam War. I just thought it would be interesting. As it turned out, nothing much happened. The SDSers marched up to the front door of the main administration building with their set of "non-negotiable" demands: abolish ROTC, abolish the Liquid Crystals Institute—which had developed some kind of sensor used in Vietnam, I think—abolish the university law enforcement program, and so forth. But the campus police wouldn't let them in. There was a brief tussle, but nothing serious, and then everyone walked away.

Later I found out that half a dozen SDSers had been arrested and suspended from the university and that the administration had prohibited the SDS from operating on campus. And I couldn't believe it. I thought, what's going on here? It can't be because of what happened at the administration building. They didn't do anything.

So when I heard that the university planned to hold hearings at the Music and Speech Building to decide the cases of the suspended students, again I decided to go along. Even though the proceedings were officially "closed," there were a lot of us who wanted to see if the SDSers would get a fair hearing. But the whole thing turned out to be a classic setup. As soon as we were all inside the building, the campus police chained and padlocked the doors and then called in the state police to arrest us. Fortunately, though, most of us—something like 200 out of the 250 trapped inside the building—managed to get out through a basement exit before the blue hats started fingerprinting and booking people.

The next day several hundred students got together at the old Student Union and formed a broadly based coalition to protest the university's actions. A steering committee was set up and I was elected chairman, mainly because I seemed to be the only person who knew anything about parliamentary procedure. We took on the name "Tri-C," short for Concerned Citizens of the Kent State Community, and began to challenge the university peacefully. Our basic position was that we wanted the administration to adhere to "due process" as defined by the Student Code. We didn't necessarily agree with the SDS but felt that if the university wanted to kick them off campus, they should do it properly.

While all of this was going on, I got a call from Harold Kitner, an art professor who also served as the university ombudsman. He asked me if I would be willing to sit down and talk with him and Lou Harris, the provost. I said, "Sure, no problem." Then Kitner started asking me about myself. I immediately understood why. I mean, here I was, heading up this group that was becoming a real political force on campus, and nobody knew who I was.

So the next night I went to Harris's house and talked with him and Dean Kitner until around one in the morning. I said, "Here's where I'm coming from" and basically laid out my life story. I said, "Look, I'm an average middle-class American guy. I'm not a radical. I don't want to overthrow the government; in fact, I'm very patriotic. I'm not a violent person, and I won't be a violent person. But I think that what's been going on is wrong, and I'm going to do everything I can to stop it." Both Harris and Kitner were satisfied with what I told them about myself, and Kitner in particular seemed to agree with me about what the university was doing. He didn't like it.

The next day we had a steering committee meeting to decide if we were going to hold a protest march or first put the issue to a campuswide vote. And while this debate was going on, some guy burst into the room to tell us about a story in the campus newspaper claiming that undercover state police had identified me at a regional SDS meeting in Akron the night before. The article was on the front page—"Tri-C SDS Linked"—and all but accused me of being an "outside agitator." Which was funny, because there were people on the Left who thought I was an FBI "plant," a *provocateur*, because my father was a police chief.

Again I couldn't believe it. From the very beginning the hard-core radicals had told me I was a fool to believe that the administration was going to allow me or any group to change their policies. And now it seemed that they'd been right. Because the source of the story was a member of the administration—not Kitner or Harris but the vice president for student affairs, Robert Matson. He was trying to discredit us by charging that the SDS controlled the whole movement.

The irony, of course, was that I couldn't possibly have been at the Akron SDS meeting because that was the night I was with Harris and Kitner. Matson didn't know that. But when I told everyone in Tri-C where I'd been, there was no longer any disagreement about what we should do. We immediately decided to call a rally and march and to challenge the administration to publicly debate the facts of the matter any time and any place.

The march was a huge success. We went around the campus shouting, "Join us! Join us!," and thousands of students came pouring out of the dorms. I gave a fifteen-minute speech and basically just said, "Look, it's bullshit. What's happening is that they did something illegally that we're against, and now they want to shut us up. Well, they're not going to shut us up." After that we organized a campuswide referendum on the major issues—should the SDS be kicked off campus, etc.—and got the largest turnout of any vote in the university's history.

In the end most of the issues were never resolved. Charges against most of the students arrested at the Music and Speech Building were dropped, and I think the SDS was allowed to operate on campus again. But the suspended students weren't allowed back, and the SDS demands were never met. The only important thing that happened was that a lot of middle-of-the-road students became politicized, and there was a lot of mistrust of the university administration. And that set the stage for what happened a year later.

The following fall was very calm on campus. I went down to Washington, D.C., in November for the Moratorium march, which was the first major protest I'd ever participated in. I remember thinking that it looked like the capital of some South American dictatorship—tanks, personnel carriers, machine-gun nests, buses parked bumper to bumper so you couldn't get near the White House. The government was so scared it had turned the city into an armed camp.

Steven poses with his parents, Jack and Lillian, at the Plattsburgh State University commencement in early June 1967.

But at Kent nothing much happened until late April 1970. I still remember distinctly the morning when an undergraduate history major came into my office and told me that Nixon was planning to send more troops to Vietnam. And I said, "He wouldn't dare. He'd have to be crazy to do that." I knew that Nixon was going on TV that night, but I had assumed that he would just announce another troop withdrawal. When he announced the invasion of Cambodia instead, I just went crazy. I was angry, outraged. I mean, we were already fighting one undeclared war, and there he was launching another. I immediately got together with a group of graduate students and graduate assistants, and we decided that we should hold a rally to protest this. We had keys to various buildings and access to mimeo machines, so we stayed up all night printing leaflets calling a rally the next day at noon on the Commons.

On Friday, May 1, we all met just before the rally to decide what we would do. And I said, "Let's bury the Constitution. The bastard has trampled all over it, so let's bury it." I found a copy of the Constitution at the back of a high-school history book, ripped it out, and then went down to the Commons and rang the Victory Bell. They used to ring the bell after football games, but it had already become a symbol of protest. So in a short time we had attracted a crowd. I spoke, and so did Tim Butz and Jim Geary—two Vietnam veterans who were totally opposed to the war. After we finished we dug a hole right in the grass and buried the Constitution.

As we were leaving, this young instructor several years older than me came over and said, "Don't forget, street action downtown tonight." Only later, after it was all over, did I realize what he meant.

I spent the rest of the day just enjoying the beautiful weather. It was gorgeous, the first really nice weekend of the spring. In the evening I followed my usual pattern and went down to Water Street to hang out in the bars. When I got downtown, the first thing I noticed was that there were a lot of motorcycles around. Then I noticed that there were people I knew from the SDS and YSA, and they were wearing red headbands and arm bands. I glanced to see who I knew, thought "Hmm, that's interesting," and

then went into Orville's, the hippie bar, to watch the NBA finals on TV.

After a while someone came in and said, "You're not going to believe this, but they're throwing bottles at police cars out on the street." I zipped outside, and it was wild, just wild. Some people were starting to build a fire in the street, and a police car came up and they just beat the shit out of it. So the cop car took off. Then an old couple tried to drive through, and they started rocking the car back and forth. There was only a small group doing this, and they were chanting, "Fuck the war!" and "U.S. out of Cambodia," and other slogans. And after a little while a gang of bikers, the "Chosen Few," joined in because they liked this sort of thing.

Then the Kent police arrived. And immediately they decided to close the bars. Well, I don't have to tell you what that did. Instead of dealing with several dozen fairly radical students and a group of heavy bikers, they now had to deal with thousands of students pissed off because the bars had been closed. An instant mob. So everybody began yelling and screaming, and then the people who had started this thing began moving down the street, trashing things—throwing rocks, smashing windows. They didn't hit every place; they were selective. They hit the rip-off drugstore, for instance, but not the little shoemaker's shop. They busted the windows of the bank and the gas company but left the dinette where all the students ate alone.

That's when the Kent police, backed by the local sheriff's deputies, really came in force. They started lobbing tear gas and pushed the students up Main Street toward the campus in the direction of fraternity row. The kids, of course, were running for whatever cover they could find. So the cops—they were so stupid—started gassing the fraternity houses. And immediately the jocks—these huge, crew-cut guys—came storming out of the frats, screaming, "Pigs! Pigs!" and throwing beer cans at the police. Now everybody was pissed off—the people who'd been ordered out of the bars, the jocks, everybody. Since the cops weren't allowed on campus, there was a face-off with the students on one side and the cops on the other exchanging taunts back and forth. It continued like that until a traffic light repairman got stranded in the middle of the street—a passing car had knocked the

ladder out from under him—and everybody went over to help him down. That defused the situation for the moment.

Early the next morning I got a call from Dean Kitner, asking if I would come over to his office right away. When I got there Kitner told me, "We have just had a meeting with the mayor of Kent. He has asked Governor Rhodes for assistance. If the students leave the campus and head into town again tonight, the National Guard will be sent in. The university has nothing to say about it." Then he told me that he needed people to monitor the rallies that had been called for that night and asked me if I'd round up some other graduate assistants to work with me.

So on Saturday evening we all gathered together and were issued blue arm bands to identify us as faculty marshals. Then we split up to cover the various rallies. I went to the ROTC building, where I knew the SDS and YSA were going to be, because I was real curious to see what they'd do. When I got there I went up to one of the YSA leaders and passed on what Dean Kitner had told me about the National Guard. The reply I got was, "Steven, it's got to be done. We're going to burn this fucking building down." Since I had been told that I was not to get in the middle of it, but just to do my best to influence people, I stepped back and just watched. This was like 9:00 P.M., maybe 9:30. They must have spent forty-five minutes trying to set fire to the building. They threw matches into it, rags, but they just couldn't do it until somebody threw in what I later learned was a railroad flare. And that finally did it.

That's when the police and firemen showed up. But they were so outnumbered they wouldn't go near it. Most of the students there—there must have been several hundred—were just spectators, but the firemen couldn't know that. So they were afraid. They later claimed that someone cut the fire hoses with a machete, but I never saw anything like that.

After the building began burning, all the .22-caliber ammunition the ROTC used in its drills went off, and a lot of people were happy because this old decrepit wood-frame building was the closest symbol of the military on campus. Then someone said, "Let's go to the dorms and get the whole campus and march downtown." I knew this was a grave error and told the leaders that. But they went anyway, and the students followed. They spilled out of the dorms.

This was the moment when, as I think back on it, the events of the previous spring came into play. Because I don't think there would have been that kind of widespread political anger if it hadn't been for the administration's actions in '69. The whole scene just reminded me so much of the march Tri-C had held where the students had joined us by the hundreds. But that had been a peaceful march, and this was something else.

So now you had this huge group of students, following the lead of the hard-core radicals, heading toward town. When they got to Main Street, I zipped up to the head of the column and told the leaders—I knew these people—that if they didn't turn back the National Guard was going to move in. And they just said, "We don't care. We're going." I said, "It's a mistake, man. It's a mistake."

Then I went over to the curb, sat down, and put my face in my hands. I was very upset. And that's when I heard it. Clank, clank, clank, rumble, rumble. I looked up the hill, to the right of the column that was already winding onto Main Street, and there were these APCs, jeeps, and trucks loaded with troops. As they came over the hill I could see the light of the street lamps glinting off their bayonets as they fixed them to their rifles. I said, "Holy shit, I don't want to believe this."

And down they came. They forced everybody off the streets and sealed off the entire campus. Then they started to

move onto the campus. Now, we had been told earlier in the day that if the National Guard came on campus they would recognize us as faculty marshals because of our blue arm bands. So about half a dozen of us started walking toward the guardsmen to find out who was in charge and what we should do. And one of the women next to me took out a handkerchief and said, "Yoo hoo, we're faculty marshals." The guy in charge said, "Halt!" but we weren't really paying attention. We were all pointing to our arm bands and yelling, "Faculty marshals!" And he kept saying, "Halt!" Then, all of a sudden, we saw all these soldiers pointing rifles at us, one rank kneeling, the other standing. And I just flinched. I spread out my arms, grabbed the people on either side of me, and yelled, "We're not moving! We're not moving!" And we all put our hands up. I thought for sure they were going to shoot us.

It turned out, of course, that they didn't know anything about blue arm bands. Nobody told them. And that's how it was the whole weekend. Communication was so bad.

The guardsmen asked us if we would help round up students and bring them to the dormitories. We did that, and then I went home. I lived out at Brady Lake, near Ravenna, about ten minutes from campus, and on Sunday I just stayed there. I didn't go on campus at all. So I missed all the fraternizing and flirting that went on between the students and the guardsmen—Allison Krause putting the

Sharoff (holding megaphone) decries the university administration's attempts to ban the SDS from campus. April 1969.

Standing atop the Victory Bell on the Commons of Kent State University, Sharoff (center) raises the two-fingered peace sign at a "Tri-C" rally in April 1969.

Top. *May 1, 1970. An unidentified student challenges Sharoff's attempt to bury the constitution on university property as two antiwar Vietnam veterans, Tim Butz (left) and Jim Geary (right), look on with amusement.*

Above. *May 4, 1970. Students flee up "Blanket Hill" as the National Guard moves in with tear gas to disperse the crowd. Sharoff's tall figure can be seen beneath the lowest branch of the tree at the extreme right of the photo.*

flower in the rifle, all that—and I also missed the confrontation at the library. Apparently there was some misunderstanding. Some students thought they were going to get to talk with the mayor of Kent and that didn't happen.

What really set things for what happened the next day, though, was Governor Rhodes's speech. I remember listening to that speech on the radio on Sunday and thinking what a very bad speech it was. He called us Brown Shirts and Nazis and said he wouldn't tolerate this kind of thing in Ohio, that he'd teach us something. It was very inflammatory.

I also remember that I got a phone call from my father that night warning me to stay away from the campus. He said, "I know who these people are. I've dealt with them. They don't know about riot control; they're not really trained for it." And he predicted that somebody would get killed. But I didn't heed his advice. When one of the organizers of the Friday protest called to tell me that there would be a meeting at 10:00 A.M. to decide if we should go ahead with a follow-up rally we had planned for Monday at noon, I told him I'd be there.

The next morning, Monday, May 4, I inadvertently slept late. By the time I got to campus the meeting was over, and the decision had already been made. So I met up with some friends and walked over to the Commons, where the Victory Bell was ringing and a lot of people were milling around. As time passed, more and more people joined us, many of them students on their way to and from classes. So within a few minutes we had a very large crowd—a thousand people, maybe more. The guard were there, too, strung out in a line near the ROTC building, or what remained of it, at one end of the Commons. I remember thinking at the time how strange it was to see them all standing there, rifles in hand, protecting this totally burned-out building.

Technically the noon rally violated orders. They had already imposed an evening curfew on campus—students had to be in their dorms by 9:00 P.M., I think—and they had also outlawed public gatherings. But no one knew about the ban on assemblies. The university never informed us. We found this out afterward. To be honest, though, I would have to say that even if we had known, it wouldn't have mattered because the general feeling that day was "Fuck them, who do they think they are? This is *our* campus." The issue was no longer the war or administration policies. The issue was the presence of the guard on campus. Our attitude was, how can the process of education go on with armed troops all around us? If they left, we could resolve this thing by ourselves.

After a few minutes they sent out a jeep with two guardsmen and a policeman and told us through a bullhorn, "You are hereby ordered by the governor and the commander of the Ohio National Guard to disperse. This assembly is unlawful. . . ." And immediately there were catcalls and people shouting, "Get off our campus!" Then students began to throw stones. The jeep came back. Same message, same response.

Then the guard sent out a small group armed with M79 grenade launchers. They lobbed tear gas into the crowd, and some students picked the canisters up and lobbed them back. It wasn't only the radical students. I saw clean-cut, short-haired kids, guys who had never got into any trouble in their life, tossing the tear gas back at the guardsmen. It went back and forth for a while until the troops started to move forward, forcing us up Blanket Hill between Taylor Hall and Johnson Hall. As the guard advanced, most of the people went to the left around Taylor Hall. I went to the right, into Johnson Hall, and then headed up the stairs to the roof. And lo and behold, I see Dean Kitner. He's standing on the roof of Johnson Hall with a group of other people, including some professors, and we're all watching this unfold. Then suddenly, I heard this solitary "clap." Then a pause of several seconds. Then "clap, clap, clap, clap" in rapid succession.

Somebody said, "Firecrackers." And I said, "No, that's rifle fire!" I didn't actually see the guardsmen fire, but I know about firearms. I knew that what I heard were rifle shots. So I said, "I'll go see what happened." And as soon as I got those words out of my mouth someone came up screaming, "They've been shot! They've been shot!"

I zipped down the stairs, ran around the building, and I couldn't believe what I saw. People all over the place just lying in blood, pools of blood. The next thing I knew a close friend was standing in front of me, without his shirt on, crying. "I stuffed my shirt into this girl's back," he said. "The blood was pouring out of her." A group of us then tried to get everyone away from the students who'd been shot. We formed circles around them so that when the medical people arrived they would have some room to work.

But the medical people didn't arrive for a long time. We waited and waited, but they didn't come for almost fifteen minutes. They didn't come, I later learned, because the National Guard at first refused to allow their ambulances to be used. They refused. That's why Sandy Scheuer died. I don't know about the rest of them, but I know about her. She bled to death. Because by the time the civilian ambulances arrived, she had been bleeding so profusely for so long that there was no chance to save her.

In the meantime lots of people were just standing around in a state of shock. Other people were going absolutely nuts, just raving. I remember this one guy from Tri-C came up to me and said, "I'm going home and getting a rifle." And I grabbed him and said, "No, this is not the way. Enough has been done already." Since nobody seemed to have any direction and something had to be done, I sent someone to get a bullhorn and then started to tell people to sit down. "Be calm," I said, "just sit down right where you are."

While I was doing this one of the university's lawyers came over and told me that General Canterbury, the commander of the guard, wanted to see me. I didn't want to go because I felt like shooting the guy. But I did, and when I got there Canterbury said to me, "All those people have to leave." And I said, "General, I can't do that. These people have just seen their friends shot. They're in a state of shock. It was about all I could do to get them seated." He said, "Those are my orders." I just looked at him and then he repeated, "Those are my orders." I turned around, went back, and was starting to explain that General Canterbury had ordered everyone to leave when, all of a sudden, another group of guardsmen began moving toward the students.

Everybody freaked. One minute they had been sitting there quietly, and now they were just scattering everywhere, trampling the fences at the far end of the Commons. At that point a loudspeaker truck came by and announced that the university was officially closed and that everyone had two hours to get off campus. I was still trying to calm these kids down, but I didn't have much success until the state police arrived and took over from the guard. Immediately you saw the difference between a trained force and an untrained one, just as my father had tried to tell me. The first thing the guy in charge

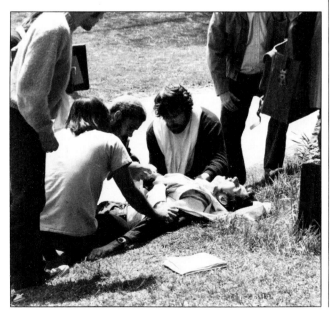

Students look after one of the wounded moments after the shootings occurred.

told me was, "We understand what happened here. It never should have happened. We don't want any trouble, but we have to clear the campus." I told him I'd do what I could, and he said, "I'd really appreciate that." Then he ordered his men to stay back while a dozen of us went around and told everybody to go home. Then I went home and burst into tears.

During the weeks that followed I was interrogated by the FBI, and I testified before the Scranton Commission on Student Unrest. I told them that the shooting of thirteen unarmed students was unnecessary and unjustified, that a trained police force never would have done it, that it was murder. I told them that I was politically pretty moderate when I came to Kent and that I was fairly radicalized now. I said, "You made me what I am, and there are hundreds of thousands of people around the country just like me." I said that it had to stop. I said that some intelligent people had to come along and do something about this shit or there would be more craziness in the streets, and more bloodshed, and more killing.

The strongest feeling I had, and still have, about what happened at Kent is: what a waste. It didn't have to happen. Those four students didn't have to die. And I have the same feeling about the war. We could have had the same peace terms that we eventually got four years earlier. Instead we wasted 25,000 more American lives and tens of thousands of Vietnamese lives. We continued to destroy Southeast Asia, and we continued to tear apart the social fabric of our country.

So I haven't really changed my views about the war. I think those who opposed it on moral and constitutional grounds were right. And in the course I teach now I still make the same case. Most of my students are American military personnel, and they seem to enjoy the course. In fact, one of the things I've found is that the guys who are my age, the guys who fought in Vietnam while I was protesting against the war, share many of the same feelings I have.

Sometimes, looking back, I think that I should have gone, too. I'm not sure why. Maybe it's a kind of survivor's guilt. Maybe it has something to do with Jack's death. But then I think that if I had gone, I probably would have been killed. Just another wasted life to add to the total. ∎

John Forbes Kerry

Swift Boat Commander
U.S. Navy, Phu Quoc Island
1968-1969

John Kerry was born in Denver in 1943 but spent much of his childhood in Washington and Europe, where his father held several important posts in the Foreign Service. From his parents Kerry gained a "sense of commitment to country" that he carried with him through St. Paul's School and Yale University.

By the time of his graduation in 1966, he had already signed up for the navy. From December of that year to July 1968 he served on a destroyer, the U.S.S. Gridley, spending several months patrolling off the coast of Vietnam. In November 1968 he returned to Vietnam where he participated in the river war of the southern delta, earning both the Silver and Bronze Stars for heroism in combat. Upon his return to the United States he became active in the antiwar movement as national coordinator of the Vietnam Veterans Against the War.

After graduation from law school Kerry spent three years as an assistant district attorney and two years as lieutenant governor of Massachusetts. In 1984 he was elected to the United States Senate.

Up until Vietnam I wasn't defined as a person. I was just a kid coming out of college. I played sports, I took exams, I graduated and there I was, full of hopes and aspirations but essentially unformed.

I was already committed to the navy, but I didn't even have any strong feelings about the war. In fact, prior to signing up I had been somewhat supportive of our position in Vietnam. But slowly my attitude changed to one of skepticism. It was, "What's going on here? What are the real facts? Do we listen to the traditional voices of public rectitude that we've listened to in the past, or do we figure this out for ourselves?" I was beginning to ask some questions—about an American foreign policy that seemed to be without any rationale, about a draft which was being used to provide the big stick for that foreign policy—but I hadn't answered them at that point. The war wasn't personal to me yet. It was an abstract foreign policy adventure that the United States was engaged in that I was thinking about in abstract, schoolboy terms.

Then in Vietnam I saw life and death on a daily basis. I got shot at and I shot back at people. And because of the kind of war it was, because I didn't like it, because I felt I had to speak out against it, because I had to define my own moral feelings about it and put them into a public context as I opposed the war, it came to define me absolutely. It demanded that I go against the grain in many ways. I mean, the easiest thing in the world for me to do when I came back would have been just to be quiet and go about my business, operate in the traditional channels and not stir the waters at all. But I wasn't happy with myself doing that. I couldn't *not* speak out against the war because I thought it was wrong.

For quite a while after I joined the navy, however, my connection with the war remained pretty tenuous. During my first tour on the Gridley we were quite removed. I went into Da Nang for eight hours one day and got to see the accouterments of war, but most of the time we were just steaming around in circles behind aircraft carriers out in the Gulf of Tonkin. Occasionally we'd have a readiness alert when North Vietnamese MiGs flew toward us from the mainland. But they'd always back off, it was really just a game of chicken. I had no contact with the Vietnamese people. I wasn't talking to grunts who were out in the field. I didn't have any real feel for what the heck was going on.

The first trip to Vietnam did give me a heightened curiosity by virtue of having been so near and having been part of the support operation. But volunteering for the Swift boats had nothing to do with my curiosity about the war. They attracted me because it was the one thing you could do as a junior officer and have your own command. In fact, when I signed up for the Swift boats they had very little to do with the war. They were engaged in coastal patrolling and that's what I thought I was going to be doing. Although I wanted to go back and see for myself what was going on, I didn't really want to get involved in the war.

I started out in Cam Ranh Bay, but about two weeks after I arrived they changed the policy on Swift boats. Originally, our mission was to interdict the flow of arms along the coast. The Swift boats formed the inner ring of a triple perimeter with destroyers on the outside and Coast Guard cutters in the middle. But a lot of swifties started getting really bored, you know, running around up and down the coast, so some of the guys began to venture in close to shore or went up the rivers shooting their guns in free fire zones. Then one day a boat made a run through the tip of the Ca Mau Peninsula. They came in on the Gulf of Thailand and exited on the South China Sea. And the captains and admirals in Saigon thought this was just terrific, the navy getting involved in the war, being right in there where the action was.

So I got transferred to Phu Quoc Island off the Cambodian coast to be part of a new program called Operation Sea Lords—Southeast Asia Lake, Ocean, River, Delta Strategy—that called for the Swift boats to start operating in the rivers. For the next five months it seemed as though we were in and out of every river in the southern part of the country. We even went on missions up the Mekong into Cambodia.

We were given patrol areas along certain stretches of river where we'd stop junks or sampans and search them if they looked suspicious. We also did a lot of work with ground troops. We once moved a whole ARVN division upriver to the jump-off point for an operation. We inserted SEALS, the navy commandos, we inserted Lurps, the long-range reconnaissance patrols. But most of the time we were going into the rivers and free fire zones and shooting targets of opportunity or waiting to be shot at to return fire and prove to the enemy that they didn't own that region. Our mission was defined as an effort to show the Vietcong that they couldn't operate in that part of Vietnam with impunity. We were literally there to shove the American flag in the enemy's back yard.

But it didn't seem to me we were accomplishing very much at all. You'd randomly stop a boat among the dozens that were going up and down the rivers and maybe you'd come up with some weapons. But for the one or two you stopped, hundreds of others went by and you knew weapons were slipping by you. Oh, we had individual victories here and there. Occasionally we'd stumble on to something that was happening. But our engines could be heard from five miles away. We never surprised anybody. We were constantly getting ambushed. As you rode along you could see bunkers built right into the riverbanks. They had .50-caliber machine guns, B40 rockets, the whole deal. There was a kid named Harwood who lost the lower part of his leg to a .50-caliber, and one of my best friends took a B40 right in the stomach. His whole boat just blew up and beached. And here you are traveling along in a quarter-inch aluminum boat waiting to get hit. It was just a joke.

With Lt. Kerry's PCF-94 in the lead, a line of boats sets out on a patrol through the Ca Mau Peninsula, February 1969.

There were countless problems. Countless problems. The ARVN were untrustworthy and didn't want to fight. A number of them were obviously VC. They knew most of the operations we were going on before we did. There were no defined lines of demarcation between "us" and "them," no specific territory to be gained and held. It was just this random process of fear here, fear there, tearing up these rivers with two 500-horsepower diesel engines booming away. If your goal was to win the hearts and minds of the people, we certainly weren't going about it very intelligently by thundering through in our boats and shooting the place up. And when you did get ambushed you usually lost more wounded than the other guys. So what have you gained?

There were twenty ways of doing things more intelligently, and we tried to suggest them endless times. We worked very hard from within to get people to understand that we didn't think what we were doing made sense. In fact, on one occasion they stopped the war on our behalf and flew us all up to Saigon for a big briefing. Admiral Zumwalt came and General Abrams, and they gave us this big spiel about what we were doing was so valuable, blah, blah, blah. Maybe it was just the navy's way of getting in on the war. I don't know.

But I was already beginning to feel that the war was a waste. The first patrol I went out on one of our men cut the nets of a Vietnamese fisherman who happened to be in a "prohibited zone." Here we were in another country, telling this fisherman who clearly wasn't bothering us in any way where he could and couldn't fish and destroying his livelihood in the process. Those nets were expensive. They weren't easy to come by, and there was no reason to cut them. There was no harm being done, no big problem. We were simply defining what was and wasn't permissible. There was something that just ran against my grain about us in our big boat with our guns ordering around the people we were supposedly there to help. And that kind of thing happened constantly.

With a one-year tour of duty you came, you did your thing, you left. You didn't bear any ultimate responsibility. You knew if you just made it through you could get out, so people started taking short cuts. For example, the B-52 strikes.

It was clear that places were targeted within our area of operations that weren't heavily VC. But they got bombed anyway. Or free fire zones. You came to understand by virtue of the fact that you went through them that a lot of these areas were not as cleared of people as we had been told, a situation that was subject to great abuse. Those with the guns were those who ruled. There was a recklessness and arrogance to the way we were fighting the war by everyone over there.

I'd lived abroad some of my life. When my father was stationed in Paris for a while I used to play in the old German bunkers outside my grandmother's house. From listening to her stories I got a vivid impression of what it was like to live in an occupied country, and that's what I felt I was in. I'll never forget the day I arrived at Cam Ranh Bay. There were dozens of Vietnamese scurrying around picking up cigarette butts after American GIs. There were Vietnamese waiting on tables at the officers' mess, Vietnamese making the beds, Vietnamese cleaning the latrines. And there we were, sitting around like kings running the war. We were the occupiers. And you can't win in those situations unless the population is supporting you, unless the indigenous troops are supporting you. And again and again and again we saw instances where the local troops, the Ruff-Puffs, the ARVNs, whatever, were unwilling to fight, had their own deals worked out with the VC.

Don't get me wrong. There were individuals, there were good units that were willing to fight. But not enough of them had a stake in it. Most South Vietnamese soldiers didn't feel they were fighting for their country because their leaders were unable to provide sufficient political motivation. The stronger infrastructure was on the other side, and they knew it.

It seemed to me that you had a classic insurgency in Vietnam in which the Communists were exercising governmental functions within the villages like taxation and so forth, a situation where the chief's head would appear on a stake and then a couple of days later if other people hadn't come on board they would start disappearing. You had to turn that process around. You had to secure territory, build your own political infrastructure, engage in the psychological contest for the population. But that wasn't taking

place, and quick forays into an area in which you simply tried to engage the enemy and then exit only wound up exacerbating the situation. It only increased the people's willingness to say, "Okay, we're really better off with the VC because at least they stay behind and work with the people."

The Vietcong were given a purpose. They were finely tuned in their understanding and commitment to a goal. They believed they were fighting for the unification of their nation and rightfully kicking out a foreign aggressor. It was a very powerful rationale and one we never really seemed to understand. The simplicity of their goals just made a great deal more sense in the agrarian, peasant world that surrounded us than the complicated geopolitical framework we were attempting to impose on them.

When I left Vietnam I was very proud of my personal service, of the men I'd served with, of their caliber and their qualities and their caring about each other and what they were trying to do. About the goals and definition of our mission I was furious. I was outraged. I was very, very angry that people were being asked to perform senseless tasks at great risk to such little purpose, unless harassment and interdiction had a great purpose. And this was a feeling shared by most of the men. They had become very disgusted with what we were doing. It was a subject of constant wardroom discussions and late-night debates.

We all felt betrayed and disillusioned. I think that for a lot of us the traditional assumptions and expectations of Americans of our age in that period were crushed by what we discovered were falsehoods, outright lies, and chicanery. The body-count process. The way the war was being sold versus what it really was. Admirals telling you things were happening that you knew weren't true. The idea that we were fighting against communism when it clearly was primarily a nationalist struggle. It was burst bubble after burst bubble. There was just a kind of stench to the whole war.

I came back from Vietnam with a basic commitment that I was going to try and save the lives of some of my buddies and not have more people killed. I didn't think people should be silent about it. I saw a special responsibility, moral and personal, to tell what I had seen. I thought

I had a perspective that was important to people's ability to understand what was happening over there. Because I'd seen it, I'd been there, I knew firsthand.

I intended to go to law school when I came back, but while I was still in the navy I participated in the Moratorium against the war in October 1969. I had negative feelings about the sort of hard-core guys—the real trashers, that wing of the antiwar movement that was out there for the kick and the shock value. I didn't have a lot of use for that. I thought they were all on ego trips, frankly, and I thought they had a different and more cumbersome social agenda than just ending the war. But the average people who I saw marching in protest—the kid in school, the housewife, the parent who had lost a child in Vietnam—I found it extremely moving and supportive. It was very liberating to know they were there, that they were just standing up in opposition. That was really a turning point for me. It was the Moratorium that coalesced my feelings, that answered a lot of questions about whether there was a way to communicate what I felt. After the Moratorium I knew there was a way to do it and that was to go out and work and organize against the war.

I was able to get an early release from the navy and I became very active all around New York City just speaking as a veteran and saying, "Look, here's what's happening." At one of these gatherings I met somebody who was involved with a group called Vietnam Veterans Against the War, and that's how I really became part of the antiwar movement.

Over the next year the VVAW staged a number of events including the Winter Soldier Investigation in Detroit where 150 veterans testified about war crimes they had seen or participated in. Winter Soldier was a terrifically important statement, but nobody heard about it. The *New York Times* didn't even cover it as a matter of fact. And it was my frustration over the lack of attention that led me to conceive of our march on Washington that eventually took place in April 1971. I was working on a book at the time, but I felt so strongly that we weren't getting our message across that I dropped what I was doing and became a full-time organizer. I was named national coordinator of VVAW and for the next twelve months devoted an enormous amount of energy

Testifying before Congress, April 1971. "How do you ask a man to be the last man to die in Vietnam? How do you ask a man to be the last man to die for a mistake?"

to raising funds and trying to pull together the whole effort of the march.

We called it Dewey Canyon III after the American operation code-named Dewey Canyon II in which U.S. forces supported the South Vietnamese invasion of Laos. There isn't any question in my mind that Dewey Canyon III was the moment when veterans of the war as an entity broke through the national consciousness. The image each night of veterans conducting mock search and destroy operations in the streets of Washington, the encampment on the Mall, the confrontation with the Supreme Court over our right to demonstrate, the emotions of the medal-returning ceremony when some of the vets took their decorations and threw them on the steps of the Capitol—the whole thing made Americans realize that there was a group out there besides the "peaceniks" who had a view about why Vietnam was wrong.

Some people argue today that the antiwar movement actually prolonged the war by alienating the majority of Americans, but I think that is absolutely false. If there had been no antiwar movement the war would have gone on for a much longer period of time or been escalated to a much greater degree. The war ended because congressmen and senators raised hell—ultimately when middle America raised hell—because people began to perceive that it was not what it was cracked up to be. And the reason that people began to see that was be-

Kerry announces the decision of the veterans to defy a Supreme Court order banning them from sleeping on the Mall during Operation Dewey Canyon III, April 1971.

cause there was a group of people there to call the country to conscience over a long period of time. And it took a long time to break through all the barriers. When you have the president and the Congress and the traditional rhetoric of patriotism and all the rest to call into question, it's very hard to break through with a minority perspective. The antiwar movement, including the VVAW, educated this country about what was happening over there and what was at stake. It limited the options available to Nixon and Kissinger. Without that pressure they would not have Vietnamized the war and gotten our troops out.

Unfortunately, the VVAW has a very mixed reputation today. There are still veterans who condemn VVAW, who will tell you that while they were fighting in Vietnam this group was back here being unpatriotic. And that is *totally* untrue. There wasn't a Vietnam veteran who was part of the VVAW who didn't do what he did because he believed he was trying to save the lives of his brothers in Vietnam and for no other reason.

The fact is that the VVAW accomplished a lot of things that most people are completely unaware of. VVAW was the first group in the country to set up rap sessions for veterans to begin the process of reassimilation. It was the VVAW that called attention to the inadequate services which veterans were receiving on their return. We were the first to expose problems with the VA, to talk about the is-

sue of lack of benefits. No other veterans group—the VFW, the American Legion—ever touched it. The first post-Vietnam stress syndrome efforts with the psychiatrist Robert Lifton at Yale University were started by VVAW. It was VVAW which began working on the question of Agent Orange long before anyone else was interested. The VVAW performed some extraordinary services that no one, including vets, has ever given them credit for. We set the agenda which Vietnam veterans groups, whether it's the Vietnam Vets of America or the Veterans of Vietnam, or the Vietnam Era Veterans, are still working for today.

And succeeding. I think they've been pretty effective in giving a legitimacy to these concerns, in making Congress aware of vets' issues. The gains have not been enormous, but there has never been the kind of conglomerate Vietnam lobby in the way there was at the end of World War II and Korea. When guys came back from Vietnam they wanted to disappear. They wanted to get out of uniform and forget about it. I mean, they just wanted to hide. Especially those who came back from '68 on, the real antiwar years when people in this country weren't praising their service but condemning the war. That made it tough for a lot of guys, no question about it. It devalued those years for them and it's only now that a lot of people are finding a desire, or even a willingness, to come together as vets.

That's why every Vietnam veteran in Congress owes it to veterans to speak out for them. Because I think the veterans of this generation got about as bad a deal as any group of veterans in the history of this country. There are still a lot of vets out there who need voices in Congress that are raised on their behalf whether it's in terms of post-traumatic stress disorder, or drug and alcohol dependency, or chronic unemployment, whatever. A lot of folks still are having difficulty getting back into things—even now, fifteen or twenty years later. And as long as they're out there I think we owe all of them that effort. There has never been the kind of energy on behalf of veterans of this war as a group that was given to veterans of other wars, and I think one of our missions in Congress ought to be to provide it.

There's more possibility for that now because in the last few years a lot of Americans have realized they didn't even

A Vietnam veteran throws his medal on the steps of the Capitol during Operation Dewey Canyon III.

say thank you to the men who served in Vietnam. When the hostages were returned from Iran a lot of people suddenly spoke up and said, "Wait a minute, these people are being treated like heroes. What about the guys that came back from Vietnam?" And the Vietnam Memorial has been extremely important. It's not only brought a lot of visibility to the problems that vets are having, it's also acted as a catalyst. It's helped a lot of people get to the point emotionally where they want to share being a veteran again, to feel proud of their service. I think veterans of Vietnam ought to feel as much pride as veterans of any other war. They fought under the most difficult circumstances in every single respect. Difficult in terms of home support, difficult in terms of the kind of war they fought. There isn't a veteran who shouldn't be proud, no matter what.

They say time heals a lot of things. But I think for many veterans it's always going to be a little bit too little and a little bit too late. There are a lot of vets who simply will never get over the scars of those first years. They appreciate the thank yous, it makes them feel better, but it's not a cure. It's never going to take away the memory of what it was like when they came back or the kind of war they fought in.

I don't disagree with those who refer to Vietnam as a noble cause. I think it was very noble that we sought to help the South Vietnamese. And there is nobility in a young man dying on behalf of his country. For a young soldier who loved his country and who decided he should support his president, who went to Vietnam and died there, that was not a death in vain because that person gave himself to something he believed in. And that's the most you can do in life. That's as noble as it gets.

But things that are noble may not always be realistic or well designed or well implemented. It wasn't a war we were determined to win. That was what enraged me and so many others when we returned from Vietnam, that there was a terrible expense of human life that added up to nothing. That's what I was trying to say to people. Don't ask those you call upon to serve to have our patriotism used that way. You owe us more than that. ■

Raymond G. Davis

Commanding General
3d Marine Division
May 1968–April 1969

Commissioned a Marine second lieutenant in 1938, Ray Davis went on to see action in three conflicts and rise to the rank of four-star general. In World War II he fought at Guadalcanal, New Guinea, and Peleliu, where he earned the Navy Cross and Purple Heart. As a battalion commander in Korea, Lieutenant Colonel Davis received the Medal of Honor for conspicuous gallantry during the Chosin Reservoir campaign of 1950. He drew up contingency plans and chose landing sites for the first combat units to land in Vietnam while assistant division commander of the 3d Marine Division in Okinawa in 1964. After a stint at the Pentagon, where he was assistant chief of staff, G-1 (Personnel), of the Marine Corps, General Davis assumed command of the 3d Marine Division in Vietnam in May 1968. He also served as assistant commandant of the Marine Corps until his retirement in 1972, after over thirty-three years of military service.

When I was at the Marines' basic school in Philadelphia in 1938, my company commander and instructor was Lewis B. "Chesty" Puller, one of the last of the Marines who had real experience in the guerrilla wars in Central America in the twenties and thirties. In our course called "Small Wars," he would come in and put his lesson plan on the lectern and look at it only briefly. Then he would close the book and say, "They made me make up a lesson plan, but we are going to talk about the real things. We are going to talk about the fighting, the war." Then he would get into the details of the minute-by-minute, day-by-day, week-by-week campaigning on the trail, the actual combat. I found that this was the best way to find out about the war business: to listen to the people who have experienced it.

I managed to be exposed to Chesty Puller on and off through the years, and he had a great influence on my career and outlook on war. The Puller outlook was one of total dedication to the proposition that you go out and find the enemy or guerrilla and destroy him. He never once thought about trying to protect an area and displacing people or winning the hearts and minds. All that was totally secondary. I think if we started with that premise in Vietnam, it would have been over very quickly. Instead we had a total disaster.

In early 1965 the decision was made to launch forces into Vietnam. I was in Washington for the next two and a half years, watching the whole thing develop. I sat through endless meetings at the Defense Department and reviewed our manpower with the secretary of the navy.

The army had ten divisions and the Marine Corps three, ready to go. But all the back-up was in the ready reserve: the heavy transportation, tanks, communications, doctors, everything. By design, everything to sustain the active divisions in combat was put in the ready reserve. This was a McNamara plan. It was budgeted that way by the Pentagon and Congress.

Initial estimates were that 550,000 troops would be required to do the job in Vietnam. But we started out with less than 100,000. When it came time to send the divisions, the ready reserves were not sent with them. They had to rebuild those back-up forces by the draft, and it took three and a half years to rebuild a force that they had destroyed, in effect, by not sending the reserves in 1965. We had Marine reserve units virtually demanding to be called up, saying hey, this is what we're here for. Let's go. But our political leaders were able to convince themselves that it wasn't good politics to call them. The decision cost President Johnson his place in history, I'll say.

The military knew it was disastrous not to do it. In fact, I heard at one time that General Harold K. Johnson, the army chief of staff, was going to resign over it. His cards were on the table. He said, "I have ten army divisions ready to go. I cannot send them without their back-up. I need these units of the army reserve. They're already there, equipped and on the payroll. Give them to me and the divisions can go." They would have had a major force in Vietnam by the end of 1965 that would have changed the whole outlook of the war.

Instead the forces deployed were inadequate. All they could do was push and shove, with nothing to show for it. Casualties were flowing constantly, but the progress was nebulous. This undermined the public support needed to build the forces to where they could become effective. So it was a vicious cycle: the longer mobilization was delayed the less support it had, and less support meant slower deployments. That's what killed us in Vietnam. If one decision had to be picked out as the major cause of the disaster in Vietnam, it was the decision not to use the ready reserve but to replace it in three years through the draft. It was the most tragic thing anybody could imagine.

In February 1968 I arrived in Vietnam to become deputy commander of Provisional Corps, Vietnam, in I Corps. General Bill Rosson, the Prov Corps commander, and I were the best of friends. He invited me out there to be his deputy and was anxious to show me around. Along with the 3d Marine Division, he had the two best divisions in the army: the 1st Cav and the 101st Airborne, really top-quality divisions. They had all the material support, all the helicopters, the best commanders. And Rosson pushed them, pressed them, and kept them out after the enemy. That was the key.

I could feel that Rosson was concerned about the immobility of the Marines in Quang Tri Province. One time when the North Vietnamese came down with two regiments just above Dong Ha, he was somewhat incensed that the Marines didn't apply all forces to the situation. And I agreed with that. I tried to understand that when forced into a defensive situation involving the manning of strong points for so long a period, one can fail to exploit the alternative of aggressive pursuit and destruction of the enemy.

I learned a lot during those few months with Rosson. The most important thing was airmobility. I was at Quantico after World War II when one of the answers to the atomic battlefield was the helicopter. You might say that Marines "invented" the troop-carrying helicopter, but we failed to fully exploit it. The army came along with the large numbers of helicopters and had greater airmobility. They could really exploit the mobility of the helicopter, combined with the highly mobile air power and artillery and engineering equipment. Being oriented toward helicopters already and watching this with Rosson, I learned the lesson of operating with helicopters on high ground as opposed to the way the Ma-

Lieutenant Colonel Raymond G. Davis receives the Medal of Honor from President Harry Truman at the White House on November 24, 1952. He earned the award for leading a relief column against Communist forces in North Korea. Davis' son, Miles (foreground), later served under his father in Vietnam as a Marine lieutenant.

rines had been doing it in flat landing zones. Out in the mountains in the western part of Vietnam there were no flat landing zones, so through necessity the army started knocking off the tops of hills and hummocks and making places for helicopters. This was an entirely different concept, and I picked it up immediately. I wrote an article about helicopter operations for the *Marine Corps Gazette*, and it became the bible for the first few months of my command.

On May 22, 1968, I assumed command of the 3d Marine Division at Dong Ha. Before I had even arrived there, I sent a message that I wanted all the staff and regimental commanders assembled there at two o'clock. At the meeting I didn't ask or plead with them. I ordered, "Before dark, these things will happen." I just laid out the scheme, what were later called my "before dark dictates."

I already had permission from my commanders to violate the McNamara Line concept. McNamara's brain trust had come up with a defensive concept of putting manned strong points across the demilitarized zone, with all these megabuck sensors in between, to keep the guerrillas out. Well, we weren't fighting guerrillas. We were fighting NVA divisions. So the concept was faulty. The strong points were too far apart to protect the line, and it was a tying down of forces.

So I directed that each of the four or five forward positions where we had a battalion holed up—or hiding out, as I called it—would now have only one company, and the other three companies and the headquarters would deploy as a mobile force to seek out the enemy. So they moved out on the offensive.

I also wanted to bring back unit integrity. I couldn't believe what I found out there. In the Marine Corps, even though we had fixed regimental organization in our tables, we had a shambles as far as organization on the ground was concerned. This whole business of rotating units in and out of the fixed positions just served to disrupt the organization, all under the guise of flexibility. The regimental commander didn't know his own regiment at all. With four of my regiments, half their battalions belonged to them and the other half were down at Da Nang.

When I reduced forward positions to company size, a mobile force of several battalions was organized. It became easier to put the regiments and battalions together with the engineers, artillery, communications, and everything that belongs together and keep it together. Unit integrity is essential for high-mobility mountain warfare—very complex, very fast-moving operations where you must depend on people knowing each other and being able to respond. It was crucial to the kind of war I wanted to fight.

To make the unified forces more effective, I also started the division on greater mobility. Fortunately, I arrived at a time when our resources were fully generated: the new model of the CH-46 helicopter was becoming available, with greater power and lift capacity. Soon we were knocking the tops off little mountain peaks, putting our forces up there to move down against the enemy.

When I was in ROTC at Georgia Tech in the thirties, I did a presentation on Stonewall Jackson's valley campaigns in the Civil War. The thing that impressed me about Jackson was his mobility: he would mount his horse and ride to the sound of the guns. I thought of that in Vietnam when we finally got enough helicopters. The division commander could mount his horse, so to speak, and ride to the sound of the guns. The army provided me with a super-powered helicopter so I could operate in those mountains with safety. I would fly out to firebases and forward units in the field every day.

I learned from traveling around that the troops were delighted by my orders.

Provisional Corps commander Lieutenant General William Rosson (left) bids farewell to his deputy, Major General Davis, on the latter's departure to assume command of the 3d Marine Division in April 1968.

General Davis fires the first shot from one of the Marines' new 175MM guns near Firebase Vandegrift in Quang Tri Province, February 1969.

They had been holed up for months, and now they were doing what Marines were supposed to do. So they took to it. And pretty soon the North Vietnamese accommodated us by launching down in there to get themselves clobbered. In my area we destroyed five NVA divisions in four months. They didn't realize the force we had in terms of Marines with helicopters and mobile firepower, so they just ruptured themselves. We intercepted radio reports from these units as they marched back up toward Hanoi. They were reporting complete destruction: all the officers and NCOs killed, weapons all lost, no supplies. Not one of these five divisions came back south for the next two years. We had butchered them. We were out looking for the enemy—and winning.

General Abrams taking over as COMUSMACV also helped us. Abe was my kind of guy. I guess we had initially stuck to the position defense and McNamara Line because the forces were inadequate for effective operations. But now that the forces were in place and we had the capability to do things differently, the whole attitude changed. I remember I was flying around up by the DMZ with Abrams. I was complaining about the fact that there were 162 NVA cannons up there that could open up on us anytime, and I wasn't permitted to do a thing. His answer was, "General, don't you worry. We're not going to let them shit on us anymore."

With that he accepted a design, a new generation of computerized fire direction and control. He even had college professors out there working on it. With every enemy cannon that would open up, the computers would tell our eight-inch guns where to shoot. In thirty or forty days we had air reconnaissance pictures showing that every cannon that fired on us had been turned over or knocked out.

The result was that the North Vietnamese said, "Let's have a cease-fire across the DMZ. If you don't shoot at us anymore, we won't throw rockets into the cities." Well, we had just captured 3,500 of their rockets in the mountains so they didn't have any rockets. But we were so anxious for some sort of agreement that we grabbed that.* We gave up our advan-

* On October 31, 1968, the U.S. announced the cessation of bombing of North Vietnam, in return for a pledge by the enemy not to attack South Vietnamese cities or violate the DMZ.

tage and let them up. This is unmilitary. It was not pursuing success, as you do in the military. It hurt our ability to pursue the war to a successful conclusion— namely, defeating the enemy.

Once those divisions were destroyed and we had seized all their bases, we were able to destroy the Main Force regiments of the Vietcong that were supported by the NVA. Then we were able to go into the villages and get the cadres out. So we had total pacification. In the early days we didn't have enough forces to protect villages. We ended up in a major displacement of the population into smaller areas where they could be protected. That was backwards. Lewis Puller taught me that you spend your full time, day or night, pursuing those guerrilla forces. That's the way to pacify the countryside. You don't sit around trying to protect the population. The guerrillas can only work when they are supported by main forces; the only way to get guerrillas is to destroy main forces and their bases of support.

When we went back and cleaned out the villages, Quang Tri Province became totally secure—so secure that I felt safe in any village out there, day or night. That was my challenge to the newsmen, to get them used to the idea that this place was secure. In the helicopter I would say, "You can point anywhere in this province, day or night, and we'll land there and I'll take off my pistol and we'll walk around there alone, to show you how secure it is." I said many times that Quang Tri Province was safer than the streets of many American cities.

To keep the enemy out, and to collect intelligence for the mobile forces, we had sixty four-man reconnaissance teams throughout those mountains. Twenty of them would be on the ground all the time; the others would be getting ready to go or they would be coming out and getting refurbished. Every day at our staff briefing, my officers knew I would ask the same question: "How many patrols do we have on the ground?" If we had less than twenty, they would have until noon to get twenty on the ground. That's how we kept track of hundreds of square miles that we were responsible for. We kept people in key spots all the time to report on enemy activities, and when they located supplies or concentrated forces we could go and get them.

There were a lot of enemy supplies and men over the border in Laos, but I wasn't permitted to go over and get them. We had an ambassador in Laos who was committed to protecting the "neutrality" of Laos, as he called it. Hell, the place was full of North Vietnamese troops and trucks by the hundreds coming down the trail at night with ammunition to kill Americans. He screamed like a stuck pig when a company got over into his territory during Operation Dewey Canyon. But the North Vietnamese didn't know where the border was and didn't care.

We even had plans to seize the lower sixty miles of North Vietnam. I was totally in favor of that, because it would have called their hand. If we seized a significant portion of their territory, they would have expanded their army to try to throw us out of their country, and that would have brought the whole thing to a close. We had plans for doing it. We had plans for everything.

But soon after my arrival in Vietnam, the decisions were made to withdraw U.S. forces. I knew that this was premature. The South Vietnamese were not ready to take over the whole country. They couldn't expose their capital city to the threat from Cambodia, so they kept their forces down there and pretty much limited their effort up north. Even though we had total security when I left in April 1969, we hadn't really tied up the loose ends enough to say, "We are going to turn them over to you." I could see the handwriting on the wall. The thing was really going to fall apart.

But by that time it was too late. Our people at home had had enough. Three and a half years of suffering, and they were ready to quit. The only trouble was that our success came so late that Walter Cronkite and the press had already told us to get out, that we were beaten. Nobody was interested. And you can't fight a war without popular support. World War II had full support. In Korea we had full support, until late 1952 when we had our forces committed to a position defense where the casualties were flowing with no progress to show for it. When you get yourself into this kind of situation, support at home erodes quickly. That's the situation we got into late in Korea and early in Vietnam.

From the beginning the United States made several "deadly decisions" that led right down the trail to the most tragic disaster in our history in Vietnam. I witnessed most of them: Not providing adequate funding. Failure to call up the ready reserve. Allowing the enemy sanctuaries. Calling bombing halts and cease–fires that allowed the enemy to rest and regroup. The enormous waste of the McNamara Line. Other decisions were only minor, but they contributed to the idea of limiting our ability to win. The military decisions, of course, were influenced by the overall problem of having an inadequate force and operating under restrictive ground rules that favored the enemy. We could not destroy the enemy, which is the only correct role for military forces.

This was against my military training. But what were my choices? My choices were either make do or resign. What good would it have done to resign? I felt capable of making do better than others. I had a lot of war experience under my belt. This was my third war. I could have gotten incensed and stomped around and just resigned. But nobody cared. They wouldn't pay any real attention. So I'd make do.

You can't go to war unless your objective is to destroy the enemy and win. Otherwise the cost is prohibitive. The cost of winning the war in Korea would have been much less than the cost of maintaining the Korean situation as we have since 1950. The Chinese didn't want to talk until they were whipped. The same with the North Vietnamese. I'm convinced that the agreement with the North Vietnamese came only because they had had enough. They would have agreed to just about anything. But at the same time, we had had enough.

There is no substitute to going for the jugular. If the military doesn't do that, there is no way to succeed. But in Vietnam we weren't allowed to do that. That's what defeated us. We carried out our orders, and the orders we carried out could lead to nothing but a tragic disaster. ∎

Top. *American and South Vietnamese commanders meet with General Davis at his headquarters at Dong Ha, 1969. Left to right are Lieutenant General Hoang Xuan Lam, General Cao Van Vien, Davis, Major General Ngo Quang Truong, and Lieutenant General Richard G. Stilwell.*

Above. *Mrs. Knox Davis pins a fourth star on her husband's uniform as General Leonard Chapman (left), commandant of the Marine Corps, promotes General Davis to the post of assistant commandant in Washington, March 12, 1971.*

Jacqui Chagnon

Administrator
Catholic Relief Services, Vietnam
1968–1969
International Voluntary Services, Vietnam
1969–1970

Jacqui Chagnon grew up in comfortable, conservative surroundings in Meriden, Connecticut. "My father was consumed with his business, and my mother took care of the children. They were never involved in peace issues or social action. Girl Scouts, Boy Scouts, that was more their style. We had never even talked about the war up to the time I decided to go to Vietnam. When I told them what I was going to do my parents were aghast. My mother thought I was crazy. If I wanted to see the world why didn't I become an airline stewardess or an ambassador? My father was even more upset than my mother. He'd served in Europe during World War II, and he knew the realities of what I was going to see."

But Chagnon discovered in Vietnam a culture that captured both her imagination and her concern. Since the end of the war she has returned to Indochina several times on fact-finding, relief, and development missions. Today she lives in Washington, D.C. with her husband, Roger, and her daughter, Miranda, maintaining her close ties to Vietnam through her work as associate director of the Asia Resource Center.

When I was about six or seven years old my family moved into a new house. My parents unpacked all sorts of boxes and put things on shelves, including a collection of photographs my father had taken during World War II. One day when they weren't home, my brother and I went through my father's collection.

I will never forget those photographs. There were horrible pictures of the concentration camps and also pictures of destruction from the fighting. They were very chilling to a young child and absolutely memorable. Here was the real thing, the real effects of war on human beings. My parents, and probably generations of parents, would hide these things from their children when in fact that's probably what we should have been learning about. If we were faced with the reality of what war does to people's lives, perhaps then there wouldn't be so many wars.

By 1968 I was studying international relations at George Washington University and getting very frustrated with my course work. All through my school years I had been struggling to find out what happens to people in a war, the effects of war and its aftermath on families and societies. It had intrigued me that we learned a lot about battles and we learned a lot about dates and figures, but we never really learned about what happened to people. I was always questioning, always asking my professors, but they never seemed to be able to give me much in the way of answers. I had almost completed my B.A. when I decided I desperately wanted to go overseas and see what war was all about. So I applied to various voluntary agencies, including the Catholic Relief Services, and they sent me off to Vietnam.

I was twenty-one years old, a very naive, inexperienced young woman with a purely academic interest in political matters. I had never talked about the war with my friends, I had never participated in a demonstration. If someone had asked me I would have said, "The United States is conducting a war against the Communists." Period. End of sentence. End of paragraph. I simply had very little idea of what the United States was doing or why it was doing it. I thought I was going to help the South Vietnamese people so they could become stronger economically to fight communism. I expected to find a lot of poverty and a lot of opportunity for me to "do good."

So imagine my surprise when I was taken from the airport in Saigon to a big building on a main street and shown my apartment on the ninth floor—parqueted floors, two bedrooms, two baths, all furnished including silverware, everything. Then I was introduced to a woman who was going to be my "maid!" And, except for the maid, it was all free. I didn't have to pay anything. The Agency for International Development provided it to CRS as part of our contract with the government. I couldn't believe it. Here I was thinking I'm going to be going into a very poor situation, and I find myself in an apartment far better than I could ever have afforded in the United States. There I was on this amazing gravy train compliments of the American government.

I soon discovered that well over three-quarters of CRS development money, and almost all relief money for Vietnam also came from the U.S. government. CRS wasn't operating on donations from Catholic individuals in the United States. It was U.S. government money being funneled through a private agency. And this I found disturbing. But what really upset me was that CRS was clearly tied into the U.S. military effort.

The agency was receiving AID "Food for Peace" goods—rice, bulgur wheat, flour, oil, milk—and storing it in the CRS warehouse. Then American civic action teams, Korean civic action teams, Filipino, Australian, Thai, New Zealand civic action teams, you name it, would march in there and requisition these goods. Then they would take the goods back to their areas of operation and distribute them. They were using the food for military purposes, not out of genuine humanitarian concern or for legitimate development efforts, but for war purposes. It was a very simple equation. When you bomb an area you have to remove the people from that area. When you remove the people you create refugees, and you can't create refugees unless you can feed them. The voluntary agencies became the main service for feeding the refugees, and the more we fed the refugees the more refugees the military was creating.

The local CRS leadership didn't see anything wrong with it. Their defense was, "Look, the civic action teams are helping the people. They're feeding the people, and the people need to be fed. They have more trucks than we have and more distribution systems so let them do it." In fact, since the midsixties our main purpose had become helping the U.S. government fight the war, and we cooperated in part because it helped us build up our coffers. I saw an enormous corruption of responsibility and integrity in allowing ourselves to be used that way. We were supposed to be acting in the capacity of a humanitarian, private relief and development agency and not to be part and parcel of American military operations.

The issue provoked heavy, *heavy* debate within the agency. Heavy arguments. Firings all over the place. That's what finally spurred me to leave the organization, but it was really an accumulation of things: their paternalistic attitude toward the Vietnamese in general and the Vietnamese who worked for us in particular; their discouragement of cultural and language training; the closeness to U.S. military programs and policies—I wouldn't even say "closeness" but "virtual identity"; and a realization that Vietnamese Catholics didn't necessarily approve of what Catholic Relief Services was doing. It was coming to my attention that there was a growing feeling in the Vietnamese Catholic community that CRS was just like the U.S. government, overloading Vietnamese life, dictating what was going to be and what was not going to be by virtue of the fact that we had money and goods and power, an attitude that was greatly resented by the Vietnamese Catholics.

So I resigned my position and went to work on the administrative staff of the International Voluntary Services. IVS was the predecessor to the Peace Corps and operated very similarly. I had come into contact with some IVS people a few months earlier. On the average they were much younger than the staff at CRS, more my age. They were also a lot more questioning, and some of what they said shocked me. They were the first ones who told me about what had happened at My Lai, for example, and a lot of what they had to say made me think. No one had made me think about what the United States was doing in Vietnam before. I put a lot of credence in what they were saying because unlike most Americans in Vietnam they were speaking in Vietnam-

ese to ordinary people. They were out in the villages doing development work, living in Vietnamese houses, eating Vietnamese food. They weren't hobnobbing with the Ministry of Education officials or the Ministry of Social Welfare officials. They could give a damn about those kind of people. They were talking to the local teachers, the local farmers, the local doctors, the refugees.

The ironic thing was that IVS got *all*, 100 percent, of its money from U.S. government contracts for the Vietnam War. You see, in 1966 Hubert Humphrey had written about IVSers, calling them "shirt-sleeve warriors." And that was how the U.S. military in Vietnam looked at a lot of voluntary agencies, not just IVS. They were going to provide the "good" image of American involvement in Vietnam—sort of civic action teams without the military cloaking. But as IVSers started speaking out against the war it became a very schizophrenic situation.

On the one hand we were saying, "You give us this nice contract, 'you givva me,'" we used to say. And on the other hand we were saying, "naughty, naughty, naughty" and demonstrating in front of the U.S. Embassy, writing letters to Congress, and so forth. It really took a toll on the psychological well-being of volunteers and staff. But at least I felt that IVS was struggling to get itself out from underneath that bind, and I think it made the whole organization a very alive place.

"I was the IVS 'A-Cop'—'Administrative Chief of Party'! My job was to take care of all the nitty-gritty basic needs involved with processing personnel in and out of the country, overseeing their general welfare, paying their monthly stipend, assisting them in finding housing, and making sure they weren't flipping out."

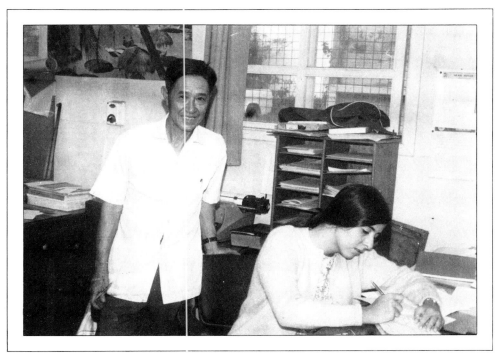

There was a lot of deep thinking being done by volunteers and staff alike about what we were trying to accomplish.

Although IVS people were considered the "hippies" of the voluntary agencies, they were by no means "hippies" in the strictest sense. Many of them were very conservative when they came to Vietnam. But they were young, some came out of peace churches—the Mennonites, Quakers, Brethrens, Disciples—and about half were serving with IVS as conscientious objectors. It was a real mix. There were a lot of Yale, Harvard, Princeton, Smith graduates, politically sophisticated people, well-read, aggressive, outspoken. They were primarily involved in education and community development. Then there were a lot of small-town farming people from the Midwest. For some of them the first big city they'd ever seen was when they came to Washington, D.C. for their training. Those people were our agriculturalists. They were much quieter than the Ivy Leaguers, they listened more than they talked. They weren't the ones to be out on the protest line in front of the embassy so much, but when they got angry, when they got concerned, it was very, very intense.

They tended to operate on the basis of simple, straightforward common sense. And that's why when they started to change their political views I really listened to them. It wasn't a lot of rhetoric they'd picked up at college. I was still trying to figure out what my thinking was on the war, and I found I could relate to them better than the others because they were coming at it from a much more neutral position, like me.

When they first arrived, many of these people felt they had come to help build a nation. But after being there for six months or a year they usually came to the conclusion that nation-building could not be done in the midst of war.

For one thing, IVS was constantly being called upon to go and help with emergency evacuations of refugees. So a group of volunteers would go up and work in the refugee camps temporarily and disturb all their other programs. But the more we helped, the more refugees the U.S. Army created and the more AID was pressing us to do relief instead of development work. It was a vicious, unending cycle. Moreover, it's a very difficult thing to do relief and development work simultaneously because you create an incredible dependency mentality among the people. You are constantly undercutting your own efforts because if you provide handouts you take away an important component of development, which is to foster a sense of competence and confidence among the people you're working with.

But it was more than that. You simply couldn't have somebody developing new strains of sweet potatoes when their test crops are being defoliated. You couldn't help build schools and develop teaching staffs when the village could suddenly be designated a free fire zone and all the people had to move out. You couldn't do projects relating to family planning when people are constantly losing children to the fighting.

The war just drained so much of people's energies. There was constant worry, constant fear. There was always the realization that you could be moved out tomorrow. Bingo. Gone. And your whole project goes down the drain. Life was so uncertain that the Vietnamese were reluctant to work towards the future. They held back from doing things that otherwise they would just have gone right ahead and done.

What you eventually came to realize was that real development was virtually an impossibility. I would say that in terms of straight development—building schools, improving agricultural yields—we were less than 50 percent effective. And if you want to ask how effective we were in terms of improving people's lives and bringing them one step further economically, socially, into being able to cope with the difficulties of life, I would give us a low mark. There was some improvement in the English-learning level. Because of IVS there are more teachers who could teach English today. And there's a little bit more knowledge about agricultural co-ops and credit systems. But there weren't a lot of solid, lasting things. Yet we were more successful than other voluntary agencies.

The other thing you realized was that the cost of the war to the people of Vietnam was staggering, and the worst consequences weren't always the most visible. Some areas were obviously devastated. A significant portion of the center of Vietnam, both north and south of the DMZ, was destroyed: forests, fields, villages, bridges, roads, everything. And along with the destruction came enormous disruption of the economy. The best lands were ruined by the breaking of the dikes along the sea and the salting of the earth. The fields were filled with shrapnel, antipersonnel bomblets, grenades, mines, so it became almost impossible to work them. People are still being injured today from unexploded ordnance. The United Nations estimates that Vietnam has the most serious handicapped problem in the world by a factor of two. In a very real sense it's become a nation of cripples.

Farther south on into the delta the destruction was more spotty. But it wasn't easy to determine from the road how many bombs had dropped in the forest or how much defoliation had gone on. And what you could see from an airplane didn't necessarily tell you either because you had to ask the people what was there before. Sometimes crops were destroyed and a weed crop grew up, and to the inexperienced eye it wouldn't look like there had been any damage. But then you ask the villagers, and they tell you there used to be a big banana plantation there or a mangrove forest.

One of the things that I feel we as Americans don't understand because we haven't experienced it in recent years is the problem of rebuilding after a war. We talk about war in terms of battles and firefights and numbers of soldiers killed and numbers of civilians lost and that kind of thing. We forget what it all means after the war. We don't realize that in that kind of tropical area the fallow fields cannot remain fallow very long without being overgrown, and how hard it is to put them back into production when the shooting stops. We have no idea the enormous labor required to rebuild dikes and canals without a lot of heavy equipment. We don't know what it is to fill a bomb crater by hand. We don't even know how big a bomb crater is.

And the war didn't mean just physical devastation by any means. It meant literally millions of people driven from their homes, taking all their possessions and moving down the road a bit. And then moving another time and another time until you're finally so far away from your native village that you wonder if you're ever going to get back. It meant an unnatural flight to the cities because the cities were less likely to be bombed. It meant massive unemployment that continues today because there was no native industry to support the refugees. It meant unbelievable overcrowding with houses growing on top of houses growing on top of houses until it seemed like life was being smothered. It meant prostitution, skyrocketing rates of venereal disease, and the development of new strains of venereal disease that today are killing women in their thirties, forties, and fifties and leaving their children with severe retardation. It meant an epidemic of drug addiction, delinquency, and mental illness. It meant a growing population of Amerasian children. It meant babies deformed from chemical spraying that today has left behind a rising incidence of liver ailments and various forms of cancer. It meant the destruction of village life, the disintegration of traditional Vietnamese culture, and, most important, it meant the dissolution of the family.

Every family, *every one*, was torn apart by the war. I have never met a single Vietnamese whose family was intact as it was before 1954. Families were disrupted by separation between those who went north and those who stayed south under the Geneva agreements. They were divided between those in the family who fought with the Saigon government and those who fought with the Provisional Revolutionary Government. They were diminished by premature deaths caused by the fighting. They were dislocated by removal from their ancestral lands. And all of it was devastating because, unlike in the United States, for the Vietnamese the family is the center of existence. And by family I don't mean the mother, the father, and the children. I mean the grandparents and the aunts and the uncles and the cousins and all that those people bring to the family.

I don't think I can find words strong enough that most Americans can under-

Chagnon (third from left), and IVS Director Hugh Manke (second from right), protest American policy in Vietnam at an informal meeting with U.S. pacification officials, August 1969.

Don Luce, former Director of IVS, Vietnam, and founder of the Indochina Mobile Education Project, during a U.S. speaking tour in 1972.

Traveling with the Indochina Mobile Education Project in Springfield, Missouri, Chagnon signs copies of a book of Vietnamese poems she co-edited with Don Luce.

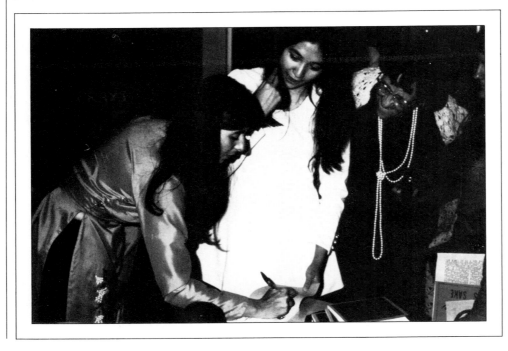

stand. It's a hard concept for us because we are so mobile, so independent-oriented in our lifestyles. But it is the key factor in understanding why the average Vietnamese was so desperate to end the war. More than anything else, the war was destroying the family, the very fabric of their society.

By the end of 1970 I knew it was time for me to leave Vietnam. I could no longer just sit by and let these things go on. I had to go back and do something because I knew that the war was not going to end in Vietnam, it could only be ended in the United States. I had come to realize the truth in something a Vietnamese priest told me when I first arrived in Saigon. He said, "Don't think that you're going to do anything for us. The best thing that you can do is to learn, to learn as much as you can about us and then go home and tell other Americans." I didn't know how I was going to do that, I had absolutely no conception at all of where to start. I just knew I had to get back.

When I returned to the United States I took some time off to sort through all my memories, to go through and figure out what it all meant to me and what I should do. Then in November 1971 I joined the Indochina Mobile Education Project.

The Project, which had been created by Don Luce, a former director of IVS in Vietnam, was a combination of exhibit and speakers. The exhibit consisted of forty-four huge panels of photographs that portrayed the different peoples and cultures of Indochina, with the last section devoted to the war. And then along with the exhibit were a speaker and an organizer who kind of managed the whole thing. We had a person in Washington whose job was to get hold of people who were concerned about the war—ministers, student leaders, businessmen, vets, housewives, everybody and anybody—and ask them to sponsor the exhibit in their own communities.

The most popular place was shopping malls, but we also had the exhibit at universities, churches. One time we set up at the USO in Fayetteville, North Carolina, where there was a big military base. We'd have interviews with the local press, go on radio and TV, prepare Vietnamese dinners and stage cultural programs, talk to high-school or college classes, church groups and civic organizations. From November 1971 to November 1974, I traveled with the Indochina Project nine months a year. By the time I was through I had been to forty-four states, giving on average three to four talks or interviews a day.

What I talked about was what I had seen and what I had experienced in terms of people. I didn't use statistics, I didn't talk about bomb tonnages, I tried to make the audience visualize the destruction in everyday terms. I would tell them about the Vietnamese family that I'd lived with, what that family meant to me and what they said to me. That was the most important thing—what people had to say about the war. One of the messages that everyone involved in the Project was trying to communicate was that our Vietnamese friends had said to us over and over again, "Just tell the Americans we are people. We are not bomb statistics. We are people, we have families, we are tired of this war, we want it to end. We don't think that continued warfare is going to solve our problems."

When I came out of Vietnam I was very depressed because I couldn't understand why the United States was doing what it was doing. Were we Americans simply bad people? And it was touring around that convinced me that Americans were not bad, we were ignorant. We were ignorant about what our government was doing and had been bamboozled into thinking that the war had some greater meaning to us than it did. I felt it was crucial for us to regain our democracy in foreign policy. We had given it up during the fifties and sixties and seventies. "Foreign policy? That's up to the politicians. It's none of my business. I have too many things to think about in my own life." So we forgot about it until it began to encroach upon our family, until we began to see our sons and daughters fighting or protesting on TV. Then Americans began to realize that it wasn't just something that politicians should take care of, it was something we all had to be involved in.

So maybe we learned something from Vietnam. But the price was high and all of us, Americans and Vietnamese, will be paying it for a long time. In 1972 I was at a shopping mall in Florida with the exhibit. A Vietnam vet who had heard me speak at a local school earlier in the day came by with his wife. She went off shopping, and he sat down and talked to me about Vietnam. He'd done two tours there with the Marines and had seen some very heavy combat. Then he went off and his wife came looking for him, and she asked me if her husband had been there long. When I told her that we had talked for two hours she was just stunned. She said, "You know, my husband has never said one word to me about Vietnam. He's been very depressed and having terrible problems getting jobs. I'm very worried and I don't know what to do." I was shocked. It was the first time I had come up against the enormous weight of anxiety, the helplessness that people who had been in Vietnam and their loved ones were going through. And I suddenly realized that leaving Vietnam was not going to be a simple process of getting on the plane and coming home.

Six years later, on a trip to Vietnam in 1978, I met a woman who I had first encountered when I visited North Vietnam in 1974. She was a southerner who had left her home in 1954 and not seen her relatives in many, many years. She seemed like such an indestructible person, so incredibly strong. Though her husband had been away at the front for years, she managed to keep going on. I asked her, "If there's peace right away, what's the first thing you're going to do?" And she said, "Pack my bags and go south to find my family." When I saw her again in 1978 I found out that after the end of the war she had done just that. And I asked her how it had all turned out. Had she found her relatives in Saigon? "Yes," she

said, "and for the first few hours it was very happy, and then it got very difficult. They realized I was a Communist, I had been labeled 'the enemy.'" And as she told me this she started to cry, this woman who had suffered so much and endured so much, because she knew that after having longed for decades to see them she was going to have to live for the rest of her life never again being really close to her own family, always having this incredible barrier between herself and those she loved.

Those are the kinds of things we don't think enough about, the terrible things that go on and on after the war is over, the bitterness and pain. We make a serious mistake in the United States in the way we understand war. It's not just the shooting and the bombing and the battles. War doesn't just kill people and destroy property. It's the whole business. I don't think you can talk about the war in terms of gains and losses. I think everybody lost, everybody, on all sides. And that's it. ∎

In 1974 Chagnon returned to Vietnam, this time visiting both North and South in an attempt to gauge the damage the war had wrought since her departure four years earlier. She is pictured here with two American companions in front of the War History Museum in Hanoi.

Vietnam Voices

For 4,000 years the people of Vietnam have cultivated a rich poetic tradition. The poems collected here, as well as the extract from the journal of a North Vietnamese soldier, are glimpses of the war seen through the eyes of people on both sides of the conflict.

The Mother's Chant

Sleep well, sleep well, my son.
Tomorrow you become a young man
You'll carry sword and gun.

Sleep well, sleep well, my son.
When you become a young man
You'll kill your friends and brothers.

Sleep well, sleep well, my son.
When you become a young man
You'll become an officer instead of a patriot.

Sleep well, sleep well, my son.
Tomorrow when you become a young man
You'll not sleep well again.

> —Do Nghe
> Saigon

Americans Are Not Beautiful

They are called My
Which my brother says means beautiful.
But they are not beautiful;
They have too much hair on their arms
    like monkeys,
They are tall like trees without branches,
Their eyes are green like eyes of boiled pigs
In the markets during the New Year.
Their hair is blonde and not black
Their skin is pink and not brown,
Their cars frighten cyclists in the streets,
Their "flying machines" and
    their "dragonflies"
Drop death on people and animals
And make trees bare of their leaves.
Here, Americans are not beautiful.
"But they are,
In their far away country"
My brother says.

> —Hoang Son
> Saigon

The Dream Which Has Withered

The day I grew up,
Near my father, near my mother,
Near my sister, near my brother,
I only knew how to plant mulberry trees,
And cultivate rice;
And then one day war by chance came
And trampled on my native village.
People in the name of the fatherland,
People in the name of humanity,
People in the name of happiness,
Spy on each other, destroy each other.
My father went up into the mountains,
My mother waits and waits,
My brother resists the war,
My uncle is a nationalist;
People teach me how to hate,
People teach me how to kill, to cut off heads—
All in the name of love,
Philanthropy, compassion;
Fathers, mothers, wives, children,
    whole villages
Turn into strangers, and become strangers,
And become enemies.
People teach me to bear grudges, to resent,
But I only want to be a husband,
A father, with a wife, with a young son
Who knows how to say the two words:
    Viet Nam—
From Cao Bang to the seas of Thailand,
But my dream is a small trifle,
Dim, uncertain, as the days pass.

> —Hoang Minh Nhan

Thirteen

Once mother told me,
"You were born in the Year of the Dog
And when the next Year of the Dog comes
You will be thirteen and strong enough
To help your father in the ricefields."

Now I am thirteen
But have seen no dogs in our village:
"They would disturb the guerillas at night,"
My mother said, softly.

Nor have I seen my father:
"He gave his life for the mountains
    and rivers of Viet Nam,"
My mother said, weeping.

    —Le Minh Thu
    Provisional Revolutionary
    Government

When the war has ended and the road is open
    again,
the same stars will course through the heavens.
Then will I weep for the white bones heaped
    together in desolate graves
of those who sought military honors for their
    leaders.

    —From a diary of an unknown
    North Vietnamese soldier, 1965.

"I Will Enjoy a Peaceful Spring"

This is an excerpt from the diary of Luong Trong Tan, an infantryman with the 320th North Vietnamese Division. He was twenty-three years old and had already been in the army and away from his family for two years when it was written.

Feb. 7 [1972]—The battalion gathered to listen to an orientation briefing by a cadre from the political staff. I felt a distaste for life. Probably everybody at home now is busy making preparations for Tet. Instead, we are getting ready for combat. Tomorrow our country will be unified and I will enjoy a peaceful spring.

Feb. 25—The early morning rain made the trenches wet. I felt very sad and an extreme hatred toward the war. All comrades were ravenous but could find nothing to eat. For a week we have had nothing but some bowls of rice gruel.

March 1—During the night enemy B-52s continuously bombed around the hill where we are camped, and I couldn't sleep all night.

March 8—At 9:00 A.M. my unit received the order for withdrawal and to destroy trenches before we left. Oh, what a dreadful thing for me. As I was destroying trenches, a helicopter flew in so low that I thought it was going to land on the hill. But it circled the area twice and then flew away. As I was lying flat on the ground, I could clearly see an American in the helicopter looking down at the hill; how panic-stricken I was at that moment.

March 10—I stayed in the trench all day. How miserable I was; I was very hungry and did not have enough to eat. All I could do was to lie down or sit with my head on my knees. How pitiful it was for those whose rice was stolen. They had nothing left to eat. That this critical shortage resulted from theft was a surprise to me. If I had concealed food in another place it might not have been lost. How I detest war.

March 18—The unit received orders to make preparations for a major attack. I felt very worried writing down this note.

This was the last entry in his diary.

Later Years
1968-1975

For the Americans, the years that followed the 1968 Tet offensive brought profound changes in the character and conduct of the Vietnam War. On the home front, a growing majority of Americans registered their opposition to the war with their voices and their votes, forcing policymakers in Washington to embark on a program of gradual disengagement. On the battlefield, military leaders sought to reduce U.S. casualties by modifying tactics, abandoning the large-unit operations of the past in favor of small patrols and an increasing reliance on raw firepower. Among the ranks of America's Vietnam army, growing disaffection manifested itself in racial turmoil, drug abuse, and increasing hostility towards both the Vietnamese and their own officers. Whatever sense of purpose had first led the United States into the war seemed to many to have disappeared. With the government no longer committed to winning, with the fate of South Vietnam increasingly in the hands of the Vietnamese, American soldiers now set themselves a purely personal objective: staying alive.

U.S. troops patrol through what is left of Saigon's District 8 during the second battle of Saigon in May 1968.

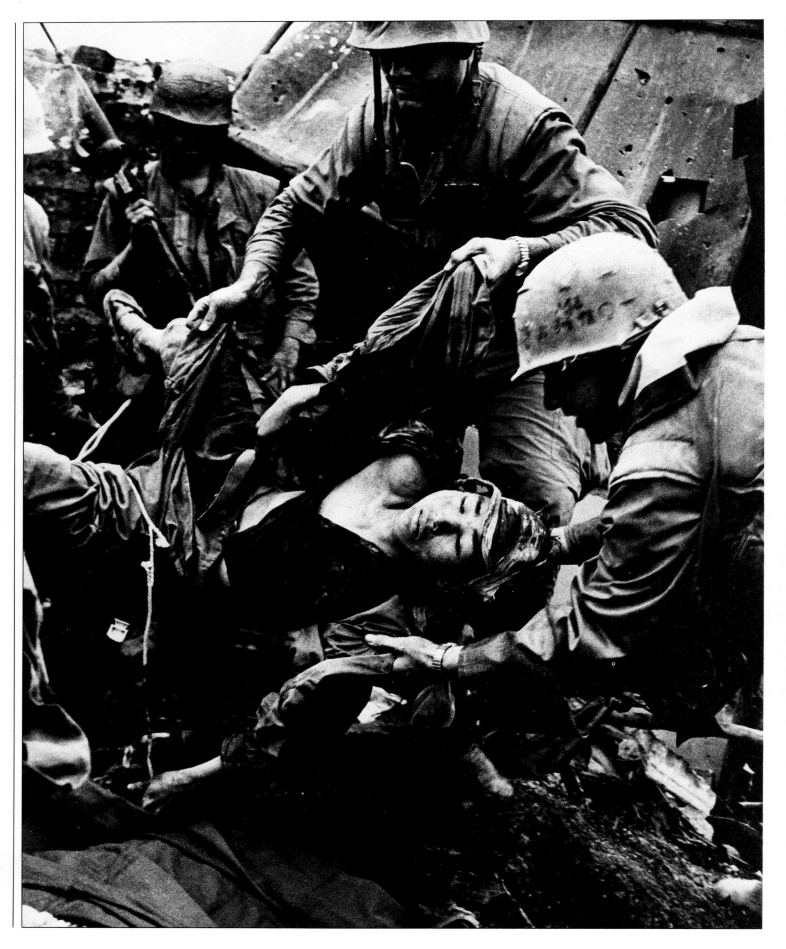

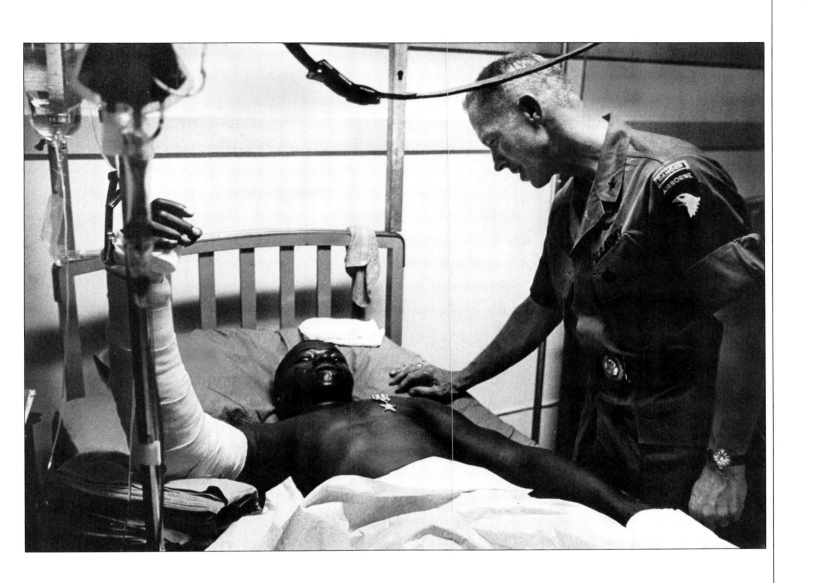

Opposite. *A wounded North Vietnamese soldier is dragged out of a foxhole by U.S. Marines during the Battle of Hue, February 1968.*

Above. *Brigadier General Sidney B. Berry, assistant division commander of the 101st Airborne Division, awards a Silver Star to a casualty of the May 1969 battle of Dong Ap Bia, the infamous Hamburger Hill.*

An ARVN ammunition dump at Lai Khe erupts in a spectacular series of shattering explosions during the North Vietnamese Easter offensive of April 1972. Although South Vietnamese forces fought tenaciously in this major test of ''Vietnamization,'' only American air power and logistical support prevented defeat.

Opposition to the continuation of the war spawned disenchantment, demoralization, and a fledgling peace movement among the troops during the war's later years. Left. A peace symbol reflects this American soldier's ambivalence. Above. Two GIs escape the rigors of war with the help of marijuana. Right. The slogans on a Cobra gunship pilot's helmet parody the American bombing campaign.

Their tours complete, GIs board a government chartered jet at Bien Hoa airport near Saigon for the flight home in November 1971. By the end of that year only 157,000 U.S. troops remained in Vietnam.

April 27, 1975. A gruesome prelude to South Vietnam's final collapse three days later, an ARVN APC passes two corpses lying amid the wreckage of a bus destroyed by an NVA tank shell in Long Thanh on the road to Saigon.

Legacies

Though the Paris accords of January 1973 marked the end of direct U.S. military involvement in Vietnam, the test of American resolve was far from over. For two years Washington argued about continuing aid to South Vietnam while North Vietnamese forces prepared a final thrust. The frantic evacuation of Saigon as the capital fell in April 1975 was the bitter denouement to twenty years of American presence in Vietnam. But for millions of Americans and Vietnamese alike, the trauma of the war could not easily be forgotten. Many bore the scars of combat, both physical and emotional. Others had seen relatives and friends go off to war on the other side of the world, never to return. Tens of thousands of Southeast Asians were uprooted and forced to flee their homelands. Only with the passage of time would the wounds begin to heal, as each sought to make his or her own peace with the past.

An ARVN soldier takes a break after an enemy attack at LZ Lonely in the Central Highlands, April 1971.

John E. Murray

U.S. Defense Attaché, Vietnam
1973–1974

Drafted in July 1941 at the age of twenty-two as a buck private, John Murray retired from the army thirty-three years later with the rank of major general. Along the way he became one of the army's foremost logistics experts.

Murray first came to Vietnam in 1968, serving as port commander at Cam Ranh Bay and then as chief of staff of the Saigon Support Command. He returned in 1972 to help assess the impact of the Communist Easter offensive on the South Vietnamese army and in January 1973 was appointed U.S. defense attaché, Vietnam.

After leaving the army in August 1974 at the conclusion of his second tour in Vietnam, Murray went to work for ten years with the Association of American Railroads in Washington, D.C. He now lives in Fairfax, Virginia, surrounded by mementos of more than three decades of service to his country, including a montagnard crossbow and numerous plaques of appreciation from South Vietnamese military commanders. On the wall of his study is a framed quotation by Thomas Edward Lawrence, better known to the world as Lawrence of Arabia: "Better they do it imperfectly than you do it perfectly, for it is their country, their war, and your time is limited."

In the movie *Casablanca* there's a character that comes up to Bogart and asks him, "What are you doing in this place Rick?" And Bogart says, "I came for my health, I came for the waters." "But this is a desert Rick, there are no waters," says the other guy. "Well," says Bogart, "I was misinformed." It seems, like Rick, I've gone through life trying to make the right decisions based on the wrong information. And nowhere more than in Vietnam.

The information I had was that there was going to be a cease-fire, that there was going to be a one-for-one replacement of military supplies and equipment expended by the ARVN, and that if the South Vietnamese got into any kind of major trouble the U.S. Air Force was going to come in and take care of the enemy. Well, I was misinformed.

One of the things I was told my assignment entailed was not to lose any more American lives. And number two, I was to get the hell out of there in one year. The assumption was that the peace would hold. I didn't like the fact that Kissinger had ignored the 250,000 Communist troops still inside South Vietnam. But on the other hand, President Nixon had given Thieu a written promise that the United States would provide them all the support they needed. If there were any serious violations of the agreement by the Communists, we promised to respond with American air and sea power.

Now I had spent a lot of time looking over diaries, letters, and interrogation reports of Communist POWs, and I'll tell you, if they had any fears it was the B-52s and the naval gunfire. As long as that was available I felt they could never mass their forces, and I know they never could have mounted their final offensive. It never would have happened.

So the assumption was that the peace would work. Nobody seemed to be willing to consider the alternative. I remember a meeting of the MACV staff shortly before the peace agreement was signed. We were discussing the cease-fire arrangements and the plans for drawing down and getting everybody out of the country, and in the middle of all this I said, "What happens if they still keep fighting?" Silence. It turned out to be a contingency we weren't prepared for.

We weren't prepared and neither were the South Vietnamese. I was shocked to discover that they had no gen-

eral reserve. All thirteen of their divisions were fully committed. We had left them without a general reserve. My God, how could we do that? Where was our generalship? Because this was the main problem that General Vien had from the beginning. As chief of the Joint General Staff I talked with him all the time, and he always brought this up. He knew that when the Communists concentrated their forces for an attack, the only way to defend the situation would be to pull divisions from someplace else in the line and open up a hole that they could pour through. And that's of course what ultimately happened. How could we be so dumb? The only thing that I heard from our side was that U.S. air power was a reserve. Well, if it was such a thing, it was pulled away by the Congress of the United States when they passed the Church-Case amendment five months after the peace agreement was signed.*

And what we did leave behind wasn't a hell of a lot of use to them either. Right before the cease-fire we loaded them up with about 13,000 tons of equipment, mostly aviation stuff. It was ridiculous. The Vietnamese didn't have the men to fly the planes, and they didn't have the mechanics to maintain them. It was like stuffing a giraffe into a telephone booth.

What they really needed more than *anything* else was ammunition. Because of the '72 offensive and all the ammunition they had fired off, their stockpiles were low. Now I had requisitioned the ammunition to get them up to what they needed. We had six ammunition ships steaming toward Vietnam carrying 60,000 tons of ammunition when, suddenly, the peace agreement was signed. We were never told when the cease-fire was going to come into force. I wasn't told the date and neither was MACV. If they had sent someone to tell us, we could have increased the steaming and got the ships in there earlier or held off the signing date till the ships arrived. But nobody bothered to tell us so we had to turn the ships around. Sixty thousand tons of ammo. It was unbelievable.

Of course the South Vietnamese had

* The Church-Case amendment, named for Senators Frank Church of Idaho and Clifford Case of New Jersey, prohibited any U.S. military action "in or over, or from off the shores of South Vietnam, Laos, or Cambodia." Joined to a Defense Department appropriations bill, the measure passed both houses of Congress on June 29, 1973.

plenty of problems of their own making, but the ARVN never got the credit it deserved. I feel very strongly about that. Their soldiers in many cases were better, and more dedicated considering the resources that we gave them, than our own. All during 1973 when they were getting supported they were full of gusto, very competent. They were opening roads, regaining territory. It had a lot of effect on the population and the army itself in terms of morale. When the Communists tried to attack something that was crucial to them, like the port of Sa Huynh south of Quang Ngai, the South Vietnamese reacted very well. The Americans had pretty much left certain areas to the NVA and the VC because I guess we thought we couldn't do it. You take the Tri Phap area in the central delta. Or the Seven Mountains region along the Cambodian border. I talked to our army historian and he claimed we took it. Like hell we did. Those Vietnamese had to go back in there and clean it out. They were good. As long as we were supporting them they were very good.

And then we took away that support. It was December 7, 1973, when I got a notice on the wire from the army that there was no more money for any supplies till the end of the fiscal year in June. I was stunned. I was never told, *never told* there was going to be any limitation on money. There was never any shortage for the Vietnamese when we were over there. You asked for it and you got it. And according to the peace treaty they were permitted a one-for-one replacement of equipment and supplies. That was part of the agreement; whatever they lost or used up we could replace it. It was right in the peace agreement.

I immediately called up people I knew and said, "What the hell *is* this?" But it was no use. I was told that there just wasn't any question about it—there's no more money. And it wasn't enormous, the consumption wasn't enormous—about 2 percent of what we put out to support ourselves when the American troops were over there.

Anyway, I made the mistake of telling Ambassador Martin that I was going to inform the Vietnamese, and he ordered me not to tell them. This is kind of a stupid thing because if you don't tell them they're going to keep requisitioning supplies and expecting to get them in 120 days, which

was the normal time it took. So I tried to tell the ambassador that 120 days is going to be like falling off a cliff. But he wouldn't listen. He said they couldn't stand the shock, and I told him, you know, Jesus, they're shock proof. Then he said that President Thieu asked him not to tell the Joint General Staff. Well, that was just a lot of bovine excrement. It was impossible for Thieu to know about it when I talked to the ambassador because I was the first guy to know. And if he *had* known about it he would have talked to General Vien, and Vien would have told me. Generals talk to generals. We all have our suspicions of the fellows in the striped pants.

But Graham Martin was the kind of guy that you never really knew what his motives were, except they always somehow had to be related to the benefit of the United States of America. He was a super patriot. If anybody should be dressed up in an American flag, it's got to be Martin. And as far as the war was concerned, on a scale of one to ten he'd have been ten plus as a hawk. He was also one of the most devious guys I ever knew. He could stand in the shadow of a corkscrew. He used to say he never told a lie, and he lied all the time. He made stuff up. Martin was like Fibber McGee—a wonderful memory for things that never happened. He's the only man I ever met who said he never did anything wrong, and believed it.

On the other hand, he had some admirable qualities. He suffered from emphy-

When John Murray first arrived in Vietnam in 1968, enormous quantities of U.S. military supplies were distributed around the country in airplanes, trains, trucks, and boats such as this utility landing craft carrying rations and spare parts from Cam Ranh Bay to the port of Phan Ranh.

sema, and in that sense Martin was heroic. He was in awful pain, you could tell, and he didn't sleep much. Some of the best meetings we had were at three o'clock in the morning back at his mansion. He'd take his tie off, and he'd sit down and relax and have a few drinks and we'd talk. When he dropped his ambassadorial front he almost became human. He was a very well-read man, a brilliant guy in many ways. One of the strangest men I've ever known, and the most interesting. I considered dealing with the ambassador a spectator sport.

All he cared about was what happened to the United States. He didn't particularly care about the Vietnamese, about what happened to them. His approach toward them was pretty much laissez-faire. He never really gave them advice or tried to put the squeeze on them, and there was definitely something to be said for that. If you're talking Vietnamization and our ultimately getting out, then they had to learn how to do things and suffer from their own mistakes. They just couldn't rely on us to make their decisions for them. But not to tell them that the money was running out?

Martin and I had a fundamental difference. He believed, as a professional diplomat, that his job was to insure that the United States withdrew from Vietnam without damage to our reputation. My view, as a professional soldier, was that I wasn't being paid to lose a war. As a result, our whole coordination with the Vietnamese was just very poorly done. The ambassador was saying one thing and I was saying another. You see, once the money began drying up the biggest problem was ammunition, and in that one area I really didn't follow what the ambassador told me. I immediately informed General Khuyen, their chief of logistics, that new supplies of ammunition weren't going to be coming at least until the new fiscal year. Just the ammunition. But he soon began to suspect the rest of it. They would requisition stuff and the requisition would be rejected, and our guys would tell them there'd been a glitch in the computers. Khuyen was smart enough to recognize that this was more than ammunition. I didn't have to tell him anything.

Meanwhile, I was protesting to Admiral Gayler at CINCPAC, I was protesting to General O'Keefe at the 7th Air Force, I was protesting to an assistant secretary of the army who came to pay me a visit, and finally I got orders from Gayler to inform the Vietnamese what was going on. So I told them there wouldn't be any more money at least until the end of the fiscal year. But it was hard to convince them because Martin kept telling them not to worry. I guess he thought that reassuring them would stimulate their morale. I don't know. The ambassador could be in hell and the devil would have a blowtorch up his ass and he'd still be optimistic about the situation. I never saw him pessimistic about anything. He was always upbeat.

But it sure made for a lot of confusion. I remember he ordered me at one point to tell General Vien that he was going to get everything he needed. So I went to General Vien and I said, "The ambassador has instructed me to tell you that you're going to get everything you need." Vien looked at me and he said, "What do you think?" And I said, "I don't think you are." But it took him a while to come around to it because Martin persistently kept telling Thieu that he was going to get everything he needed.

Khuyen understood quick enough, though. The ARVN was going to have to tighten its belt until Congress came up with more funding. We stopped using ammunition that wasn't killing anybody, the stuff you throw up just to light up the sky at night. We cut out practically all sandbags. We said, "You got a shovel? Then start digging dirt and fill a bag." Barbed wire, lumber, construction material, housing for soldiers' families, anything you didn't need to fight a battle we eliminated. We cut out combat rations, too, which was an awful mistake, but we had to do it.

Some of the stuff we eliminated wasn't all that vital. We were spending a million dollars a year on winter underwear. What are you doing with winter underwear in the tropics? Well, you find out a lot of our fighting was up in the mountains, some high-altitude places. So what I did was cut that in half. I figured these are little guys, they can walk around with bare legs, but we'll give 'em the shirts. Or toilet paper. At U.S. flag commercial rates it would cost us ninety-nine cents a roll to ship that stuff from San Francisco to Saigon. It was crazy. So I said, "Well, what did they do before they had toilet paper?" And I was told banana leaves. So I said, "That's what they're going to do now."

The fact was we had Americanized them. They had gotten used to our inventory and our way of reaching in and getting anything we wanted. It was like giving kids ice cream at every meal and suddenly saying no more ice cream. Except that most of the stuff we were cutting back was a lot more important than ice cream. By January 1974 supplies and equipment of every kind started dropping off, and after that it never recovered.

In May, Congress appropriated more money—$1.1 billion for fiscal year 1974, all but about $300 million of which we had already spent—but it wasn't enough. The NVA had launched attacks all over the country and the South Vietnamese were running out of supplies. All the while Martin kept telling them you're going to get everything you need. So Thieu tells Vien, "I want you to make up a shopping list of what our needs are. And I want you to write it up and take it back to Secretary of Defense Schlesinger." Then Vien comes to me and says what do we need, and I wind up drawing up the list and writing something up for him to say, and both of us head off to Washington.

When we got to the Pentagon General Wickham, who was Schlesinger's military assistant, asked me what I wanted to talk about. So I gave him the script I wrote for Vien. Then Wickham says to me, "Well, what should the secretary say?" So I sat down and wrote out about three pages for him. The next day we came into the secretary's office and there he was behind his desk puffing away on his pipe. He used the tobacco smoke as a sort of camouflage, because while Vien was delivering his message, which the secretary already knew he was going to deliver, Schlesinger is glancing at a bunch of three-by-five cards he was holding in his right hand with notes from the reply I had written for him. When we're all done—they had a lot of brass there and I was the last guy to leave the room—the secretary winks at me and says, "How did I do?" Then Vien, who spoke English and had read his paper in English, he took me aside and said, "You know, I have to report back to my president and the secretary talked too fast. What did he say?" So of course I gave him a copy of what I had written for Schlesinger. But I was beginning to wonder whether I ought to write soap operas or something instead of being an army officer.

Naturally, Schlesinger told him the same things I'd been telling him all along: you have to tighten your belts and belt anybody who doesn't. But since it was the American secretary of defense who was saying it, the message got back very strongly. After that they finally decided, Jesus, we've really got a problem.

You know, I spent my time in the army with most all of the secretaries of defense and I think Schlesinger was the finest one, the best trained and the best qualified. I was responsible to him for everything in Vietnam, and I took advantage of that. Whenever I wanted to see him there was no question about it, and he made decisions that were in our favor. But he was one of the few people at the Pentagon that seemed to understand what was going on. After it was all over I saw General Woolwine, the chief of logistics to the Joint Chiefs of Staff, and I told him I didn't understand why something hadn't been done, why people hadn't reacted to our warnings. You know what he told me? He said, "John, we didn't believe you." They thought I was a lunatic. They thought I was just being suckered in by the South Vietnamese. There wasn't a hell of a lot of empathy for the Vietnamese from the American military.

The United States Army likes to think it fought a big war in Vietnam. It didn't. When we were fighting the heaviest action was probably battalion-sized combat, sometimes maybe a division. But in 1974 the ARVN was engaged in corps-sized battles and they were fighting without air support, without any of the support that the U.S. Army was used to. And the weaponry that the enemy put in there, all the tanks and the 130MM guns and the 120MM rockets and the Strela missiles and

all the antiaircraft stuff. When you've got to go up to 15,000 feet with those obsolete aircraft they had to avoid getting shot down, what good were they?

The Pentagon could have done better. It could have done much better. They were charging the South Vietnamese for obsolete ammunition that the U.S. Army didn't need that they could have issued free. They were charging them for excess supplies that they were giving away free to the Koreans and the Taiwanese and the Thais. Stuff like that. When the money was being reduced the Pentagon comptrollers were looking at the cost of the war and they're saying, "You're firing 6,000 rounds a day of 105s. So let's take that 6,000 rounds a day and multiply it by 365 and that's what you're going to need in the way of ammunition." Well, that's crazy. We had a thousand 105s in the

February 1973. Murray (left), and General Dang Van Khuyen (center), the South Vietnamese chief of logistics, discuss billeting arrangements with the Polish delegation of the International Commission of Control and Supervision. A multinational team of observers, the ICCS monitored the cease-fire agreed upon by the U.S. and North Vietnam in January 1973.

"What I found on my first inspection tour was that our U.S. supervision stunk." At Bac Lieu a shipment of lime is left in the open without any protective covering.

Murray, Khuyen, and General Nguyen Van Chuc confer at Tan Son Nhut airport in December 1973. Although neither ARVN commander knew it at the time, the flow of supplies from the United States was about to be drastically reduced.

A year and a half after the declaration of ceasefire, South Vietnamese forces were under attack throughout most of the country. In July 1974, Murray (third from right) and several other U.S. officers are briefed on the deteriorating situation near Quang Tri.

country. That's only six rounds per gun per day. In the '72 offensive they fired 200,000 goddamned rounds in a day, and they had the support of the B-52s and the F-4s and the navy gunfire. Six thousand rounds a day might be enough when the enemy was fairly quiet, but it was crazy to suppose that would be enough in the face of a major offensive.

And by the summer of 1974 that's just what was happening in South Vietnam, although few enough people seemed to notice it. Nine months earlier during the Yom Kippur War in Israel, American newspapers were writing about how the Israelis had lost a thousand of the flower of their youth. Big headlines. Jesus Christ, the South Vietnamese were losing a thousand men a *week*, and there weren't any headlines. Everyplace I went they were asking for more supplies, more support. What a military force needs above all is what it takes to move, shoot, and communicate, and they didn't have enough to meet any of those needs.

They had lost their mobility. They didn't have enough fuel for their helicopters or their tanks. Most of their trucks were up on blocks because they didn't have the gasoline to run them. They didn't have enough batteries for their radios. They were short of spare parts, boots, socks, the ponchos they used as shelters to keep them dry in the monsoons. They were running out of medicine—there were soldiers in the hospital who couldn't get morphine when they were having their

legs amputated because the South Vietnamese didn't have the money to buy it. They had no food. The soldiers were getting a bowl of rice a day, and they had nothing for their families.

I remember visiting a military hospital that had a ward containing maybe forty quadriplegics, guys who had lost the use of all four limbs. They were in slings with a belt across the middle, facing the dirt floor. They had no air conditioning or anything like that, and all they could do, literally, was sweat. But they had their wives and sisters and families sitting below the slings wiping the sweat from their faces. The hospital administrator told me he was going to have to keep the families away. And I said why, because in Vietnam it was customary for family members to take care of their relatives even when they were in a hospital. And he said, because they're giving their families all their food. Their families are eating their rice.

And the lack of ammunition, that was the big thing. Their ammunition supplies were just low as hell. It had forced them into a completely defensive position. They had cut back severely on artillery fire and had almost rationed hand grenades out of existence. I visited one ARVN unit that summer commanded by General Nguyen Khoa Nam, a good fighter. His men used to carry eight to ten grenades apiece into battle. Now they carried two, he said. "One is to throw at the enemy, and one is to pull the pin on yourself," which is what he did, when all was lost.

The final blow was the congressional action in August on the appropriations for fiscal year 1975. I figured that if they got $1 billion a year, that would sustain them as long as the fighting didn't get any worse. But Congress gave them only $700 million, and when shipping, administrative, and other costs were deducted they really ended up with about $500 million. I couldn't believe it. I couldn't believe we could be that stupid on what really amounted to such a small amount of money. My God, when the American troops were there we were spending $14 billion a year just to support the bombing!

The last time I saw Generals Truong and Toan and the rest of the corps commanders it was hard for them to believe what was happening. They were all very literate men. They were reading *Time* and *Newsweek* and all that, all the doom and gloom and you're not going to get any more support and that sort of thing. They had a dead view of the future. It was just sad, very sad, very depressing.

I thought that if I had had the opportunity to talk directly to the Congress of the United States they would not have made those decisions. Because in my mind I could not imagine rational people, even with the politics of Watergate, not listening to what the hell was really happening in South Vietnam. When I returned to Washington I met with Secretary Schlesinger and he said to me, "You should talk to the press and you should talk to the Hill." So people set up appointments for me, and the first one I was supposed to see was Senator Mike Mansfield. But Mansfield refused. He said he didn't want to talk to any more army generals, that son of a bitch. That no good Pontius Pilate son of a bitch.

There were a few congressmen willing to listen to me, but not many. Most of them were listening to the mobs in the streets. Democracy's got some horrible flaws. If it is a fact, as they say now, that most of the people in the country were against the war, all I can do is recall Montaigne, one of his essays where he says it's a sad thing to uphold the belief of a multitude as a test of truth. It's one of the great, great failures of democracy.

The big lesson of the Vietnam War to the rest of the world is don't trust any kind of negotiations with the United States of America. Because you can't count on us. And the Constitution is really a nefarious document when it comes to the rest of the world. The president can make agreements and you think you've got an agreement and you haven't, because the United States Congress has got to support it. And they can in effect put through what you might call an ex post facto arrangement.

I don't think we made a mistake getting involved in Vietnam. Not at all. I think freedom is an unfinished business, and I feel basically we are involved in that business. Our mistake was not in getting involved. Our mistake was lack of will. Our mistake was not hanging in there. But it was a mistake somebody else had to pay for, the people of South Vietnam.

We cut their throats. All of us, the military, the Congress, the president, the media, and the people of the United States. We made them promises we didn't keep. The collapse in 1975 was the direct result of the cutback in support. There is no question in my mind about it. Even if the end had not come so suddenly it wouldn't have made any difference. They were going to lose. Given the supplies they had on hand, they had at best about sixty days to live. Without the support of the United States they simply didn't have the resources to keep fighting. Just as well they didn't try to endure. Just as well. ∎

Not only battlefield defeats, but also economic hardship contributed to the demoralization of the South Vietnamese army during the war's final years. The houses provided to soldiers' families, like these at Dinh Tuong, were often little more than hovels with open ditches for sewers and running water only when it rained.

Thomas H. Stebbins

Missionary
The Christian and Missionary Alliance
1957–1975

The son of missionary parents who met on the boat to Da Nang in 1918, Tom Stebbins was born in Hue in 1933. The Japanese occupation of Indochina forced the family of nine to flee to the United States, but Tom was one of six Stebbins children who eventually went back overseas as missionaries. He went on to spend eighteen years in the land of his birth, with only occasional sabbaticals in the United States. As a pastor for The Christian and Missionary Alliance, the first Protestant mission in the predominantly Buddhist and Catholic country, Reverend Stebbins, along with his wife, Donna, "planted" native churches in and around Tuy Hoa, Da Nang, and Hue. He later served as CMA field chairman in Saigon, and was one of the last Americans evacuated from the capital as the country fell in April 1975. Currently a pastor in Omaha, Nebraska, Reverend Stebbins often travels around the country to speak to various Vietnamese groups.

The last thing I wanted to be was a missionary. I had had boils while on the mission field as a child and almost died of malaria. I knew what the heat was like in Vietnam and I knew what it was like to live in a foreign culture. I really wanted to be a professional tennis player. But when I was in high school in Florida, I heard a message that challenged me to become a missionary. I really felt God needed me overseas. So in 1951 I enrolled at Nyack College, New York, the CMA training school.

At Nyack I did a study and found that there were fewer missionaries per million people in Vietnam than in any of our mission fields around the world. And I wanted to go to a country where there was a lot of pioneer work to be done. I had that natural love for the Vietnamese people and some background in the language, so I felt I'd have a head start there. And then of course I had some family members there: my parents and sisters had returned to Southeast Asia.

My wife and I arrived in Saigon on February 15, 1957. My mother was really anxious that I would come and work in Hue with them, but I didn't want to do that. I asked the mission if I could go to a province where there was very little missionary activity to plant churches. So I went to Tuy Hoa, about a day's trip south of Da Nang.

I would spend five days a week out in the villages. The first couple of months the Vietnamese pastor and I would go out on bicycles to the villages, sometimes wading through rivers that were up to our waists, and sleep in villages. I had forgotten the language from my youth, so I didn't speak much at first. I would play my trombone and sing Vietnamese hymns and the pastor would do the preaching. Gradually I learned the language, then I began to do more preaching. The people said I spoke Vietnamese like a Vietnamese, probably because of my childhood roots in the country.

I actually started preaching to the children at first. You could make mistakes in the language and they wouldn't laugh at you or make fun of you. I felt very comfortable preaching to kids, and I found hundreds of them would gather around to hear me speak to them. Then after I got comfortable speaking to the kids, I noticed that the adults were starting to crowd them out. So I said to the pastor,

"Hey, I think I'm ready to preach to the adults now."

When I preached, first I'd talk about God and give them evidence of our belief in there being a God. I'd talk about His love and how it was manifested in Jesus Christ. I'd usually show slides of the life of Christ with a kerosene projector. Then we'd answer questions. They'd say, "Well, if I become a Christian, do I give up worshiping my ancestors? What about my idols?" Or, "How much rice will you give me? Is Christianity an American religion?" Things like that.

I was told that on many occasions there were Vietcong in the audience when I was preaching. Of course, they didn't expose themselves, so you didn't know when you were talking to people in the villages which side they were on. But they would ask questions and you would say to yourself, "I bet this guy is a Vietcong," because of some of the questions he would ask.

As conditions became more dangerous, we were cautioned about traveling at night. In 1961, Tuy Hoa was surrounded and rocketed by the Communists. One time they caught a Communist and beheaded him and put his head up in the middle of a field in Tuy Hoa, to kind of warn the people, hey, if you follow the Communists, this could happen to you. The Communists would also chop off the heads of village chiefs and leave them behind as a kind of retaliation.

I really felt that we were in danger, but I believed that I was doing God's will, doing His work, and that He would protect me. Someone once said that you're eternal until your work is done. I felt that as long as I was doing God's work and taking reasonable precautions, He'd watch over me. But at the same time both my wife and I faced the possibility of death in the course of our mission.

In our second term, from 1962 to 1967, most of our work was limited to the cities because of the increase in enemy guerrilla activity. We began to see a greater presence of American troops after the build-up in 1965. Being American, we maintained a really good relationship with the American forces. Many of our missionaries served as unofficial chaplains in areas where there weren't military chaplains. In fact, every missionary's home was open to the GIs and we'd have them over for meals.

The soldiers would volunteer to bring in medical help. I remember one time dentists and doctors from one of the navy ships came in and examined all the neighborhood kids. Guys came in and painted part of our house and built a doll house for my child. And they would get involved in building schools for our churches. I remember one occasion in Da Nang when the Marines built a beautiful children's hospital that they eventually turned over to the church to operate.

We accepted these things as long as there were no strings attached politically. The Communists portrayed us as being spies, agents of the American government, which, of course, was totally false. The National Church of Vietnam had a neutral stance in that it believed in the separation of church and state. You might say they ministered to the Communists at night, whenever the guerrillas might be in the village, and then in the daytime they would preach or relate to the South Vietnamese free people.

Our church went on record as being nonpolitical. From time to time I would have embassy personnel drop by and ask my evaluation of the political situation. But I seldom gave any opinion. I never really got involved. I think that's one of the reasons why, even though I was working out in relatively dangerous areas, I was not attacked or killed: because I think the Communists saw the stand that our church took politically.

From 1965 to 1967 we lived in Hue, my boyhood home. Being a Buddhist stronghold and the imperial capital, it was very resistant to the Gospel. After all the years of my dad's labor, they had only one small church in the city and a couple out in the country. So the challenge for my type of work was a lot greater.

Hue was an educational center, so we rented a large French villa near the university on the more western side of the Perfume River and made a youth center out of it. We had ten Vietnamese Christian students living with us, and they helped us organize English classes. We taught probably as many as 2,000 students and government officials English during those three years.

Our house in Hue was across the street from my boyhood home, which incidentally had become the CIA headquarters. We didn't know until later that we were living across from the CIA, but I guess that's one of the reasons our house and area were frequently rocketed by the enemy. We had lots of narrow escapes. I remember one night I had a dream that we were being attacked by the Communists. I could hear machine guns firing and rockets were falling. Then I woke up, and it was real. I could hear machine guns down the street a couple of blocks, and rockets were falling all around. So it was getting pretty scary.

I also went up to Quang Tri Province to visit a church at Gio Linh, which is right on the DMZ, within eyesight of North Vietnam. Once the army flew me in a helicopter right to the church because the road was full of mines. The amazing thing to me was to see the church just packed to the doors. Even though there was war and battles all around, the churches were packed to the doors and people were responding to the Gospel. I think that in time of stress like that they were much more open to eternal and spiritual things.

In late 1967 we went home for furlough. Actually, I wanted to stay for another year; our work was just going so great, having such good response. And

Mrs. Mary Stebbins with her seven children during a speaking tour of the United States with her husband, Irving, in 1937. Left to right are Harriet, Elizabeth, Tom (front), George, Mrs. Stebbins, Robert, Anne (front), and Ruth.

we were enjoying ourselves at the youth center, planting churches, and working in the military hospital. But my wife persuaded me to leave. There was no missionary to replace us at the time, so we just left the house, with our pictures on the walls and books in the bookcases, so that missionaries could come up from Da Nang and stay the night.

I had a strange feeling that last time I went across the Perfume River before leaving for the United States. I was riding with a Vietnamese pastor, and I had this strange feeling that Hue was in for a really terrible experience. I said to him that I felt Hue was doomed for some real tragedy.

When Tet broke out I was concerned for my sister, Ruth Thompson, and her husband, Ed, who were at the mission in Ban Me Thuot, working with the Mnong people. I didn't know who was being hit in Vietnam until someone called me early in the morning and said, "Have you heard the news?" So I turned on the news and it said that our Ban Me Thuot station had been attacked and that six of our missionaries had been killed. Two of them were my sister and her husband.

When we came back in the summer of '68, Hue was rubble. Our house was riddled with bullets. The North Vietnamese had taken over our house to attack the CIA headquarters, and all our possessions, even our beds, everything, were taken by either the friendlies or the enemy. My library was all dumped on the floor. We came back to a big mess, but we were thankful, because we knew that had we stayed there we would have been among the 5,000 that were killed.

When I returned I felt the enemy really made a mistake in what they did. They turned the people against them by the atrocities they committed. Before Tet the students at Hue would sometimes defend the Communist position. They'd say, "They're really going to bring equality. And they will do away with a few people holding all the wealth." But when I came back, their attitude had totally reversed, 180 degrees, and you never saw anybody more anti-Communist than the university students in Hue. So for three or four years, because of the increased presence of the U.S. military, plus the people's hearts and minds being turned against the enemy because of the atrocities they had committed, at least in the I Corps area, I felt

that the situation had improved and I was really quite optimistic.

In the summer of '69 I was elected CMA field chairman and moved to Saigon. There were about 100 missionaries in Vietnam at the time. Of course, the responsibility for them was weighing heavily on my mind. I was really concerned that they would not take any unnecessary risks and go to dangerous places where they didn't need to go. So I had a few sleepless nights thinking about the missionaries. I'll be honest, I didn't want to be field chairman. But when your colleagues give you a strong vote like that . . . I felt I should do it.

Saigon at that time was jammed with refugees. I'll never forget, about two blocks from my house, adjacent to the Cambodian embassy, were some storefronts. There was a crack in the wall about a yard, a yard and a half wide. Some refugees had gone and built a two-story shack in that crack. They lived on the top floor, and on the bottom floor they had a sewing machine and they built a little shop. That was indicative of how people jammed into every little nook and cranny that they could find to live. They crowded into their relatives' houses, so that instead of one family living in a home you had three, four, or five families. You had people sleeping on mats on the sidewalk at night. Then they'd roll up their mats and pull out a piece of canvas and open a shop on that sidewalk in the daytime. Saigon became the most crowded city in the world, I think, during that time. With all those people, the number of churches grew rapidly; we had over forty churches in Saigon.

When I got back from a furlough in July 1974, I became pastor of the International Protestant Church in Saigon, two blocks from the American embassy. By then I began to sense that the Vietnamese questioned the Americans' loyalty and support of them. Basically they were still pro-American. They understood the Americans' exasperation at how the war dragged on and the loss of so many of our guys. They understood why we were backing out but at the same time I think a lot of them felt we were sort of betraying them, that we made a commitment to stand with them and now were backing off. To see us go back on our promises was rather embarrassing to me as an American living there.

The whole situation in Vietnam kind of seesawed. You'd have times when it looked like it was going down the tubes, then there would be a total reversal, and there seemed to be a great improvement in the whole situation. So at the end I didn't know if maybe we were in one of those low points, about to have another reversal. I didn't think the fall of Vietnam was that imminent.

But in the spring of 1975, as I began to hear that one after another of the provinces had fallen, I saw people become very anxious and wondered how much longer Vietnam would have. I guess the day that really showed a turn for us was April 8, when North Vietnamese planes bombed the presidential palace. You couldn't believe the droves of people that were evacuating from the center of the city. There were police and soldiers in jeeps shouting over their bullhorns, telling the people to quiet down, that everything was going to be all right. But people were just fleeing in droves for the suburbs.

The CMA was evacuating all of the wives from Vietnam, and most of the men would soon be leaving. My wife was getting ready to fly out that day when the bombs fell. I said to Jack Revelle, our field chairman, "I'm taking Donna to the airport." He said, "Well, you'd better get on that plane and go with her." So we took a Pan Am jet over to Manila. We thought we'd be returning, that it was just a temporary evacuation.

On Friday, April 25, Jack called to tell me that he had left Vietnam and that there were no more of our missionaries there. When I relayed this message to our mission headquarters in Nyack, they asked me to fly back to Saigon to help around 600 members of our church who were high-security risks: Vietnamese who were in some way connected with the U.S. or Vietnamese government. It took a cable from the White House to get me a flight on April 28. The pilot of the C–130 thought I was off my rocker because people were clawing at fences and doing everything to get out, and here was some crazy preacher flying back in.

After I got off the plane in Saigon, I headed straight for the embassy. The deputy ambassador said that if I would get a list of the people, they would get them on some airplanes to fly out. When I got to the International Protestant Church, there were probably 200 or 300 people there waiting. They about swallowed me alive. I was their only hope, you know, to get out. I started on a list of people, but I could see in the confusion I couldn't get anything done. Just as I was walking to get back into the embassy taxi, enemy planes started bombing the presidential palace and the airport. The C-130 I flew in on never took off. So I figured, well, I'm on my own now.

We went one block in the taxi, but there was barbed wire across the road. I jumped out, made my way gingerly through the barbed wire, and ran the remaining block to the embassy. The gates were closed and the Marines were nowhere in sight, so a Vietnamese guard helped me climb over the wall. I spent the night on a cot in the embassy clinic. I tried to call our mission headquarters but the lines were all busy.

When they opened the gate the next morning, the twenty-ninth, I went across the street to the World Vision headquarters. I drew up a list of people to sponsor to get out, but the embassy personnel said they would not be able to get out the large numbers of people that they had hoped. Since I spoke Vietnamese fluently, I said, "Look, if I stay behind and interpret for you guys so you can get all your interpreters and Vietnamese personnel out, if I stay until the end and there's still time, would you be willing to take my people over at the church?" So that's why I stayed until the very end.

Dr. Eben Dustin, the embassy doctor and a member of our church, told me that there was a ship in the harbor that would take all of my people if they would go over there. So I called over to the church and told the people to go to the ship. I said, "Don't wait for me to get you out by helicopter because it doesn't look very hopeful." But I was told later that the leader of the group just didn't know how secure the streets were, so he advised them to stay and hope that I would get them out on helicopters. Only one pastor and his family drove across town to the ship and made it to Guam.

By late morning there were a few helicopters landing on the roof and they started taking people out. In the outer embassy compound, people were climbing the chain-link fence to get inside. I stood at the gate of the inner compound, counting the people as they went through, interpreting for the Vietnamese, and giving

them instructions as to how many people could get on the next helicopter. For the rest of the day I stood at that gate. We evacuated about 2,000 or 3,000 in about fifty helicopter loads.

Finally, about midnight on the morning of the thirtieth, Dr. Dustin came to me and said, "Pastor, the ambassador is leaving on the next helicopter. You'd better get on this one that's coming in."

At 12:30 I phoned the church one last time. I told them I had been ordered to leave on the next flight. The pastor at the other end of the phone said, "Two hundred of us are here and have prayed and wept all evening. It would have been better for us to stay home. Our neighbors know we've tried to escape. Now it will be very difficult for us to return." I replied that I was extremely sorry, that we just had not enough time to get them out, that we'd tried everything possible, and that I'd leave a letter with the ambassador reminding him that they were at the church if anything could be done at the last minute. Then I went to the top floor of the embassy and got on the helicopter at 1:00 A.M. It was jammed. I didn't think we were even going to get off the roof. I also thought the enemy might shoot us down.

As we were flying across the treetops, I was very broken up. I was saying goodbye to the land of my birth. I had a lot of friends there. I buried my sister there. This was my boyhood home, where I'd spent twenty-six years of my life. I considered Vietnam my country.

Reverend Stebbins (center) and Glenn Wagner (right) of the Pocket Testament League present a New Testament to Major General Nguyen Chan Thi, ARVN I Corps commander, at Da Nang on October 8, 1965.

Top. *Evacuees are loaded into a helicopter in the U.S. embassy parking lot on April 29, 1975, in this photo taken by Stebbins. He left early the next morning by helicopter from the embassy rooftop.*

Above. *On Guam in June 1975, two Vietnamese pastors wait in the water to baptize refugees at a service conducted by Reverend Stebbins (in white).*

We landed on the deck of the U.S.S. *Vancouver.* I stayed on the deck until about six or seven o'clock in the morning, waiting for more helicopters, hoping that some of my people would have escaped. Finally, I was told that the ambassador had left, and it dawned on me that they hadn't escaped.

As I stood on the deck of the carrier looking back at the coast of Vietnam, I was a little bitter, kind of angry at God. Why would He allow Vietnam to fall after all of our prayers and labor? Why would He allow my people to go through this blood bath they were about to face? That was what probably caused me more grief than anything: the imponderable "why?" that you wrestle with at a time of crisis like that.

But about five years later, after working in Guam and Hong Kong with Vietnamese refugees, trying to forget this grief and trying to find some kind of solution, I spoke on the fall of Vietnam at a meeting of our CMA National Council in Hartford. Then I said, "I think I'm finally beginning to understand the 'why?'—for a number of reasons."

One of them was that the National Church was ready to be severed from the missionary presence of the CMA, so that they would become more independent and mature. There wasn't the blood bath that we expected in Vietnam; the church is actually growing more rapidly now than when we were there. Also, through the fall of Vietnam, many of our Vietnamese Christians were scattered to about forty countries, and they're having a witness all over the world that they had never had before. I said that through all of this trauma and tragedy, many, many people have sought God and found salvation in Christ. As the Psalmist says, "Surely the wrath of man shall praise Thee." Through that great hour of suffering, many people have come to experience God's salvation.

So the "why?" began to be answered, and today I've found comfort in a resolution to that bitterness that I felt at that moment on the deck of the *Vancouver.* I know it sounds like an oversimplification, but if any good can come out of war, I would say it's of a spiritual nature in the hearts of men and women. My heart is divided: I grieve for the people of the North and South and all the suffering they've gone through, and at the same time I'm thankful that there is some good, some gold that has come out of the fire. ∎

Cuong Van Nguyen

Deputy Province Chief
Lam Dong Province, Republic of Vietnam

Cuong Van Nguyen was born in 1941 of Buddhist parents but attended a Catholic boarding school. In 1954, when the school staff left for South Vietnam, he went with them to complete his high-school education. His mother followed three years later leaving behind all that the family owned. Cuong graduated from the University of Saigon's law school and the Faculty of Letters. He was then selected for the National Institute of Administration. Upon graduation in 1964, he was appointed a civil servant in Lam Dong Province along the southern border of the central highlands about 100 kilometers south of Ban Me Thuot. After serving in the ARVN as an infantry lieutenant, Cuong returned to civil administration and by 1975 had been promoted to deputy province chief.

By 1975 my own feeling was that something very bad was going to happen. Especially when I heard on the BBC that the U.S. Congress didn't approve the military aid. But at that time, President Thieu still believed in the written promise by President Nixon that, "We're not going to abandon you." He was naive to believe that because Watergate had happened, which signaled that maybe President Thieu had lost his support in the United States. Also, the U.S. had let Cambodia fall and it really affected the South Vietnamese fighting spirit because we knew if America didn't intervene in Cambodia, then they probably wouldn't intervene in Vietnam again.

We kept a very close eye on the battles in the central highlands because if they are lost, we are lost. But at the same time I felt that we had strong forces and fighting experience. I didn't think that the North Vietnamese could win that war. That's why I was still living in my province and kept my wife there. As the number two in the province I drove her around the downtown areas so the people know I'm still there. But then it's just like a domino; Ban Me Thuot, Quang Duc, Pleiku, Hue, and Nha Trang were lost, all the way down to the south. And I'll tell you one thing, that right now I don't know why. It is still a big question in my life. You heard about the Tet offensive of 1968, you heard about what we called the bloody summer of 1972. We're the South, we don't lose. I still can't believe we fought for twenty-two years and then we lost the whole country in just a few weeks.

I finally gave up when my boss evacuated his family. I was pressured by all kinds of relatives to help them escape to a safer area, so I sent my family to relatives in Saigon. One thing I'm proud of is that I stayed until the NVA took over my residence. I waited in my office. I was one of the last to leave the province headquarters on the day before Easter.

I had a very courageous district chief. I told him to leave but he said no and stayed. When I reached the boundary of Tuyen Duc Province I had my last radio communication with him. He reported his RFs and PFs were still fighting and had destroyed four T54 tanks. At the border we were stopped by the neighboring province chief. He didn't like it that we were leaving. I said, "Look, we have

10,000 civilians with no soldiers to protect them. You can't let them stay here and wait until the Communists send the mortars." Finally they let us through to Da Lat. It was the saddest experience I'd had up to that time. As I evacuated the whole province with me, people were dying along the road from hunger, thirst, and all kinds of mishaps.

I went on to Phan Rang and finally north to Nha Trang, where the government was trying to organize a defense with everyone under forty-five years of age. I stayed in Nha Trang for a few days until a friend of mine in the Vietnamese navy got me a place on one of their ships. I arrived in Saigon with only my black pants and shirt, my M16, and a little Browning pistol. I met my family and then reported to the interior ministry and was assigned to work in immigration, but after two days all the big bosses disappeared. I didn't know what was going on by that time and was really confused. I had an American friend who'd promised he would take my family out, but at the last minute he disappeared and I was left behind.

At that time I had seven children whom I was worried about and hoped I could find a safe way to get them out, but early on April 30 the last choppers left Saigon. I looked at the embassy roof and saw all the choppers leaving and said, "That's that." But my wife pushed me to find a way out, so that morning I moved around the Saigon port, but all the boats were either gone or their motors were broken down. There was chaos everywhere so we went back to the house just as the first North Vietnamese group came in. My wife sat down on the curb and cried, "I will lose my family, I will lose my husband." I was trying to keep my spirits up, but when I saw the NLF flags and all of the Buddhist monks head to the Independence Palace I said, "Now they have our capital. That's the end of the world."

I had a relative who lived in the North and came south with the NVA occupation forces as an official. When he came to our house and saw me, the first thing he did was give me a blow ... hit me. He said, "Why didn't you get out? Why didn't you get away?" It's unbelievable. Thanks to him I learned how the North Vietnamese program was going to work. The Communists would say those people working for the former government should attend the reeducation program. The longest will

Well-to-do South Vietnamese, with family and belongings, await passage on the last remaining commercial flights out of Saigon on April 29, 1975.

jet can't go faster than these rumors, and that's what makes people survive. I think the rumors were a good thing because after the fall a lot of people committed suicide, even those who never got involved in government activities but who were scared about the Communists. Some were businessmen who were wiped out when the currency was changed. Others killed themselves after the new government assigned them to economic development zones in the jungles where there was malaria and all kinds of diseases, malnutrition, bad conditions—like clearing minefields with bare hands or filling in bomb craters with no tools—and constant insults from the Communists. Many decided that I don't want anybody to destroy me. I'll destroy myself. The reeducation program is a blood bath without using a single bullet.

For two months after I left my family, I studied and planned to get out as soon as possible with a group of people that had worked for the government and military. We made all the false papers because some were still working and could borrow the papers from other people. They could look at the seals and then imitate them because in our group were some artists. You have a fresh potato and then you cut it and carve it and make the fresh seal. We did that since you can't move around without permission.

We got a big fishing boat, but the first time we failed to get out because of bad timing. The boat couldn't get close to the area we chose because of all the rocks, so we had bought a small boat as transportation from the beach. But the small boat couldn't locate the big boat and we aborted the trip. We had brought together 150 people for the escape, but we had to disperse and reschedule the trip.

After the first attempt, however, everyone felt this was a good organization and some began to pass the word to their relatives. Without notifying me they got people into the escape group that were not prepared and not trained. Someone attracted the secret police. The Communists followed us and waited until we got in the boat and then surrounded it and arrested the whole group. They tied me up to the root of a tree separately because a lot of people say that guy there, they pointed at me, he's the leader.

First they robbed us of every single thing we had, and then for three days

be three days or one week. But this was not true. Some of my superiors are still in the reeducation camps.

So I didn't report to the new authorities. I was really scared, because I knew that if they found me, they would arrest me, put me in jail, or maybe shoot me because I had citations from when I was a deputy district chief. I had commanded a unit that defeated a Communist force and received the Gallantry Cross with gold star for the number of enemy that we had killed. That night I left my wife and all my kids with my in-laws and I started moving. I feared that some of the neighbors had been working for the Communists and might denounce me. Like the cyclo driver that lived at the corner. He's always polite and greets you every day. But now he's changed. He's a boss, the chief of the quarter. So who do you trust?

Rumors helped us survive. They were like food, nutrition that helped you to live, to struggle with life. The rumors are that South Vietnamese troops are hiding and fighting in the jungle or humorous stories about how the people from the North try to raise fish in the flush toilets. And those rumors go fast, you can believe that. The they questioned us. They sentenced me to death for four things. First, because they said I worked for the CIA, then because I worked for the former government, then because I had served in the army and was therefore an enemy of the people, and last because I tried to take the property of the people abroad. Finally they moved the rest of the group and I thought, well, that's the end of my life. They will kill me sooner or later. But a spirit of survival raised in me and I started thinking about escape. I leaned against the tree and pressed my ropes against it and finally, piece by piece, I broke the root of the tree I was tied to. I waited as the sky turned darker and darker. Two of the guards were asleep, one was talking, and the other guy was walking around nearby. I attacked the one that was moving around. It was a miracle. The guy had an AK47 and could have shot me, but instead he hit me with the rifle and split my lip and broke my front teeth. I felt the blood blow all over but I thought, if I die, you die. I knocked him down and ran and jumped onto this barbed wire fence and somehow got over. I was bloody all over but I kept running and they missed me when they shot. I ran and ran until I fell unconscious.

When I woke up a couple was shaking me, a couple who were living in the jungle, cutting wood, and making charcoal to sell in the market about fifteen kilometers away. I told them I had a motorcycle and I was robbed and then beaten because I tried to resist. The old man cleaned my wounds with a bottle of alcohol, gave me something to eat, and showed me the way to get out of the jungle. I finally reached the highway, but because I had no money I had to ride standing on the rear bumpers of buses. When we got close to a security checkpoint, I would get off, walk around the guard post, and wait for another bus.

Finally I got to Saigon and went to the house of a friend for help. He said, "I want to help, but you can't stay here." He told my relatives I was back, but I didn't attempt to meet my wife. Most of the time I slept in the bus stations because they were so crowded, or covered up with a piece of newspaper in the parks or abandoned houses. I survived on junk food I found in the streets. To communicate with my wife, I would go to a friend's house and leave a message. Two days later she would come over and pick it up and leave notice of what the next step would be. The reason I couldn't see her was that

South Vietnamese refugees scramble for space on the small boats leaving the coastal city of Nha Trang.

A barge, heavily laden with refugees on their way to Saigon, goes ashore at Nha Trang to refurbish its supply of fresh water.

the authorities might follow her. After we were caught on the boat, she was in jail for a long time, and even after she was released they ordered her to report weekly. Because the authorities might interrogate the children, my wife told them I had already gone to the United States. Finally she left word for me to try to get away by myself if I could.

I tried ten times in 1977 to get out over land, but each time I failed. The last time I was with a group of ten people, special forces, air force, government, businessmen, who were armed with a few hand grenades. The guy that had been in the special forces had been along the Ho Chi Minh Trail in Cambodia and Laos and knew the route through the jungle. Traveling in two groups of five, we would use the same road the NVA used to penetrate the South to cross into Thailand. What we didn't know was that there were still engineers working on the road and they were guarded by military units. The first group ran into one of the NVA units and were all killed. We ran. I think that we five ran for twenty-two days in the jungle. We were bitten by insects and drank muddy water, but we kept running.

I was very discouraged. However, after returning to Saigon, I discovered that my wife had met an aunt while trying to sell some things on the black market. Her aunt was trying to find someone to take her family out of the country. She told my wife, "I can trust you because you are my niece. Help me, I got money." So my wife

left a message for me saying, "I've got financial help. You can make a plan now. Spend whatever you want."

So I started to reorganize my group and make a plan, but this time I kept it a small group, just thirty-seven people including my wife and children. Because I had been in the civil service school in Saigon during the Diem regime, I was familiar with the economic development areas south of Saigon. They had built artificial canals to improve the area, and I decided to use them to get to the sea. I divided the group into sections of three or four people and had them wear the wide Vietnamese hat but with colors painted on the top so I can recognize my group. Then I had them leave Saigon a section at a time and move to pickup points along these parallel canals.

Meanwhile, I had four guys in a big fishing boat regularly going out to sea through the Communist patrols. Upon returning they would always turn in whatever extra fuel and rations they had left to prove they were honest people, that they were not leaving Vietnam. I also bought a small boat with a double hull to pretend we were transporting rice and sugar cane along the canals. When we came to our people at the end of each canal, they called out for help saying, "It's late and we need a ride to the other canal." We say, "Well sure," and then we take them into our boat, give the kids sleeping pills so they don't cry, and hide them in the second bottom. Then we hid the boat in the bushes. Everybody tries to get out at night, so I decided to get out in the daytime. I had decided that we would all either be free or die. I went right in front of the security patrol and showed them we had just enough water and rice for two people for two days' sailing. Then we sailed out and met the big boat in the open sea. We transferred the people from the small boat, sank it, and hid them where the fish are stored in the big boat. Then we sailed into international waters, and five days later we reached the southern province of Thailand. The authorities didn't allow me to stay there so I made another attempt to land at Songkhla, Thailand. There was already a group of refugees in the town, and I was allowed to stay and report to the government. I requested political asylum in America and was interviewed. Since I had a sister in Oklahoma City and had been an official of the South Vietnamese government, I was allowed to leave after about two months. I reached Seattle, Washington, on November 11, Veterans Day, 1977.

It was kind of rough here in the United States because the standard of living was so high. But I wanted to be a productive person and I accepted everything they offered me. I took a job at $2.65 an hour stripping the covers from discount magazines and papers. Later I became a fork lift driver and worked for two years in receiving and shipping. Finally I got a job as an assistant credit manager and got the chance to get back into paperwork. I worked there awhile and began to feel better. I could plan my future and started working on an MBA. Then in 1979 General Motors opened a plant in Oklahoma City. I was one of the 30,000 people who applied for a job, and I was hired. I've been working there ever since, first as a paint mixer and later on taking care of the spraying equipment.

But with seven children we couldn't survive with one income. The kids grew up and the demands increased. So my wife started working first for an American restaurant and then an Oriental restaurant learning how to cook. One day she said, "I want to be my own boss and open a restaurant." I said, "But we don't have any money." However, I was president of the Vietnamese Catholic Communities of Oklahoma, and I have a lot of friends who know who I am. I told them about my intention and they said, "Go ahead, I can loan you money." So somebody gave me $200, some gave me $500, some $2,000. Finally I got about $20,000, and in 1982 we opened our restaurant. Now my wife works sixteen hours a day, and I switched to the night shift so I can help her.

I have told my children that other families try to pass on their fortune, but because of the Communists I tried to do that and failed. They took all my possessions. Now my philosophy is to educate my children and transfer my fortune to them that way. My investment is to give them a good education because even the Communists can't steal that. With knowledge, you can still survive because nobody can rip out what you have in your brain.

My oldest daughter just started school at the University of Oklahoma and has said she will not marry until she graduates. My oldest son will go to college next year. I told them that "I can pay for you,

but then it will be your turn when you complete your education and you can support the younger ones."

But I also told them, "If one of you wants to join the army I am for it." Because if you don't fight, one day the Communists will rule the world and that's the end because they don't respect you as a human being, no. They violate human rights. Nobody talks about the thousands and thousands they have killed in the re-education programs. You have to prevent the Communists from expanding. You have to beat them as far away as possible. It's just black and white. You must choose either freedom or communism. ∎

Top. *A woman passes by the body of a child trampled to death during the panic to escape from Nha Trang as North Vietnamese forces close in, April 1, 1975.*

Above. *The Songkhla refugee camp in Thailand in July 1979 where international relief efforts provided food for the many and political asylum for the fortunate.*

Ernest E. Washington, Jr.

*Infantryman
Charlie Company, 1st Battalion, 1st Marines
February–October 1967*

Ernest E. Washington, Jr., was born and raised in Roxbury, Massachusetts, a section of Boston. "I was educated in Boston public schools, and divided and segregated as they were, I got a decent education. I also received a strong Christian foundation from my parents."

After graduating from high school in the spring of 1965, he worked for a year in a printing shop before enlisting in the Marine Corps in September 1966. Upon completion of his military service in 1969, he earned a bachelor's degree in management at Bentley College and then went on to obtain a master's degree in public administration at Northeastern University. Currently a project manager with the Massachusetts Port Authority, he spends much of his spare time working as treasurer and board member of the Vietnam Veterans Clearing House, an organization that provides outreach services to veterans in the black community.

It was called Operation Brown. Late June 1967. It was a battalion-sized sweep west of Da Nang, and my squad was sent out in front to scout out this ville that was supposedly empty. I was a grenadier at the time, so I walked the tail end, carrying my M79 blooper. As soon as we all got into the village, which was surrounded on three sides by these thick hedgerows, the enemy opened up and pinned us down. We had a weapons squad behind us, just outside the ville, so immediately we got some support. But it wasn't enough because one of the M60s got knocked out and the other 60 was some distance away.

So one of the officers called in an air strike. Only somehow he fucked up. Threw the wrong smoke and gave the wrong coordinates so that when this Phantom arrived a few minutes later he dropped all the shit on us. Mainly 20MM cannon rounds. The first ones hit some of the hooches, and they just burst into flames. Even though we were still taking hostile fire, a couple of guys stood up and started yelling and waving their arms at the Phantom. But there was too much smoke, and he was flying too fast to see anything. Other guys ran into the burning hooches—anything to get away from the destruction that goddamned plane was dealing out. He made six passes.

I was lucky. I saw this stone wall and ran to it and hugged it, so when this round hit the wall I took a big piece of shrapnel in the right shoulder and some smaller pieces in the back, but I survived. Eight of the guys in my squad were killed. Eight out of fourteen—all, as far as we could tell, by "friendly fire."

When the medevac chopper came in they squeezed all of us on together, the living and the dead. I'll never forget the pain of that ride. At that point I'd been in country four months, and I'd been in firefights almost from day one. But I had never seen the enemy up close, and I had never seen a dead Marine. Other platoons in our company had taken some KIA, but not our platoon. We'd only had some guys wounded. So there I was on this helicopter, staring at my buddies, guys I'd been rapping with just a short time before. And their eyes were still open, and their wrist watches ticking. I remember that especially—their watches ticking. I was only nineteen years old.

That's where the trauma of Vietnam began for me. It got worse a few weeks later. I was in the hospital at Da Nang, recuperating from my wounds, when I got a letter from my sister telling me that Sonny Davis had been killed up at Con Thien. And I couldn't believe it. I wouldn't accept it. I thought, "No, not Sonny. It couldn't happen to Sonny." Then I managed to scrounge up an issue of *Stars and Stripes* to try and confirm it, hoping that I wouldn't see his name. But his name was there. And I cried. I'm still crying today.

Sonny Davis was my best friend. We had grown up in the same neighborhood in Roxbury, and our families belonged to the same church. We didn't go to the same high school together, but from junior high school on Sonny and I did a lot of hanging out together. We were always at his house or my house, we competed against one another in sports, we even got into trouble together a few times, though it was never anything serious. Just part of growing up in the city.

I was proud to be Sonny's best friend because he was the kind of person that everyone else looked up to, the kind of person who was good at everything he did—a real good athlete with a good mind who was also very sensitive to other people. A lot of that had to do with his upbringing. His family, like my family, was very close-knit and supportive. His father, who was a businessman, commanded respect. And his mother was the same way. They were models for a lot of black kids in the community.

So it wasn't surprising that when we got our draft notices, Sonny and I decided to go in together. And Lavelle, too—Lavelle Williams, he was the third member of our high-school trio. This was in September of '66, the time when the draft just swept through the black community and took all the young males. My buddies from the same block, from across town, the guys I competed against in basketball games—we all got our "Greetings" at the same time and went down and took our oaths in batches. They took us in batches.

Later, when I started talking to black veterans from other places, I found out that the same thing happened in their communities. But at the time I didn't think anything of it. It just reinforced what my father, who was a navy veteran, had always told me: that it was every young man's responsibility to register for the draft and that when their time came they should go and do their duty. Since it seemed like everybody's son was going, I just thought my old man was right. It had to be the correct thing to do. I also thought of it as something exciting. I mean, I had gone from combat comic books to GI Joe to an all-male school where most of my classmates aspired to the military. The whole macho thing was part of my mentality, and I wanted to let some of that out.

But all three of us realized that going into the military was better than staying where we were. We'd been out of school for more than a year and we had jobs, but the work was shitwork—fifty or sixty bucks for a forty-hour week. And there was nothing else out there. So we all thought about going in as our alternative to chronic joblessness.

The one thing I didn't want to do, though, was go into the army. I wanted no part of the army. So I went and talked to the navy people, and the air force people, and eventually I found out that only the Marines would let you enlist after you got your notice. We talked with the Marine recruiter, and he told us about the "buddy system" and how we could go through the whole experience together. We listened to all this bullshit and fell for it hook, line, and sinker. He even showed us a list of schools and signed us up for computer training. What a joke that was. None of us ever saw a computer the whole time we were in.

After we took our oaths we reported to the train station for the trip to boot camp at Parris Island, South Carolina. I remember looking around and noticing that a large percentage of the guys getting on were black. There were a lot of working-class white guys too. But again, at the time I didn't think too much about what that meant. I guess I was just very naive. Then the train moved south and stopped in Hartford, and the majority of guys who got on there were black or Puerto Rican. It stopped in New York City. Same thing. And all the way down—Baltimore, Washington, D.C., Richmond—it was the same.

Even before we left, Sonny, Lavelle, and I had made plans. We knew that everybody didn't make it out of Parris Island. We knew that you had to be in good shape mentally and physically to make it in the Marine Corps. You had to show them something. So our attitude was that we were going to show them what Boston was made of, what Roxbury was

Ernie Washington (second from left) and several members of his company at a temporary field HQ south of Danang in Quang Nam Province, April 1967.

made of. We were going to be the best. And it seemed like everyone else had the same thing in mind.

And we did a good job of maintaining the Roxbury reputation at Parris Island. As a matter of fact, Sonny was the outstanding Marine in our training battalion. I mean, there were recruits at P.I. from everywhere east of the Mississippi—from as far west as Chicago and as far south as New Orleans—all trying to see who's better than the next guy. And Sonny was the very best. He was good at everything—the rifle, hand-to-hand, the drill, the whole works. Lavelle and I were both very good, too, in our own rights. All three of us were able to get rank, to get our PFC stripes, during our training. But Sonny was the first because he just stood out. He was an inspiration to everyone—not just myself and Lavelle, but everyone.

It was at Parris Island that we first started hearing about Vietnam. Up to then we had just thought about joining the Corps and becoming Marines. We didn't think about what would happen after that. Now they were talking about "gooks" and "Victor Charlies" and preparing us for what it would be like over there. At the time I didn't understand the reason behind a lot of the calisthenics and that kind of physical brainwash stuff. I didn't really know why they had everybody saying something at the same time, and doing things at the same time, and having strict responsibility for certain things. I didn't see the relationship between the drilling and discipline and the combat situation until I got in my first firefight. Then the truth came to light. Because you've got to do what you're told to do. There's some discretionary thought but not much. There's one person that's responsible, and you have to listen to his instruction and grasp it immediately. And that's a function of mindset and discipline, which is what they give you in about twelve weeks at Parris Island. It makes you mad at the time, but it pays off. Because what it boiled down to in Vietnam was that if you did what they told you to do, you lived. You try to do something that your mind told you, you may not live.

I wasn't certain that I was going to Vietnam, though, until the day we were issued orders. This was like a week before we graduated. The drill instructors brought us all together, called out each individual name, and said what your MOS was. Mine said 0311, Westpac Ground. Everybody knew that Westpac meant Western Pacific, and that meant Vietnam. Everybody knew that 0300 meant infantry, which was broken down into, I think, four subgroups—0311, which is rifleman; 21, which is machine guns; 31, mortars; and 51, rockets. Of the ninety-two in my class, ninety of us got MOS 0300. The other two were truck driving and mess. Lavelle was one of the lucky ones. He got truck driving. We all got Westpac.

After Parris Island we went to Camp

Lejeune, North Carolina, for weapons training. What I remember most about that experience was the racial turmoil there. I mean, there had been some of that at P.I.—you know, name calling and singling out of black recruits to outperform everyone else and that kind of thing. But at Camp Lejeune it really intensified. It seemed that white and black Marines just couldn't get along with each other. Everybody seemed to have either an I-don't-like-you-because-you're-black attitude or an I-don't-like-you-because-you're-white attitude. It was reciprocal. It got so bad that we had to stay in the barracks, couldn't go to the movies at night, couldn't even walk around the base at night because there were so many racial skirmishes. Two guys jumping on one, three guys jumping on one, five guys jumping on one. And this was on both sides. It turned out to be much the same way in Vietnam whenever we came back to the rear. You'd be out in the field fighting the enemy for a couple of weeks and come back and have to fight some more.

After Camp Lejeune we went to California, and that's where the three of us first started to split up. Lavelle went to Okinawa, to motor transport. Sonny and I went to Vietnam. On the way over we still had a lot of enthusiasm. In fact, we couldn't wait to get there and kick some ass because that's what we'd been trained to do. We had also talked about how we were going to approach the crossed rifles, which is lance corporal, and how we were going to get them. Even though Lavelle wasn't with us, we were still a team within a team.

Our attitude began to change, though, right after we landed in Da Nang. This was in February 1967. When we got off the plane, we went into the transit center and were billeted with guys going home. And I was shocked to see the condition these guys were in. I mean, these guys couldn't have been that much older than we were, but years and years were in their faces. They looked beat tired, and lost. It was then that the fear kind of got to me for the first time. I was nudging Sonny and saying, "Look at these guys. Look at them. They don't look anything like us." And I thought, these guys are the survivors. If I'm lucky enough to survive, I'm going to look like that. And eventually I did look like that. Going home.

But Sonny was cool. If anyone started

"Sonny was the very best." William W. "Sonny" Davis, Jr., stands at attention outside his parents' home in Dorchester, Massachusetts in January 1967, shortly before his departure for Vietnam.

to fall to pieces it was me. "Hey, man," he said, "if they can do it, we can do it. They can go home, we can go home." That was him, though, all the way. If you were down thirty points in basketball or twenty to nothing in a football game and there's two minutes to play, Sonny would say, "Hey, we can still win." That's what he brought to anyone he was around all his life.

So we talked to these guys that were leaving. And they teased us, saying things like, "Next week you're not going to be alive if you don't get your shit together and listen to us." They seemed to feel it was their responsibility to school us. And you wondered whether you should listen to this stuff or not. Later we learned that we ought to have been listening to every word. Because they were preaching the gospel, the gospel according to Vietnam.

After that experience we went to an assignment office where you gave your name and service number and they told you what unit you were to report to. And that's where Sonny and I got separated. He was assigned to 1/9—1st Battalion, 9th Marines—and I was assigned to 1/1—1st Battalion, 1st Marines. And I argued and bitched. I said, "Why can't he go to 1/1? Or me go to 1/9." The man said, "No. Davis goes to 1/9. Washington goes to 1/1. And that's that." So I got on the truck and went west while Sonny went up north to Quang Tri.

It wasn't until then, after I joined my unit, that I first started to really notice the incredibly disproportionate number of black troops in the field. I should have seen it coming long before that—in boot camp, at Camp Lejeune, or at the transit center in Da Nang. But when I got out into the field myself, I couldn't help but notice. I started looking around and listening to the brothers and they said, "Check it out for yourself. Count the number of white Marines in this company." There were ten whites in Charlie Company. In the squad I was with when I got wounded, there were thirteen blacks and one white. And the white was the squad leader.

Even then I tried not to think about it too much because we had a job to do. The job was "Chan," as in Charlie Chan. That's what the brothers used to call the enemy at that time. It had more of a ring of respect to it than "gook." Because after you've been out in the field ninety days or so, you find out that the Vietcong and the NVA aren't as slipshod as you were led to believe in boot camp. I mean, you think it's going to be a piece of cake with this guy, that you're going to chase him all around and kick his ass. Then you found out that he could kill you, too, pretty much when he felt like it, because this was his own back yard. And you'd see all the shit we dropped on him—the bombing runs and the gunships and the napalm. There was no way really to prepare for that. So you had to develop a respect for him. And it didn't take long.

During my first few months in the field we operated in the area south and southwest of Da Nang, in and around Marble Mountain and midway between An Hoa and Da Nang. There was a lot of guerrilla activity around there, so we dealt mainly with the VC. Sonny, meanwhile, was dealing mainly with NVA regulars up north near the DMZ. We wrote letters back and forth, just like we'd promised when we'd separated at Da Nang. Then, around the middle of June, his letters started to trail off, and the next thing I heard was that he had been killed at Con Thien. July 7, 1967. Rocket attack. He got a direct hit right in his hole, so there was nothing in the casket. No remains. Nothing but a framed picture on a casket.

Even when I'd recovered from my own wounds, I still couldn't get over Sonny's death. Somehow I still didn't believe it. I kept thinking it had to be a mistake. So after I got out of the hospital I disappeared for a while. The military calls it AWOL, but I just didn't report back to my unit right away. I hitched a helicopter ride from Da Nang to Phu Bai and went to visit a friend who was in administration, a guy who now lives right up the street from me. And he hid me out there for a couple of weeks while I tried to get my head together. When I finally reported back to Charlie Company, I found out they hadn't even missed me.

Then, shortly after that, in early October, my father died. So the Red Cross got me out of the field and got me home in ... shit, it must have been something like fifty hours. And I distinctly remember coming in without any feelings. I didn't cry. It was like just another job I had to do. My mother and sister were sedated most of the time, so they weren't any help. So I came in, took care of the funeral arrangements, got him in the ground.

It wasn't until just before it was time to go back that I finally became human again. I said to myself, "Goddamn. What are you going back for? Why don't you just disappear? They'll never find you here now that you're back." But my mother talked me out of it. She said, "Listen, that's not what you're supposed to do. I've been talking to this one and that one, and I think the way we ought to pursue this is through politics." You know, she wanted to talk to the McCormacks and the Kennedys and Senator Brooke to see if they could get me out as the sole surviving son. But it didn't work. I don't know if we just didn't have the influence or what. So I still had to go back.

After I left, my mother went to some people at the Catholic church and I guess they were able to do something, because right after I got back to Vietnam I got a humanitarian transfer to a duty post in Japan. Only by then I didn't want it anymore. I didn't want to leave because I had just found out that I was going to go up to Con Thien. In fact, the transfer came through the night before we were supposed to get on the trucks. And I was looking forward to it. Because one of two things would happen. In the best case I would get revenge for Sonny's death; in the worst case I would see him again. And I would have gone if the staff sergeant hadn't pulled me aside and said, "Hey, man, get the fuck out of here. What are you thinking about? You're going to Japan, to choice duty. Finish your time out there. I'll kick your ass if you think about doing anything else." Staff Sergeant George W. Grundly, Jr. If it wasn't for him, I might have done something stupid.

So I went to Japan, finished out my tour, and then came home. I got back to the United States on April 4, 1968, the day that Dr. Martin Luther King, Jr., was assassinated. I heard the news when I landed in California, so by the time I got to Logan Airport in Boston the rioting had already started. I tried to get a cab home, but none of the cabbies would go into the black community. So I had to take the subway. And back then, you know, it wasn't easy going for military personnel. All these people were giving me these strange looks because of my uniform, compounded by this attitude of, "What's wrong with you people in the black community?"

When I did get back into the community there was a lot of turmoil, a lot of confusion, and a lot of anger. I mean, after Dr. King was killed, all those people that had been keeping from crossing the line into active civil rights, they crossed it then. It was liberation time for black people. It wasn't a situation where you were in or out of that game. Everybody was in it.

And that's what a lot of black veterans came home to. What made it more confusing was the attitude of most of the liberation movement leaders. These were mainly guys who had gone to college for a few years and didn't go into the service, the few who were left behind when the draft took most of the young men in the community. To them the fact that we'd gone off and risked our lives in Vietnam didn't mean a thing. To them the only issue was the struggle at home for black rights. I remember my friends saying to me, "You joined? Then you got what you asked for." End of conversation. None of those people are my friends today.

But at the time a lot of black veterans just joined in the struggle. When they got out of the service they immediately joined the Black Panther party or De Mau Mau or some other paramilitary organization, trying to do something for their community in terms of information and programs. It was natural for a lot of veterans. I myself didn't participate in it very much. I just wanted them all to know I supported them across the board.

As for myself, by the time I got out of the military a year later, in April '69, I had my own little plan. And part of that plan was to get an education, get a little more big-picture oriented than I was when I first went into the service. I'm sure Vietnam had a lot to do with it. And Sonny's death. Because when I got back I was just so energized, I had so much rage, I wanted to turn it into something positive. I wanted to make a statement.

So when I heard about this program for veterans at Bentley College—no SATs, just come in on probation, and if you can maintain a C average the college would pay for the rest of your education—I jumped at it. You have to understand that this was unheard of at the time. Veterans were still in the begging stage, trying to get the state to do something, anything for them. And all the state did was to offer a "bonus" of 300 bucks. That was it. So after walking the streets for several months, in September I got a job and started going to Bentley at night. And I did pretty well.

Graduated with about a 3.3 average. I was proud of myself.

I also got married. That was part of the plan, too. One of the things I thought I ought to do when I got back—you know, find a woman, get a wife, have a child, early on when you're supposed to. I did all that, only it didn't work out as well as I'd hoped. I brought some very evil things into the marriage in terms of my past experiences, especially my Vietnam experiences. I thought things should be a certain way, and I wasn't listening to anybody else. So I think I kind of made everyone around me miserable.

And it didn't really change until I started talking to other veterans who'd been through the same experience I had. That's the only thing that brought me around. I found out that we suffered from a lot of the same problems, like the apathetic attitude of our own community, the black community, to the issues of black Vietnam veterans. And that hatchet hasn't been buried yet. There are still people looking cross-eyed at us because they think our timing and our judgment was a little off, because we were 12,000 miles away defending someone else's freedom when we should have been home fighting for our own people's rights. And anytime we try to bring the black veterans issue to the forefront, their attitude is, "Wait a minute now. All you guys volunteered, and we've got other issues to deal with that are more important."

So one of the things we've tried to do is point out the relationship between the Vietnam issue and other issues in the black community. One of the major problems we have, for example, is a lack of male leadership. And that's directly related to the fact that the war took away so many young men. Twenty-one young blacks from Roxbury died in Vietnam. And of those who came back, there are many who can't take leadership roles, or contribute effectively to the community, because they've got bad heads, or they've got drug problems, or they're in prison. Others have seen their families fall apart because they can't hold down a decent job. They can't make the readjustment.

It's the same for a lot of working-class white communities like East Boston, South Boston, and Somerville. They were raked of all their young men too. And that's a crime, a crime that somebody should pay for. Because these guys are now in their

late thirties, some in their forties already, and if they don't get help now they're never going to be able to contribute to their communities.

In the past few years I think we've begun to deal with some of these problems, but only because the vets themselves have begun to take action. We've begun to take care of our own. Because it got to a point where we realized that was the only way it was going to happen. Like the Memorial down in Washington, D.C. The Vietnam veterans had to do it themselves.

I was there at the dedication of the Memorial in November of '82. In fact, that was *the* event of that year; everything else was secondary. I went down to find Sonny's name on the wall, and when I finally saw it I felt weak. I could only look at it so long. Then I had to go back to the hotel. I couldn't stand it. Couldn't stand the fact that the president couldn't make it. Couldn't stand Westmoreland being in the parade waving a flag. We might as well have had McNamara and the whole crew march and wave flags.

Still, I think the whole dedication did inspire me to a degree. Because when I got back to Boston I felt driven to do something I'd been thinking about doing for some time, and that was to build a memorial to Sonny in the black community. I wanted to make sure that his spirit was not forgotten. I wanted to help to produce a better understanding of the sacrifices of black men in the Vietnam War. And I wanted to educate people about the legacy of black participation in all of America's wars, from Crispus Attucks to the Red Ball Express right down to our own time. And in my mind, Sonny Davis exemplified all those things.

When I took my idea to the black veteran community, they welcomed it. Every last one of them stopped what they were doing to help me with it. And we pulled it off, even though a lot of people in the community thought it was too controversial. We went to all the heavy hitters and told them what we were going to do. We went to Governor Dukakis and said, "We're going to have William W. Davis, Jr., Day in Massachusetts, and you're going to sign the proclamation." And Dukakis signed the proclamation. Same thing with Mayor Ray Flynn.

January 29, 1984, turned out to be a big day. A big day that this community won't forget. Everybody was there.

People from the commissioner's office, from the governor's office, from the mayor's office. Television people, newspaper people. Black veterans, white veterans, veterans from the western part of the state. They all came to this memorial service. Standing room only in the church. Then we went down to the intersection of Tremont and New Dudley—to William W. Davis, Jr., Memorial Square—to dedicate the monument to Sonny. We had a very impressive Marine color guard from the naval air station. They did the ceremony—gun salutes, the whole works.

And you could see what it was doing to the Davis family. His mother and father. You could just look at them and see. Because they're old and wise and mature, and they know that people die and no one gives a shit the next day. But here were all these people who'd come together to honor their son, to let them know that he hadn't been forgotten. And that's what they needed, you know, though I think they still felt some bitterness. Because when his mother got the microphone, the first thing she said was, "It's about time." And she was right. It *was* about time—another instance where the vets had to do it for themselves.

The dedication of Sonny's memorial might have closed the book on the Vietnam experience for me—not on my veterans work but on the experience itself—except a year later, in August 1985, I was invited by a local TV station to take a trip back to Vietnam. They were doing a special piece to be aired on Veterans Day, and they wanted to take along some veterans. They had already selected two white veterans and they wanted a black veteran, and I guess my peers in the black community nominated me.

It was good to go back. It was good to visit a lot of places I'd never been before, like Hanoi, as well as some places I had. It was good to be reminded of the special relationship a lot of black troops had with the Vietnamese people—a relationship of mutual respect—and to hear someone say "Soul brother Number One" again. And it was good, too, to talk with these men who had once been my enemies, even though I wasn't sure I was ready for that before we left. One of the interesting things was that everywhere we went the Vietnamese veterans kept grabbing our belts to demonstrate how they fought us. "We were right up underneath you all the time,"

they said, "uptight, so that when you called in the goddamn air strikes they would drop the shit on you, too." And I thought about the day I got wounded, because that's just how he played the game.

The highlight of the trip for me, though, was our visit to Con Thien. The Vietnamese authorities didn't want us to go up there because it was dangerous. There's only one trail, the guides told us, and there's still a lot of undetonated explosives out there. They said, "Nobody goes up there." And I said, "That's what we came for." So we got special permission and we went up, film crew and all. The guides went up the trail first, and we were right behind. I walked the tail end. We joked about that, but I was dead serious. I wasn't walking point this time.

When I got to the middle of that firebase, I could do nothing but cry. Because except for the death and dying, everything else was still there. All the remnants of war are still at Con Thien. Concertina wire. Sandbags. Hard hats cut in half. Bottoms of jungle boots. C-ration cans. Budweiser beer cans. Still there. Just standing there, looking at the place, you couldn't help but think of the sacrifices the men there had made and what has happened to the men who did come home. I turned to the journalist who headed our party and said, "I thought one of the foundations of America was that you get back what you put in." Because it was evident that everybody there had put out. They had put out everything they had. ∎

Surrounded by a crowd of curious Vietnamese, Washington strolls along a street in Da Nang during a return visit in August 1985.

Ten years after the war's end, the remnants of battle still litter the ground at Con Thien, "The Hill of Angels." August 15, 1985.

Harry G. Summers, Jr.

Battalion Operations Officer
1st Infantry Division 1966-1967
Member, U.S. Delegation to
Four-Party Joint Military Team
1974-1975

Harry Summers began his military career in 1947 when he enlisted in the army at the age of fifteen. After serving as a combat infantryman in the Korean War, Summers received a direct regular commission as a second lieutenant in 1957. Twice wounded as a battalion operations officer with the 1st Infantry Division in Vietnam in 1966-1967, he was awarded the Silver and Bronze Stars for heroism on the battlefield. In 1974 he returned to Vietnam as a member of the U.S. delegation to the Four-Party Joint Military Team, and he was among the last Americans to be evacuated from Saigon in April 1975.

After the war, Colonel Summers worked in the office of the army chief of staff for several years before being appointed to the Douglas MacArthur Chair of Military Research at the U.S. Army War College in Carlisle, Pennsylvania. His controversial yet much-acclaimed reassessment of the Vietnam War, On Strategy, *was published in 1981 and his* Vietnam War Almanac *in 1985. In September 1985 he retired from the army to accept a position as the senior military correspondent for* U.S. News and World Report.

Was the war winnable? By definition it was winnable, because the North Vietnamese won it. But if you mean, could *we* have won it? . . . I think so. Of course, you've got to define what you mean by "win." Win has to be the realization of the objective you set out to achieve, which doesn't necessarily mean total victory as in World War II. But that's still the paradigm in most Americans' minds—you've got the good guys, you've got the bad guys, and you've got a clear, definite victory.

A better paradigm in the nuclear age is the Korean War, where your political objectives are limited and you achieve them over time. Not very satisfying, not very dramatic, but certainly Korea was a victory in any sense of the word. Because in a nuclear world the one thing we're not going to do is take the strategic offensive to seize the enemy's capital, destroy his military, occupy his territory. Not against the Soviet Union, a nuclear-armed adversary, or against a surrogate of that nuclear-armed adversary. We're just not going to do that, and neither are they. And for good reason, because the risk far outweighs any political gain either side can hope to achieve.

The point is that we need to explain to the American people the dynamics of war and the principles of military theory. Americans aren't very comfortable with theory. If you mention philosophy, the average American's eyes glaze over. But one of the things that came out of Vietnam, I think, was the realization that if your theories are wrong, if your fundamentals are wrong, then everything that follows is wrong.

If war is a political act, and I think it is, then the first thing you have to do is to establish your political objectives. You have to be very clear about what it is you're trying to do, because otherwise how are you going to determine how you're going to do it? Again, take the example of Korea. During the MacArthur hearings in 1951, the Senate asked General Omar Bradley, "What are your political objectives?" And Bradley said, "You're asking the wrong person. Ask the secretary of state." So they called Dean Acheson in and asked him the same question. And Acheson replied, "Our political objective in Korea is to repel the North Korean invasion and restore the *status quo ante bellum.*" Very clear statement of political objectives, and a very clear-cut division of labor. The State Department's job was to fix a political objective. The military's job was to try to help to attain that objective with the use of military force.

But with the Kennedy administration that all started to fall apart. There was no clear voice from the State Department. The Defense Department in effect created its own State Department with the office of International Security Affairs. So State failed to set clear political objectives, the military was meddling in that, and State was meddling in the military. As a result, instead of getting a clear division of labor, you get everybody and nobody responsible for everything. So in the case of Vietnam, we never established what our political ends were. They weren't clear.

When President Johnson first took over, he treated the war as a back burner affair. He hoped it would go away. But he had the specter of the fall of China behind him, and the specter of the Bay of Pigs, and he thought the illusory right wing would get him if he didn't stand up to the Communists. So he tried to sneak us into the war in a sense. He increased the U.S. military commitment but deliberately tried to downplay the war. The guy just didn't have any balls when it came down to it. Nixon, with all his faults, at least understood that war is a contest of wills. Johnson never understood that.

The biggest mistake that Johnson made, though, was his failure to establish the value of the war. Whether he could have sold it to the American people or not is another story. But at least the attempt to sell the value of what we were trying to do, to define the objectives we were trying to accomplish, should have been made. As Dean Rusk said, "The United States cannot fight wars in cold blood." We just can't do that. That's not what a democracy does.

If you go back to the Constitution, there are two ways the United States uses military force. One way is under Article 2, where the president commits forces under his own authority as commander in chief in response to an immediate crisis. There are 400 instances in our history of the use of force in that manner, from Thomas Jefferson and the Barbary pirates up through President Reagan and Grenada. By and large the public supports that because: one, it's short—the forces are put in quickly and withdrawn quickly; and two, the crisis is well understood. The other way we use force is under Article 1 of the Constitution, where Congress is given sole authority to declare war, to raise and support an army, and to commit forces to a prolonged conflict. Under Article 1 you have to have congressional support up front. Yet both President Johnson and President Nixon justified their use of force in Southeast Asia under Article 2. They used Article 2 authority to fight an Article 1 type war.

And that won't wash. Because the American people have a natural resistance to the commitment of U.S. forces. It's not a reflection of Vietnam. President Roosevelt could have told us that in 1939, '40, '41, when the whole world was going up in flames and he was trying to galvanize public support and we still weren't interested. Is it difficult? Hell, yes, it's difficult. But if you don't have the support of the people in a prolonged conflict, who the hell is going to pay the bill? It's their sons and daughters and their money we're talking about.

Americans are very pragmatic people. Once U.S. forces are committed, they expect us, not unjustly, to win on the battlefield. But in Vietnam we couldn't pull it off. They supported us, in fact, long after we deserved their support—"we" in the sense of the government—because we had no concept of how we were going to end it. And eventually the American people realized that. The common everyday American woke up one morning and said, "These bastards don't know what the hell they're doing." They asked the pragmatic question, "To what end?" And there wasn't any answer.

That's why public opinion shifted against the war. It wasn't because of the antiwar movement. In fact, studies of public opinion have shown that if anything the antiwar movement only prolonged the war, because however much people were turned off by the war, they were even more turned off by the antics of the antiwar movement. And it also wasn't because of the media. You know the arguments: if they'd had television cameras at Normandy we wouldn't have been able to win World War II, and so forth. Well, it's true that the media, and especially television, are good at bringing the price of war into the living room. But the price of anything, including war, only has meaning in relation to value. If the Ameri-

can public had been convinced of the value of the war, as in World War II, then the price would have been perfectly acceptable. But in the case of Vietnam ... we're still arguing today what the value of the Vietnam War was; that is, what our objectives were. So it shouldn't surprise us that the price soon became exorbitant.

Since we never clearly articulated our political ends, we never had a military strategy in Vietnam. Because a strategy, by the U.S. government's own definition, is the use or threatened use of force to achieve the political ends of the United States. The North Vietnamese, by con-

April 1975. A battle map on the wall of Colonel Summers' Saigon office indicates the positions of North Vietnamese Army units closing in on the South Vietnamese capital.

Summers destroying documents of the U.S. delegation to the Four Party Joint Military Team in late April 1975.

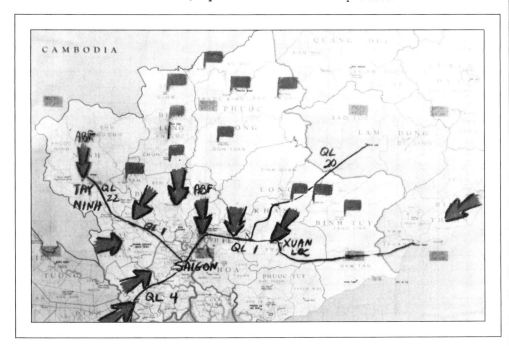

167

trast, had very clear objectives. Their goal was the unification of Vietnam under their auspices and, eventually, the total conquest of Indochina. They made no bones about it.

But we didn't even see *that* clearly. We continued to view Vietnam as essentially a guerrilla war long after it ceased to be such. In fact, one of the things I don't emphasize strongly enough in *On Strategy* is the duality of the war. There were two wars going on simultaneously in Vietnam. One was the war in the countryside, the war in the villages of South Vietnam. The other was the war against the North Vietnamese regulars and the Vietcong Main Force units. The question in our minds should have been, which war is the United States best equipped to deal with? And I think the answer is obvious. We were best equipped to deal with the NVA regulars and the Main Force units.

In hindsight, it seems that what we

ought to have done is used American troops to seal the DMZ, going across Laos into Thailand. And played to our strengths, because the United States military in a defensive position is an awesome force. And we should have left the task of pacification, the war in the countryside, to the South Vietnamese. If it was successful, we would have probably ended up with another Korea, with U.S. forces remaining there for the next thirty years to maintain the peace. It would have taken a long-term commitment; there's no doubt about that. But we would have achieved our objective, if we had clearly defined it, as in Korea, as the restoration of the *status quo ante bellum*. Would the North Vietnamese still have pursued their objectives? Probably. The North Koreans didn't give up theirs. But they're still waiting on the other side of the thirty-eighth parallel.

We'll never know, of course, whether it

A question of leadership. President Johnson meets with Generals Bruce Palmer (left), Leonard Chapman (center), and William Westmoreland (right) following his public announcement of a U.S. bombing halt on October 31, 1968.

would have worked because as Henry Kissinger once said, "History doesn't provide its alternatives." But at least it would have been an efficient use, a sensible use, of our military power.

A lot of the blame for the American failure in Vietnam has been placed on General Westmoreland. To some extent that's understandable. He makes such an attractive target because he deliberately personified himself as Mr. Vietnam. And if we'd won, he would have taken all the credit. Nevertheless, most of the criticism has been unfair. It's unfair in the sense that Westmoreland was never in control of the war. People see him as the counterpart of General Giap, and nothing could be further from the truth. Giap was the DRV's defense minister, a member of the ruling Politburo, and commander in chief of the armed forces. On the U.S. side, the equivalents were the various secretaries of defense, the president's national security advisers, and the navy admirals in Hawaii. None of these people was within thousands of miles of the war, yet they severely limited Westmoreland's authority to prosecute it; that is, limited it only to South Vietnam. He didn't even have control over the war against the enemy's supply routes. He had no control over naval operations off the coast of Vietnam, and he had a very little authority over air operations in North Vietnam and Laos.

Westmoreland, of course, accepted these limitations. But if he were being candid I think Westmoreland would say that although he had a better strategy—and in fact had recommended several times that American ground troops be sent in to interdict the enemy's supply trails—he just didn't believe that we could lose the war. And he wasn't alone. Then, when the realization came that we could lose, it was too late to do anything about it because the war had become an abomination to most Americans.

Not that Westmoreland didn't have his faults. One of his chief faults was that he wasn't what Clausewitz called a "military genius." But one of his strengths was that he *knew* it. He had no illusions about his intellectual prowess. So he compensated by surrounding himself with some very able people, such as General Bruce Palmer, General Richard Stilwell, and General William DePuy. Bruce Palmer is one of the smartest officers in the American military, and so is Stilwell. And DePuy

was the finest division commander I ever served under in the United States Army.

The point is that the mistakes we made in Vietnam weren't primarily the mistakes of the tactical commanders; they were strategic errors. Yet you still hear a lot of criticism of the tactics we used. People say, for instance, that what we learned in Vietnam is that we can't fight wars of attrition; we have to fight wars of maneuver. What they fail to realize is that attrition and maneuver are aspects of a single whole—the yin and yang, as it were, of a successful strategy. Look at Grant's strategy in the Civil War. It was very simple. Grant waged this terrible war of attrition against Lee in northern Virginia while Sherman drove Johnston back into Atlanta, making it impossible for Lee or Johnston to reinforce one another. Once this was done, Sherman tore loose across the South and cut Lee's lines of supply. Attrition and maneuver—hold them by the nose and kick them in the tail. What we had in Vietnam was the attrition side of it, but we didn't maneuver against the enemy's supply and infiltration routes.

Even without the benefit of maneuver, the decision to pursue attrition against the North Vietnamese, as one analyst has pointed out, was based on a reasonable premise. That is, it was reasonable to assume that if we killed 2 percent, 3 percent, or 5 percent of the enemy's armed forces, he was going to give up. How could we know in advance that the North Vietnamese would be willing to accept losses utterly beyond our belief? Yet General Giap now admits that he took 600,000 KIA between 1964 and 1968. And that doesn't include the wounded. Proportionate to the population, that's the equivalent of 7 or 8 million American casualties. Can any American believe that we would take 8 million Americans killed for anything?

And you have those who say that we used too much firepower indiscriminately in Vietnam. To some degree it's true. A lot of our firepower was unfocused, a matter of just shooting holes in the jungle. But if Giap's to be believed, it's also true that our firepower was focused enough to kill more than half a million of his troops by 1968. So we must have been doing something right. And then there's the idea that somehow Vietnam was the most atrocious war ever fought, which is ironic since some of the supposed evidence of that—like "free fire zones"—in fact represented

attempts to limit the indiscriminate use of firepower. People forget that the entire continent of Europe was a "free fire zone" in World War II. They also forget that when the 8th Army pulled out of North Korea after the Chinese came in, we applied a scorched-earth policy—all livestock was destroyed, all food was destroyed, and all houses were burned because the Chinese army was living off the land.

Most people still don't appreciate the savagery or ferocity of the Vietnam War at the small-unit level. The danger and difficulty that the front-line American infantryman faced just isn't recognized. In part, I think, that is because the overall U.S. casualty figures for the war are misleading. But if you break those figures down by division, you find that the American Division, for example, took something like five times more casualties in Vietnam than it took in World War II. The 1st Cavalry Division took almost twice as many casualties as it took in World War II and Korea combined. Even the 1st Infantry Division, which took very heavy casualties in World War II because they went ashore at North Africa and at Sicily and at Normandy on D-day, still took more casualties in Vietnam.

And through it all, at least during the early years, the American soldier performed magnificently. In fact, the army we had in Vietnam when I was there in 1966 and 1967 was the finest army the United States ever put in the field. And there were reasons for that. They were better educated for one thing. There were more high-school graduates, for instance, in Vietnam than in World War II. They were a little younger, which means they were a little more audacious since one of the things age gives you is a sense of mortality. They were well trained and they had good spirit. They'd do anything asked of them. Volunteer for the most dangerous missions.

But again, that was 1966-1967, when we still had a sense of mission. We thought we were doing something valuable. By 1969 or 1970, that had all been lost. When we started the Vietnamization process, when we started to draw down and to avoid contact, the prevalent feeling among the troops became, "Why be the last guy to die in Vietnam?" The American soldier, too, is very pragmatic. He assesses a situation and asks himself,

Summers appearing with former Defense Secretary James Schlesinger on ``Meet the Press'' on April 28, 1985, the day before the tenth anniversary of the fall of Saigon.

Major General William E. DePuy, commander of the 1st Infantry Division, presents the Silver Star for ``gallantry in action'' to Captain Harry G. Summers, Jr. at Phuoc Vinh, South Vietnam, in August 1966.

"Is it worth it?" And if he thinks it's worth it, he'll do his damnedest. If he thinks it isn't worth it, all the propaganda in the world won't change his mind. I think if you look closely at the drug problem and the other problems the American army suffered in Vietnam during the later years, you'll find a lack of a sense of mission at the root. Poor leadership made it worse, but the lack of a sense of mission was crucial. And you can't blame the American soldier for that.

One of the things that propelled me to write my book, in fact, was the feeling that the enlisted man who served in Vietnam was taking a bad rap. Many of them were even blaming themselves for the failure, for not having won. I wanted them to see that whoever lost the Vietnam War, it wasn't them. I wanted to set the record straight and put the onus of responsibility where it belonged, on the civilian and military leadership at the very highest echelons.

I suppose it sounds a bit arrogant, but if we require our soldiers on pain of death to show physical courage on the battlefield, which we do by law, then we ought to expect the same degree of moral courage from people at the top. And that just wasn't there. The Joint Chiefs of Staff knew we didn't have a strategy in Vietnam, but they never told President Johnson that. None of his advisers did. Instead, they tried to protect him, and in trying to protect him they destroyed him.

General Harold K. Johnson, the army chief of staff during the early years of the war, later recalled that at one point he decided to go to Johnson and resign in protest because he thought the president was getting people killed needlessly and violating all the principles of war. But on the way to the White House he changed his mind and decided he could do more to change things from within than if he resigned. And as he reflected back on that lost moment, he said, "Now I will go to my grave with that lapse of moral courage." Here was a guy who as a young officer was captured at Bataan, endured the Bataan death march, and spent World War II in a Japanese prison camp. As a regimental commander in Korea he saw his regiment overrun by the Chinese. A guy who was in two wars right up front, and one of the most moral officers I've ever known. He kept a Bible and a Boy Scout manual on his desk. Yet just before his death, he told me that for five years after the Vietnam War he couldn't stand to think about it because he felt such a terrible sense of personal responsibility.

What a tragedy. Halberstam's title was so apt: *The Best and the Brightest.* If it had been a bunch of incompetents or a bunch of crooks or a bunch of evil demons, they would have been easy to deal with. You'd just get rid of them or catch them and drive a stake through their heart. But what do you do if it's the best and the brightest? What do you do with the Robert McNamaras and the McGeorge Bundys and the Dean Rusks, people who certainly had the best interests of the country at heart? That's what shakes me. That's the scariest part of Vietnam. It was the very best minds that got us into it.

∎

Rick Amber

Fighter Pilot, U.S. Navy
Yankee Station, Gulf of Tonkin
January 1970–March 1971

Rick Amber was born in Dallas, Texas, in June 1944. During his youth he developed a love for machines and speed. Sometimes he raced his '57 Chevrolet at 100 miles per hour along the city's new central expressway and dragged on the straight-away behind the high school. After a year at the University of Hawaii majoring in "girls and surfing," he was appointed to the U.S. Naval Academy in 1963. Despite a flair for engineering and seamanship, Amber chose flight training upon graduation. "I think being Jewish had a lot to do with it. The Six-Day War had just been fought, and everyone knew Israelis were the best fighter pilots going." Early in his flying career, Amber realized he wanted to pilot single-seat fighters and nothing else. After receiving his wings in 1969, the wish was realized with assignment to fly F-8s for Fighter Squadron 211 stationed aboard the U.S.S. Hancock.

Vietnam was not a big issue. I just knew I wanted to go because that was where the war was. The only fear was that it might be over before I had a chance to get there. I spent New Year's Eve 1969 in Japan, and then on New Year's Day we flew out to the *Hancock* on a helicopter. It was a 27-Charlie class carrier, the oldest and smallest attack carriers in the fleet. F-8s were always on 27-Charlies because they were smaller than F-4s and took less room on the deck. The deck looked incredibly tiny as we flew aboard. You just didn't look very far and there was the end of the deck. What it meant to me was a much smaller landing area. Instead of the usual twenty-foot clearance when I came across the ramp to catch the wire, I now had less than ten feet, a much tighter landing.

When I got off the helicopter, I was struck by the smell of JP-5, like kerosene, which to a fighter pilot is the greatest smell in the world. The deck was filthy with red hydraulic fluid, which is also good because if your F-8 is leaking that means at least there's some in there. There was gunpowder on the gun ports and that's the way an F-8 should look. The F-8 was the last of the gun-fighters. It had four 20MM cannons and there were no plans to ever put guns on fighters again. I guess it's like driving Porsches, there's something legendary about it. It was a good feeling being around real combat aircraft that were just on the way back to the line. I was there and wanted to be there real bad and was loving every minute of it. The guys were all real shit-hot fighter pilots, and I was ready to join up with them.

As soon as I hit the *Hancock* I ran into a friend of mine that had turned in his wings but had still volunteered to serve as catapult officer. That's probably the first contact I had with somebody that was dead set against the war in Vietnam, so set that he was willing to sacrifice all the training of the past two and one-half years to not carry weapons over the country. I used to eat with him, and we often talked over his decision to quit flying. I respected his position, but I couldn't for the life of me see how that could override his wanting to fly. Flying, to me, was everything.

The whole time I was flying missions off Yankee Station, the North Vietnamese just weren't interested in fighting. We had air superiority, and the Communists would not launch their MiGs. We mostly flew combat air patrols and cover for photoreconnaissance. At any given time there were dozens of American aircraft airborne over Vietnam, so even if they felt that they were good enough to shoot down an F-8 or an F-4, what were they going to do with the other ten or twelve that were on their ass?

I loved clouds. Flying among them was the greatest play time. It really gave a sensation of speed. And flying over Vietnam was something else—altogether different than flying in the States—there weren't a lot of rules and no jetways. Night flying was another wonderful thing. The launches are terrific because the F-8 loves to fly and just goes straight up. When I got out on top, over the clouds, I'd turn off the lights and between what moonlight there was and the white clouds, I'd feel very close to all the millions and millions of stars. I'd feel a lot higher than I was.

However, there's one part of F-8 flying that's not enjoyable at all and that's night recoveries. I lost a real close friend in Hawaii between my first and second cruises to Vietnam. He hit the ramp at night and ejected just as his plane exploded. But when he went out, the cockpit was tumbling, and despite the ejection he never got out of the seat. He just skipped along the deck, hit the hatch next to the catapult, and was killed. Every night approach to the back of the ship is a foreign situation. You're flying real close to the wrong side of the power curve, and the F-8 is just not stable in the groove at low speed.

When you're coming toward the carrier, the first thing you see is the wide white stripe down the middle of the flight deck and you try to put your nose right up there. Off to the left you see an orange ball—the meatball—with three green lights on either side. If the ball is lined up with the green lights, you are on the glide slope. If it rises above the green line, you're high. If it slides below, you're in deep-shit trouble. You're low, and you don't want to be low on a carrier. You make very incremental corrections with your throttle and stick to stay on the proper glide slope. Nose over and you go faster, push forward the throttle and you go up. The idea is to be right on speed while making sure your angle of attack, or nose of the aircraft, is in the right position for your tail hook to catch the wire. The line-up on the deck is also interesting because it's changing all the time. The landing deck on all carriers is angled to the left. So in addition to pitching up and down from the swells of the ocean, the deck is actually moving sideways as the ship goes forward. Therefore, as you're approaching to land, you're always making corrections to the right.

You're shooting for a specific point on the deck, the three-wire. Not the one-wire or the two-wire or the four-wire, those are last resorts. You want the three-wire and nothing else. All you think is meatball, line-up, angle of attack; meatball, line-up, angle of attack. The closer you get, the narrower the margin of error becomes. All your corrections are tiny. Finally it's just meatball, meatball, meatball. At the instant you touch down you slam on full power, assuming that you've missed and need speed to get airborne again. It takes several seconds to get to 100 percent power, so you have to go full throttle as soon as you touch down. Ideally, the biggest surprise when you land should be the touchdown itself—the jar of the wheels hitting the deck.

Despite the night landings, flying F-8s on carriers was everything I expected it would be. It was just the best thing that you could be doing, so I wasn't in a big hurry to stop. In early March I talked to my XO about extending for a third Vietnam cruise.

My last flight was the second of the day, an evening hop and a night landing. I remember it was the Ides of March, the fifteenth, 1971 in the States. I had been doing some nice precision flying with the flight leader and then had gone into the break to land when it was announced the ship's landing system had failed. But, no big deal, we could still come aboard. It's just that the LSO, the landing officer, would have to wave us aboard manually. He gets out what looks like a TNT plunger and manually moves the ball up and down because that's what we were used to looking at.

I felt like the LSO was bringing me in on the number-one wire because it allowed a smaller angle of descent, therefore you could come in with slightly more power. However, that places you closer to the ramp. I had centered the ball so I was in close when he gave me the wave-off

signal. I went to 100 percent power, but at that distance there's not enough time for the aircraft to respond. Also, there's a lot of air coming over the deck at twenty-eight knots and dropping straight down off the fantail, so there's a huge sink. Anything drops when there's that kind of wind.

All I did was scrape the ramp, I didn't really hit it very hard. I remember there being a feeling of crunching, not a sound so much as the vibration of the stick. But I thought everything was okay. The reality is that when you're low on fuel, the tanks are full of fumes, and it only takes a little bit of friction to ignite the stuff. The plane exploded. There's a fire wall behind the seat so I didn't see anything, but the blast was so violent my hands flew off the stick and throttle. It was the nearest thing I can imagine to being right on top of an atomic bomb. In that split second, I knew this was one F-8 that wasn't going to take part in naval aviation anymore, and I wasn't going to stay with it and go into the water. I reached over my head, yanked down the face curtain, and the ejection seat fired off just like clockwork.

Some of the other pilots were in the squadron ready room watching the landings on closed-circuit television. They saw the white nose on the aircraft so they knew it was an aircraft from our squadron. There was a weird flame from the underside of the aircraft, then a fireball, and I came shooting out of the center of the explosion. Luckily the canopy stayed on until the ejection, or the flames would have sucked out all the oxygen and burned me up. The rocket seat got me about a hundred feet in the air, the chute opened just perfectly, and I didn't even get singed. The next thing I remember was the chute opening, a violent pop. I thought of my squadron mate who had been killed when he went out horizontally, so I was tickled to death that I was in the air. I was feeling great, ready to hit the water, get picked up by the helicopter, get a new flight suit, and go out again the next day. Then I remembered I was at low altitude and might drop back down into the fireball. Unfortunately, when I left the aircraft it was already breaking up so I had angled up to the right, which put me in the air in front of the ship. As I was coming through my first swing in the chute, I twisted my head around to look at the deck, and all I saw was gray steel. It

was the island of the ship, bigger than I ever imagined it could be, rushing at me.

All I could do was brace myself for the impact. The ship was moving at twenty-eight knots, and I was swinging into that mass of metal. It was like getting hit by a truck at whatever that combined speed was. I must have blacked out for a second, no more. I came to hearing the air boss hollering at the flight deck crew to get the other planes away from the flames. The deck looked like it was on fire. I had missed the captain of the ship by about ten feet, smashed into a steel plate, and then, instead of falling to the flight deck, had been caught by a catwalk eight levels up. I was lucky; there were so many jagged pieces of metal that could have just cut me in two.

I could see a lot of faces. The captain and XO came out on the bridge and looked down. I knew I was hurt pretty bad and was having real trouble breathing, so I was trying to get the oxygen mask off of my face but was having trouble moving my hands when the corpsman got there. I remember starting to doze off and thinking I was dying and saying, "Oh, shit, this is it." Then I began resisting falling asleep because I didn't want to go. Something said, fight this.

I still had feeling above my chest, and everything hurt because I had broken so many bones in my upper body: all the ribs on the left side, the shoulder, and the collarbone. I heard the corpsman say we should lower him with a Tilly. The Tilly's a big crane, and that's what should have been done because the first thing you want to do is immobilize the spine. But they were really in a hurry to get me out of there, so they strapped me to the stretcher and carried me down to the 02 or 03 level. Then they decided to lower me the rest of the way to the flight deck, but in the process one of the ropes either broke or slipped and I turned completely over. My head was hanging upside down, and I knew that was bad. I don't know how well off I'd have been if that hadn't happened. They finally got me on the flight deck and then down a series of narrow ladders to sickbay and the flight surgeon. Since I was having trouble breathing they did a tracheotomy, went in and cut open my throat. I don't recommend it. If there was one thing that I hated in the next couple of weeks it was that stupid tracheotomy. No talking, a helpless feeling when you've got a million questions to ask.

They decided to fly me to the hospital ship, which was tied up to the dock at Da Nang, so they carried me back up to the flight deck and onto a helicopter. All the time the flight surgeon was breathing for me with a resuscitator bag. It was bad weather, overcast, so we had to make an instrument approach, and the helicopter hit a tree on a hillside. The pilot managed to stay airborne, but they all started putting on life jackets. I thought, if they're going to ditch that's it for sure, because I ain't swimming. But the pilot made it aboard the hospital ship. They thought there was a neurosurgeon aboard, but they were wrong. Finally, with a new chopper, I was flown to the army evacuation hospital at Da Nang. In the operating room the anesthesiologist said, "I'm going to put something in your IV to knock you out." I could have kissed him. I thought that was a wonderful idea.

When I woke up they were still drilling holes in my skull to put tongs in my head for traction. I asked to see the doctor. In neurosurgery they get pretty good at lip reading. I knew I was desperately injured, but I just didn't know how bad. I asked him what was wrong and he said, "You've got a broken neck so you're paralyzed from the chest down." I said, "What can you do to fix it?" He said, "Nothing. That's the way it's going to be, forever." So I learned real early and that's probably good.

I knew one thing, I was going to live, and that made me feel great. Then you gradually start trying to survive from minute to minute, day to day. Da Nang, however, was tough. I was in intensive care, and almost everyone they brought in died. Finally I was put in a Stryker frame. It's a bed that can be turned upside down to rotate you from lying on your back to lying on your stomach. It's real uncomfortable because you're in traction, and there are ten or fifteen pounds of weights holding your vertebrae apart so your neck will fuse properly.

I immediately developed pneumonia. So with one tube down my nose draining my stomach, an IV, a catheter, and a hole in my side to drain my lungs, I looked like I was being plumbed. Also, they were putting a red antiseptic on my head daily to keep infection from setting in where the tongs were emplaced. I was quite a show.

Shipmates around the fleet had heard I'd ejected unsuccessfully and assumed I had been killed. I considered it a real successful ejection, although there were times in those early days, when I was depressed, that I wished, fleetingly, that it hadn't been. The thought was, Why me? Why not somebody else? I didn't do anything wrong. It's a selfish reaction, but fairly normal, and it doesn't last long. They had told my mother that I was seriously injured and the prognosis was doubtful. Finally, though, I got a phone call from her so I could explain I was injured but in great shape. And I was. I was really feeling good, the trach was out and no more pneumonia.

Visitation was really important. I was really impressed with the amount of personal attention given to me throughout the evacuation process. A few days after getting out of intensive care, the two nurses that cared for me the entire time came down and visited me. They realized it's important for the patient to talk to someone on other than a professional level.

I had to go to Japan next. I was getting painkillers regularly so I don't remember much of the trip. I recall leaving Da Nang in a bus and being put into a helicopter somewhere. I was in Japan for three weeks. They started therapy by doing range of motion on my arms, legs, knees, fingers, keeping the joints active so atrophy doesn't set in quite so much. By

Amber's plane returns from a mission over South Vietnam.

"Flying, to me, was everything." Rick Amber stands before a T–2 Buckeye jet during training in Pensacola, Florida in 1968.

then I could nibble on food, and I was getting stronger all the time. About a month after I'd been injured they put me on a C-141 for home, still in that Stryker frame and still in the tongs. It seemed like we flew for days. We refueled in Hawaii and spent two nights in San Francisco. I remember one night the Stryker frame broke loose, and I was hanging from a support by one arm hollering for help. I was real anxious to get as far away from there as possible.

Then I was moved to Balboa Naval Hospital in San Diego, which was beautiful. I got there in April, the tongs came out, and I got my first haircut and shampoo. I just can't describe the great care. At any given time there were three or four people ready to help you. And I had all my squadron mates who were back in San Diego. I always had ten or twelve visitors, just a constant throng of people. I remember eating and drinking in that room till all hours, just having fun. They'd put salads on me and I'd be the buffet table. And during the daytime there was a lot of work, weightlifting and physical therapy. I wanted to stay and go through rehabilitation right there in San Diego, but they just weren't equipped for it. It was a matter of waiting for something to open up at the VA hospital in Long Beach, although my doctor at Balboa

made sure I had over four years in the navy before I was transferred. He knew it would make a significant difference in my retirement.

I was shipped to Long Beach in an ambulance in June of '71 and spent my twenty-seventh birthday there. They told me in San Diego that the one thing the VA hospital does is make you hate it so intensely you'll want to get out of there. You don't want to stay. They said it would take a year of rehab, but I left in September. It's just no place to hang out. Everybody had the same kind of injuries, which was okay because you learn a lot, but it was boring. Hours and hours of boredom. You went to different therapies, were measured for a wheelchair, and learned to drive a car with hand controls, but there were so many people going through the system and so few therapists there just wasn't enough time for individual attention. As a result you learn from other paraplegics, the guys who had been hurt five or six years. They can tell you what the real story is out there. By September, I was spending most of my time just doing things I could do myself anyway so I asked to leave. After a few days of intense practice in the chair, they checked me out one morning and I split in my car for San Diego.

The only time I felt antagonistic at all

was when I was discharged, because I wanted somehow to stay in the navy. The way they handled the discharge really sucked. In the middle of the afternoon a yeoman, they didn't even send an officer, said, "Here sign this." It all took about ten minutes. You know, for all the trouble they went to, they could have just mailed the son of a bitch to me. So now I was no longer in the navy. All handled with no formality, no good luck, no thanks, no nothing. It was just so impersonal, and I was so close to the navy. I couldn't be a fighter pilot, but I was still a damned well- and expensively trained naval officer. What antagonism I have is not over what happened in Vietnam so much as the way the navy handled the severance.

I stayed with my girlfriend for a while until I found an apartment that was wheelchair accessible. Remember, back in '71 there were no provisions for us. There weren't any curb-cuts, no ramps, and the federal rehabilitation act hadn't been passed. We were just getting started in this country making handicapped accessibilities. It's really a phenomenon of the last ten years.

We found a few restaurants we could get into, but drive-in places got a lot of business from me. At first I wasn't working or going to school because I was just not emotionally prepared to take that on, but the inactivity led to some severe depression. There was nothing specific that would trigger depression. It's just something that goes on and off. Finally, I decided it was time to get busy. I ran into another veteran, and he and I started a little health food store on Route 1 near Solana Beach, making avocado sandwiches and smoothies. We weren't challenging Coca-Cola, but it got me back into a mindset where I knew I could be productive. Soon, however, I realized it wasn't a realistic way to spend the rest of my life.

In August '72 I came back to Dallas, and while I was here a chemical research company hired me in their technical services department. I credit them with really bringing me back into the world. I also got interested in education and completed a master's degree in environmental engineering. While I was in school I met an administrator of the EPA who said they were interested in hiring veterans, so in '77 I went to work for EPA and engineered there for four years.

About the same time I married the girl

next door who, I discovered, was interested in television communications. The cable industry was just hitting Dallas, and she got me to attend a couple of classes where they were building all kinds of local programs. I really enjoyed it and by '81 I was ready to go back to school, so I enrolled in the SMU school of communications. There I met a film producer who was teaching a seminar in Los Angeles for writing, directing, and producing videos. I jumped at the chance, stayed on campus at UCLA, worked out of his offices in North Hollywood, and got a real feel for the business. In '84 when I graduated, I went to work for Dallas's cable company in the local programming arm of the community access program. We are building a system of local programming throughout the community, and I help run one of the four studios where people can produce alternative programming and have it aired. It's a highly successful concept here. We put on hundreds of new shows every single month, and Dallas has become the showcase of access programming. It has got-

ten the community heavily involved to the point they're committing their own resources.

As for the future? A realistic goal for my life is that I'll probably end up getting a Ph.D. and teach in conjunction with a lot of free-lance video tape work. You know, I don't like being injured. I was probably too cavalier about the world. You get a lot of time to think once you've been injured. I'm sure it's made a better person of me, and I've got my life in order. I'd rather it hadn't happened, but it made me mature and taught me to take life more seriously.

But you know, I still have that need to fly. If I struck it big, if I had all the money in the world, a lot of it would be spent on flying. Rigging hand controls on an airplane is no problem. And to me it's not unrealistic that I could fly in the space program. I'd love to be on a crew or even go along as a passenger. You don't need your legs in space. It would be really great to get up in the air again. ∎

Amber cruises on the campus of Southern Methodist University in his Honda Goldwing motorcycle, specially equipped with a Tomco sidecar.

Opposite. Amber's flight logbook from March 1971 includes the record of his last flight.

Stephen W. Gregory

*Infantryman
Kilo Company, 3d Battalion
1st Marines, 1st Marine Division
May 1968–June 1969*

Steve Gregory was born in Washington, D.C., in January 1950 and grew up in suburban Maryland. After several minor brushes with the law, he joined the Marines at the age of seventeen. "I was very, very naive and very, very immature," he recalls. "I thought that the service was going to teach me something and discipline me." At boot camp at Parris Island Gregory scored high marks for proficiency and conduct and made private first class in twelve weeks. After thirteen months of combat in Vietnam, he received his discharge in April 1970. Today Gregory and his wife, Susan, whom he married in May 1985, live in eastern Pennsylvania.

God, there were so many dudes that I saw get blown away. So many operations. Six major operations and three enemy offensives in thirteen months is a lot of operations. Why Oklahoma Hills stands out, I just never really figured out. You can even read it in a history book and it's a little paragraph saying something like, ". . . encountered few firefights." Well, this was no firefight we were in on April 11, 1969. It was a total, all-out battle, and it haunted me for years and years.

We operated in the An Hoa basin, in areas with names like Dodge City, the Arizona Territory, and Booby Trap Valley. It was a big, big area. Dodge City had lots of hamlets and villages, and it was real shoot-'em-up place. We were in a place called Charlie Ridge, because a lot of gooks were constantly there. Whose brainstorm it was I don't know, but on April 10 we were to dig up all these enemy graves, looking for weapons, rice, anything that might be able to help identify the enemy in the area.

We were digging up the graves and getting sniped at all day long. We had people that went down, and they kept making us dig. So we dug and dug, and medevacked and medevacked, and they kept us out there digging. We never had a chance to dig in, to prepare ourselves for the night.

No sooner did it get dark when we were hit with everything. They unloaded on us with RPGs, machine guns, the whole bit. We had no place to take cover, we couldn't do anything. Every one of our listening posts was hit. You could hear guys screaming as satchel charges were thrown into their position and as we were hit with RPGs. We medevacked people out of there all night long.

It all dwindled down about five in the morning. I know why they did it: in retaliation for us digging up their graves. If we could understand what they were shouting at us during the fight, that's probably what they were saying. So we knew the next day was going to be a bitch.

We figured that the order from headquarters would be for an entire platoon to sweep the area. When the call finally did come down at seven in the morning, they wanted only one squad to go through the area. I was the platoon radioman; I took the message and gave it to Lieutenant Christian, the 2d Platoon commander.

The squad that was chosen was Alpha Squad.

Alpha Squad at the time was led by my best friend, Johnnie Lee Anderson—J.L. We were always together. Every day we ate together, slept together, sat and talked and smoked together. We were both ornery to each other, always fighting just like a couple of old ladies. My mom would send stuff to him in my packages, and his mom would send me stuff in his packages. We were really, really tight.

After I took that message, I just had that gut feeling that something bad was going to happen. I was worried about J.L., especially because his radio man had only a couple of weeks in country. So I turned to Lieutenant Christian and said, "I'm going to carry the radio for Alpha." He said, "No, you're not. You're the platoon radioman. You're going to stay here." I just looked at him and said, "Fuck you, I'm going with Alpha."

When you're a boot officer who's only been in country four days and you look at this nineteen-year-old kid who looks like he's been through about thirty wars, with that stare that says he's been there for a while, it's very difficult to say no. Because he's liable to just shoot you right where you stand! So anyway, I disobeyed his orders and went ahead and carried the radio for Alpha Squad. I knew we were going to get hit.

There's nothing in this world that can describe an ambush. You're diddy-bopping along saying jeez, I hope I make it through this day. The guys who had been there for a while would be saying stuff like be careful, we're going to get hit, we know we're going to get hit. Then to explain the feeling that hits you and the sounds. . . . It's like the whole world is exploding around you, and you're just expecting to be thrust up into the sky and split all different ways. Some people try to describe it like the Fourth of July. I would disagree. It's ten times worse than that. If you've ever heard anything really, really loud, so loud it's frightening, that's what an ambush is like.

We hadn't walked more than a click when it seemed that the whole world just emptied on the first six of us that walked through. The balance of the eleven-man squad never got through. I automatically dove the instant the fire came. It was coming from all over. They had us in a semicircle ambush.

J.L. was about fifty or sixty feet away from me, and he got hit on the initial impact. He probably took two or three rounds in the stomach, because he was pulling at himself and rolling and yelling "Corpsman! Corpsman! Corpsman!" The navy corpsman, Doc Levi, took at least three rounds trying to go help these Marines that were down.

I had three rounds imbedded in my radio. I could not transmit, but I could receive. I could click the headset and the command radioman could hear it clicking. Lieutenant Hobbs, the Kilo Company commander, would ask me questions and I would click one for no and two for yes. They wanted a pinpoint location so I got up to pop a smoke grenade. That's when I got hit with a Chicom grenade.

J.L. was still rolling around, yelling. Three other guys were screaming because they were wounded bad. One guy's arm was nearly gone. Every time that I attempted to go to J.L., to try to give him first aid, they would shoot me right back down again. One guy tried to pull me back by the back of my neck. But I wouldn't let him. I stuck my rifle in his face and told him to let me go.

Just as I did that a Chicom landed near J.L. In his pain and anguish he rolled so much that he rolled right over onto the Chicom, and that just blew him the hell away.

After J.L. died I didn't care no more. I didn't care. I knew I was going to die, but I wasn't going to just lay down and give up without a fight. I was in there for another three and a half hours, just by myself. I went to every last one of the others and patched up those that I could patch up. I used every grenade that anybody was carrying.

Then Lieutenant Christian decided he was going to make a run in there to help us out. So he came in and got down on my left side on one knee, John Wayne-style, to throw a grenade. Luckily he threw the grenade first as he got shot right between the eyes. It was the fastest death I'd ever seen during the entire time I was in Vietnam. His eyes just closed and he flopped over and he was dead. Ten minutes later the 3d Platoon's lieutenant, Lieutenant Peterson, did the same thing on the right side of me and got shot through the face. So I got a dead lieutenant on this side of me and a seriously wounded one on the other side. I was just

bleeding all over the place, with shrapnel all through the head.

Finally I was able to fire enough rounds on a bunker to allow a couple of guys to get Peterson out. Then after they got him, there was so much intense fire that nobody would come back into that ambush anymore.

I just finally went crazy. I didn't know for sure that J.L. was dead. I mean, you know he is, but your mind refuses to accept it. There was just this chance that he was still going to be alive. So I went back into the ambush to retrieve the rest of the dead and wounded. I went to J.L. first and dragged him out. When I went back in, I just walked and fired my weapon steadily. I didn't care anymore. By the time I got to the third or fourth guy, a couple of guys started helping me out.

The worst thing in the world was picking up J.L. with nothing left of him from his chin to his crotch but a small portion of his intestines hanging out, the rest of him just totally blown away. His eyes were wide open. He died a very, very horrific death. You could see it in his eyes, he died in pure pain.

But I got him out. I was the one who closed his eyes. I was the one who wiped the sand from his face. That was the vow that we made to each other: if either one of us got into real shit and got wounded or killed, the other would make sure that his body was sent back.

But to have him destroyed like that. . . . If he had died a normal death, like Lieutenant Christian—one round through the

Private First Class Stephen Gregory at his parents' home in Maryland in April 1968, just prior to his leaving for Vietnam.

"We were always together." Lance Corporals Steve Gregory (left) and Johnnie Lee Anderson take a break near An Hoa during Operation Taylor Common, early 1969.

head, you're gone—I probably could have lived with that. But to see the horror on his face, I knew that he just could not believe that this had happened to him. I think together we always felt invincible, that there was no way in the world this shit was ever going to happen to us because we were too bad. But it did.

I didn't have any emotion anymore. I didn't care who I killed, what I killed, I had to kill something. I went back in with two guys and went bunker to bunker with hand grenades, M16s, and a .45. I pulled wounded gooks out of the bunkers and shot them in the head. I killed every last one of them that was wounded and could have been captured. There were no prisoners today. There were no prisoners for me in Vietnam, period. I called in Phantom jets and two tanks before I was medevacked out. I got the Bronze Star with Combat "V" for what I did that day.

After that no one wanted to have any conversation with me. It was really freaky because I still had thirty or so days left in Vietnam, and I never talked to anybody. I didn't go sit with anybody when it was time to eat or anything like that. I was a total loner. I never made another friend in Vietnam after J.L. got killed. It was just because anybody that I'd ever become close to ended up getting blown away.

And I never showed any mercy. If we got into sniper fire or anything, I stopped trying to pick it out. I paid them back with the max. I opened up with everything. If a son of a bitch sniped at me from a house he was in horrible shit because I just got a LAW and took out the whole damn building.

I was through with two-faced enemies, when one minute they weren't and the next minute they were. I didn't care. My standard rule after the ambush to my squad was if it was anywhere around you and it was Vietnamese, kill it. Even if it was a pig or some other animal; if you thought it had slant eyes, kill it. I never lost a single guy from my squad because they did exactly that.

To be honest, I never wanted to leave the Nam. I was so adhered to what I was doing. The day I left Nam I cried. I was standing on top of the sandbags and tears were coming down my face because it was the first time that platoon ever walked away and I wasn't going with them, and it really tore me up. I didn't want to go.

It took me an extra five days to even make it home. I stayed in San Francisco five days just getting drunk, walking around, trying to put it all together. It's hard to explain, but I was lost. When I got to Baltimore-Washington Airport, I was wearing my uniform with seven or eight ribbons. A young girl said something like, "Did you get all those for killing people?" I'll never forget it.

Then for three solid days I got together with the guys I had gone to school with. It was a total waste. It was like I just had nothing in common with them at all anymore. I was nineteen years old going on fifty. I'd seen babies born, I'd killed people, I'd seen total poverty and disease. I'd seen people in so many different ways it was pathetic. These guys hadn't seen anything. They were all so opinionated, but they didn't really know what was going on in the first place. Neither did I, for that matter, but I knew a little bit more than they did. At least I'd been there to know. I had something to base it on.

My troubles started three weeks after I got home. I was at a pool party when this thirty-five-year-old guy with long hair and a beard started giving me a whole ration of shit. He said something like, "Oh, you just think you're a real big bad Marine. You ain't nothing but a baby killer."

He made his mistake. Three weeks home with no type of deprogramming, with no real opportunity to break away from the atrocity and death of Vietnam, how was I supposed to be able to control myself from hitting somebody who says something like that to me? I laid him out. They called the cops, but I didn't try to run. I tried to explain that this guy had started it, but who do you think they're going to lock up, a nineteen-year-old or a thirty-five-year-old?

The guy pressed assault and battery charges against me. I was assigned to Quantico at the time, so I went back there to get an attorney. But they told me, "You were on leave and you were in civilian court, so you've got to use a civilian lawyer." When I finally did go back to court I had no counsel, no plea-bargain offer or anything. I got eighteen months in a maximum-security prison—for a simple fistfight. When the judge gave me the time he said something like, "You're not going to bring that war back to the United States." Like I'm the one that went over and started it and just brought it back like

it wasn't already prevailing in the United States anyway.

I did four and a half months at Hagerstown, Maryland, and made my first parole. I think even the parole board thought it was a little ridiculous that a guy would be locked up for a simple fistfight. When I got back to Quantico, they said, "You're out of the Marine Corps." They gave me two hours to get my shit off the base, and they gave me an undesirable discharge. Period. So at age twenty I had a criminal record and an undesirable discharge, and as a Vietnam veteran was considered a drug-crazed baby killer by half the nation. That's a hell of a way to start out manhood. I wasn't even old enough to buy a beer yet.

You just turned and wanted to hide. It was really confusing. I went around for a long time feeling that I was a bad person. I thought, my country says I'm a bad person, I must be a bad person. My country wouldn't lie to me. I thought I could never do anything right because of all this bad stuff that I did in Vietnam. I really believed it.

I never talked about Vietnam. I had nothing to do with any other Vietnam veterans. I could not be in the same room with another Vietnam veteran, just because of the fear that they'd start talking about it or that we both knew something that everybody else didn't know. So I just avoided it. I stayed away from the different veterans' organizations. I would never go outside of this circle that I lived within inside myself, my own little world. I would never attempt to venture outside of it or show any emotions or anything. I just stayed constantly in that small little world and that was it. It was definitely safer there. It damn sure beat all the pain and suffering that took place in Vietnam.

The ambush haunted me for years and years. I would see J.L. everywhere I went. If something good was around, like a woman or something like that, I'd find myself wishing he was there. I wouldn't let anybody get close to me. I had this immense fear that anybody that became close to me was going to be taken away and I was going to have to see those eyes and brush that hair away again. I couldn't do it.

The thoughts, the dreams, and the flashbacks got to such a degree that I tried to commit suicide for nothing more than to try to end the anguish of seeing faces and hearing the cries. For seven, eight, nine years that's all it was. We're talking two, three, four times a week of having these horrendous dreams. I would wake up and my bed would be soaked and I'd be shivering my ass off.

Two or three months after I got out of the Marines, I went to the VA for help, because I knew that I couldn't handle it. They refused to help me because I had a bad discharge. They said they would put me on an outpatient basis and they would get back to me. And of course they never called me back.

I couldn't get a break. I kept trying to do something with myself, but had companies turn me down for work as soon as they found out about the discharge and all. I tried so many management trainee programs. The first job I got that paid halfway decently I paid an employment agency for. I paid them $550 to lie, to get me a job as a bill collector. I wouldn't ever think about being a bill collector. But I paid $550 just to get a job.

I was arrested so many times for just dumb stuff. Many were for disorderly conduct, where I would fight so many guys by myself. Once I lost it, the Nam started ticking in my head, and that would be it. There was no bringing me out of that until something dramatic happened. I had to find a release for all the adrenaline. There were just a lot of minor things like that over the years. The bank was the final straw.

On February 9, 1977, Gregory walked into a bank in Silver Spring, Maryland, carrying two rifles. After shouting "This is not a holdup," he took eight people hostage.

What was going through my head when I walked into the bank? Nam, totally; the ambush, the bunkers. That's it. Nothing else. I just laid all my stuff out on the living room floor just like I was going into combat. I just laid it all out, counted my rounds, cleaned my weapons, the whole bit. When I left my house to go to the bank I wasn't anywhere in the United States anymore. I was totally gone.

A doctor later had a theory that the act in itself was little more than an elaborate suicide attempt. I have to go along with that, because there's no other explanation. I really expected to get blown away. I just couldn't handle it anymore. I was tired of the flashbacks, I was tired of the dreams, and I couldn't find any help.

I took all the people inside the bank, and they all became a squad. It was like I was protecting them from the enemy, and the enemy was all outside and they were coming in to get us. So I fired all these rounds just to keep them at bay. I wasn't aiming for anything, but anything that made any noise, like the air conditioning, the cameras, or the big clock, I shot it out. It was like in the Nam, you couldn't see the enemy so you had to have your instincts intact where you could either smell or hear something different. Anything that made noises that was around you in the Nam, you got rid of it.

I fired over 200 rounds into the ceiling and the walls. But I didn't hurt anybody; I didn't want to.

One cop who was in the Nam tried to talk me out. I don't remember half of anything that they said to me. I was gone, I mean I was wasted. When I finally put my weapons down and the SWAT team rushed in, I was yelling out radio messages. I was in there about six and a half

On June 14, 1970, shortly after his discharge from the Marine Corps, Stephen Gregory is awarded the Bronze Star.

Gregory struggles as he is put into a police van after surrendering in a Silver Spring bank, February 9, 1977.

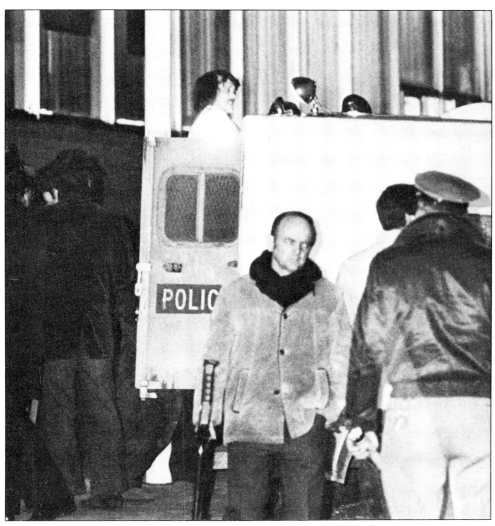

179

hours—ironically, about the same length of time I was in the ambush.

I spent about seven months in jail awaiting trial. That's when I started getting interested in writing and began to try to verbalize and communicate about the things that were happening to me. Some of the social workers, by giving me the tools to communicate and showing me that they cared, showed that there was another side to me, that these things could be worked out. They were really good to me. They cared about what I had to say about the Nam and the things that bothered me. Nobody had ever cared before. They just didn't want to talk about the Nam. When you did, nobody wanted to hear it. It was either too gross or too depressing. So you just kept it all boiling inside you.

One social worker, Ron Rose, was a Vietnam veteran, and he told me about his feelings of raw rage. That helped a lot, knowing that I wasn't the only one that thought these things and felt these things. Because for eight years, before I ever went into the bank, I always figured that I was alone, that I was the only one that was like this.

Everybody knew that it all had to do with the Nam, but my attorneys refused to use the insanity defense based on Vietnam. One of them kept saying, "The United States isn't ready for it." That was in 1977, and they weren't ready for psychological problems in relation to service in Vietnam. So they just went with a regular insanity defense. I lost and received a sixteen-year sentence. I think the judge really felt that there was more to it but just had to do what he had to do.

They wanted to send me to Hagerstown, but I convinced them to send me to Patuxent, which used to be a federal psychiatric institution and was now run by the state, because I wanted to try to do something for myself. I took college courses there and worked on the newspaper and had a nice recreation job, so I was trying. But I would try to talk about Vietnam, and the doctors and the others would ridicule me and make fun of me. So I didn't really get any help there at all.

I finally got a little bit of money together and bought a typewriter. I took all of the court papers and news articles from my trial and had copies of them made. A friend of mine sent me a copy of an article about David Bonior, one of the

Vietnam veterans in Congress. So I put all this stuff together, then sat down and wrote Representative Bonior an eleven-page letter telling him what had happened since I was in the Marine Corps.

Then one day I was sitting in the prison dining hall and some guy walked up to me and said, "You won your appeal," and showed me a *Baltimore Sun* article. I didn't even know that I had won my appeal. The court gave them four days to get me out of prison and back to jail for a new trial. I still didn't know what was going on other than the fact that I had a new trial coming.

The next thing I knew David Addlestone and Elliott Milstein of the National Veterans Law Center showed up to interview me. Apparently David Bonior had forwarded my letter to them. David and Elliott told me that they had been looking for a case like mine to present a mental defense for Vietnam veterans. I just lucked out by writing a letter.

The courtroom scene at my trial on March 2, 1979, was probably the most dramatic thing that ever happened to me in my life besides Vietnam. I pleaded guilty to reduced charges after a plea-bargain. The VA was there to say that they had screwed up on my case and that I should have received treatment all the way back in 1970 when I first went to them. Two doctors testified on my behalf. Then instead of sending me to jail, the judge gave me only six years' probation. I had walked in in chains and shackles; I walked out a free man.

Gregory was later transferred to the Veterans Administration hospital in Cleveland. Several months later he became one of the first Vietnam veterans to be awarded compensation by the VA for stress-related disability, or what in 1980 became known as Post-Traumatic Stress Disorder. While an outpatient in Cleveland, Gregory lived with another patient who was involved in drug trafficking. Not wanting to jeopardize his probation, Gregory returned to Maryland. There, in October 1979, an Ohio drug dealer who thought that Gregory was intercepting his shipments made an attempt on his life. When Gregory called him in Columbus to explain that he was not involved, the dealer "started cussing at me and said something like, 'You can't hurt anything but women and kids, like you did in Vietnam, anyway.'"

In a fit of rage Gregory flew to Columbus and got into a gunfight with the man and his bodyguard. No one was injured, but in the

subsequent car chase with police a girl was killed. Gregory was not driving but was found guilty of aggravated felonious assault and sentenced to five to fifteen years in the state prison at Marion.

After all that, what more could I ever do? I had already reached the pits. I was in one of the worst institutions in the United States. I couldn't go any lower. So there couldn't be anywhere to go but up, if I worked at it.

There were about 1,700 inmates at Marion, and about 300 were Vietnam-era veterans. About 180 had seen combat. While I was there I helped organize programs to help them out. We put out a newspaper, and I became a contributing writer for the *National Vietnam Veterans' Review*. We had the only Amvets post inside a prison, and I became commander. I wrote to the VA regional office in Cleveland about not being able to get treatment in the prison. I got forms and information on PTSD and Agent Orange. I must have gotten six guys disability for PTSD while I was there. And every last Vietnam veteran that served in combat was taken out to the VA hospital for Agent Orange testing. To me that was a great achievement.

A bunch of other Nam vets and I started what was known as the Incarcerated Vietnam Veterans Committee. We were able to get four different rap groups going three nights a week, and I acted as the leader. By working on their problems and helping them out, I began to help myself too.

By the time I got done, the United States Marine Corps and the United States Army knew who Steve Gregory was. They were constantly receiving letters for awards information from me on behalf of prisoners. My belief was that by obtaining the things that they had coming to them, they could better believe in themselves and believe that their service in the military was beneficial. It was like they were finding out stuff about themselves that they never knew. I remember one guy got a Bronze Star that he didn't even know he had earned. It made me think, wow, I did something.

By the time I was paroled in 1983, my statistics showed that there had been over 55,000 Vietnam-era veterans incarcerated across the United States. I hooked up with everybody—the Brotherhood of Vietnam Veterans, the United Vietnam

Veterans Organization, Amvets, the VFW—anybody that I could get to read a letter and receive a response back from that would give me the slightest inkling that they would be helpful. I took advantage of them, to use them to try to help the other guys who were hurting. By the time I got out, the Agent Orange and PTSD programs were established in every institution in the state of Ohio. At least they were getting something more than what they had before.

It's ironic that I found support there. Because there was no other support on the outside. I had to get incarcerated, I had to go do something bizarre to ever get the slightest inkling about what I was supposed to do to make myself as normal as possible, where I could live within the normality of society. And by God, I proved to the sons of bitches that it worked, too. I haven't had a single damn problem since I got out of prison. I'm now off parole. I leave some jobs, but I'm working at it. I don't give up. I've proven that the effort, the warmth, and having people work with me, having people understand, was all it really took in the beginning.

I'm not afraid to talk about the Nam anymore. The biggest thing that ever happened to me in my life was learning how to finally sit down and take these thoughts and feelings and put them on paper, because I could read them over and over again and analyze them and get a better picture and understanding of what was going on. Having the desire to do that and the want to know where I was in the Nam, what I really did, who I was really with ... it was like being totally reborn. Now I know where I was, what I did. I know we went through a lot of shit, but now I can feel good about it.

You can imagine how many times I've gone over and over these things within my mind in order to find answers, to try to find rhyme or reason: why me? Why did it have to happen to me? All the pride, all the loyalty. ... I think I did a good job in Vietnam. I think I was a good soldier. I maintained care and devotion and loyalty for eleven months before the ambush. I lost the best friend I've ever had and went through all of that, then made it home and look what happened to me three weeks after I got home.

I have more control over my life now than I ever had before, but it's very, very

fragile. It could be shattered and I'll be right back at a bank or in a firefight with some guy or doing something crazy. I guess I figure that I always should have been dead, and I can't understand why I'm not. I think, in all actuality, I was a severe casualty of that ambush, too. I wasn't just wounded. A great portion of me died inside there. My heart died. Most of my capacity for thinking in terms of appropriateness and logic died. They're not going to be returning that in any casket or body bag, because it's a part of me that will be buried in the sands of Dodge City for the rest of my life.

When I die, I know where I'm going to go. I'm not going to go to hell, and I'm not going to go to heaven. I'm going to Vietnam. J.L.'s going to be there, and Gallagher's going to be there, and Fats is going to be there, and Tennessee's going to be there, and the lieutenants are going to be there. A lot of the dudes that I knew that died are all going to be there. We'll be back walking down the old red dirt road and getting dusty and nasty and stuff, but we'll all be together. ∎

With his lawyers, Elliott Milstein and David Addlestone, and Dr. John Wilson (left to right), who testified on his behalf, Gregory celebrates his probation sentence outside the Montgomery County Courthouse in Rockville, Maryland, on March 2, 1979.

Steve Gregory and his wife, Susan, in November 1985.

Andrés Tijerina

Captain, U.S. Air Force
Vietnam, 1968–1971

Andrés Tijerina was born in Texas in 1945, two years after his brother Albert. Despite poverty and racial segregation, the pair excelled at school and won scholarships to Texas A&M University, at that time an all-male military institution. They were members of the Corps of Cadets and like most students expected to join the military. Upon graduation they took commissions in the U.S. Air Force and were selected for pilot training. Andrés flew C-130s in Vietnam and in the course of 150 combat missions won the Distinguished Flying Cross and three Air Medals. Albert piloted B-52s for the Strategic Air Command and then was transferred to flying CH-53 helicopters. He was killed in Laos on March 1, 1971, and was awarded the Distinguished Flying Cross and Purple Heart. His son Albert Anthony is a naval ROTC scholarship student at Texas A&M. Andrés now holds a Ph.D. and is writing a history of Mexican-Americans in Texas. He is an executive with the Motorola Corporation.

Our father abandoned the family when I was about five years old and accepted no further responsibility for us. He left my mother with three children: my brother, Albert, my sister, Sylvia Ann, and me. She took us from one town to another finding whatever work she could until finally we landed in San Angelo, where she worked at the five-and-dime during the day and a Mexican food restaurant at night.

One day the doctor called us into his office, my mother was over in the corner crying, and he told us she was going to have to be gone for an awful long time. That started an extended period of her being in the hospital, so we went around to different relatives. We stayed with an aunt and uncle to pick cotton in O'Donnell, then we would go with another aunt and uncle to pick cotton in Miles, and then we'd be with my grandparents and we'd pick cotton someplace else. Once we lived in a garage with the tractors; another time we stayed in an old boxcar that was parked in the middle of a field. Albert and Sylvia and I slept on a pile of straw covered up with big comforters: no doors, no lights, no windows.

We'd enter school only after Thanksgiving, when picking was over. But we entered with a thirst for knowledge because we were very conscious that all the other kids knew things we didn't. I remember once I walked into a new classroom and they were all talking about the word "sentence," and I didn't know what a sentence was. I went to my book and with the help of the teacher attacked it so feverishly that by the end of term I knew more than the rest of the class. That's the way we three went through school.

Then in 1957 my mother was finally out of the hospital, and we settled down again in San Angelo. We really loved our little home because we were together again. Junior high was our first opportunity to apply our energies to one school. Sylvia became an accomplished pianist, Albert collected medals for his trumpet playing, and I became the first Hispanic drum major in our junior high school's history. That was our strongest period when all of my family developed strong bonds of love and loyalty. We stayed around each other and all contributed and formed a very tight-knit unit.

It was us four against the world because even then segregation was still pretty blatant. We weren't allowed to go into swimming pools, the theater, barber shops, restaurants. I know each one of us lost friends. Sylvia had a boyfriend, an Anglo, that she really liked. But one day he said he couldn't be seen with her anymore. So she carried that scar. I had the same thing happen. Friends at some point would tell me, "I can't be any closer to you because of my parents," or someone would say, "You guys can't go someplace because Andy's with you and everybody would look at me." By high school, racism had crystallized as a factor in my life. I was not invited to join any of the Anglo clubs. I was rarely invited to Anglo functions. I began to expect that I would be excluded. I know the low-income, redneck kids from across the tracks had problems too, but the ethnic factor was superimposed over an already difficult social and income situation. Other people had problems, Mexican-Americans had an extra one.

Sylvia went to college first, but then she dropped out to earn money for Albert and me to go. Albert picked Texas A&M. The thing that impressed him about A&M—at that time all male and all military—was the military bearing, the pride, the esprit de corps. He had always read extensively and was very impressed with Douglas MacArthur's evocation of the West Point code, which my brother related to A&M and his own life: "Duty, Honor, Country." When I visited him the first time, I saw Albert eagerly diving into achievements, one right after another. He just couldn't satisfy himself and I knew without a doubt that I had to become an Aggie also, so I enrolled in 1963 to join my brother.

But I still expected to be discriminated against. My first day at A&M I almost picked a fight with my Anglo roommate. I told him that I didn't ask to be with a white man, and if he ever tried anything with me, by God, he was going to have to fight one mean Mexican. And this guy just looked at me in amazement. I said, "You know what I'm talking about. You're white and I'm Mexican." Then he said, "I just came here to be an Aggie like you." That was a slap in the face to me, a shock that any Anglo could see me as an Aggie, something that he should look up to. That was the first time I had ever been perceived as something other than a Mexican. Aggies above all else identify themselves as Aggies, and the measure of acceptance at Texas A&M is not how white you are nor even how high your grades are. They would say don't bring us your high-school rings and jackets and sweaters. Earn your Aggie ring.

Albert and I loved it because it was the first time in our lives that we'd been accepted. We were measured on the basis of proficiency and performance and we both thrived. Albert was a distinguished student the whole time he was there: a student senator all four years, president of the A&M West Texas Club, and, finally, head drum major of the Aggie band. That was probably one of the proudest moments in our lives. I went on to collect outstanding military awards and became military commander of the band.

By the time Albert was a senior in 1965, there was a general awareness that just about everyone at A&M was bound for Vietnam. We didn't feel unpatriotic, but we were already getting word back that upperclassmen who graduated ahead of us were getting killed. My commanding officer freshman year was killed flying a C-130 at An Khe. So patriotism notwithstanding, there was still anxiety about the personal threat of Vietnam.

I remember one Sunday afternoon Albert and I were sitting in this open window of his room, legs hanging out, talking about the inevitable tour of duty we were going to do in Vietnam. I said, "I can't believe that we're going to do it. There are plenty of people who aren't going to go, and I don't think that you and I should go off to a war and get killed for a society that treated us the way it has. Why should we go and fight for this country? For people who have done nothing but discriminate against us and mistreat us and try to cheat us every step of the way. They've abused us and our family. Why should we go and die for these people?"

Albert thought awhile, and then he said, "Well, we're not. We're not going for those people. We're going to fight for the people who did let us into schools. We're going to fight for the teachers who did help us and did reward us when we did well. We're going to fight for the Aggies and the people who gave us a scholarship, who let us into a major university. And we're going to fight for those people who defended our rights and allowed us to grab at the big American pie. These

are the people, and these are the institutions that we're going to fight to defend. And when we come back, Andy, you and I are going to fight side by side, and we're going to whip all those people who are abusing other Americans. We're going to defend and strengthen this nation."

That was the last time I ever doubted what I was going to do in life, because part of that understanding was not only that we were going to resist oppression and discrimination and racism in America but also that Albert and I were going to do it together. He said, "You're an intellectual and I'm going to be a lawyer, and we're going to fight together and they're not going to stop us." I remember he also said, "The commission you and I are going to get is the same commission George Washington held." It would be easy for us to say, no, not this war. We both agreed it was very important for us to be able to come back and say, "We're veterans. We fought for this flag, now it's our flag." It was a mission that we had, and that's what I went to Vietnam with.

We had an understanding between us that neither one of us would kill, or do

Andrés Tijerina stands before a T-38 jet during pilot training at Webb Air Force Base, Texas, in 1968.

Andrés Tijerina, fellow lieutenants, and their instructor (right), during training session at Webb Air Force Base in 1968.

anything that would require us to kill people, in the service of our nation. Albert went into B-52s but was assigned to the Strategic Air Command at Wright-Patterson Air Force Base in Ohio. He got into SAC because it represented all of the things that we wanted out of the military. SAC was strictly a defense, but a mighty defense. That's the way we saw the military and the way we saw flying: You have to be strong, you have to be powerful, but you don't go around bullying other people.

In pilot training I had the highest flying grades, but when the time came to select aircraft I selected a C-130 instead of the F-105, which was the hot plane at the time. The flight commander called me into his office and gave me a chance to explain that it was a mistake and go ahead and select the 105, but I didn't. I was a gung ho pilot, but I was not a gung ho fighter pilot. I didn't love flying as a means of killing.

Since I picked 130s, I got to Vietnam before Albert, in 1968. I'll never forget my first mission. We flew into Tuy Hoa on Christmas evening and then up to Da Nang for a load of ammunition the next morning. From Da Nang we were to deliver 30,000 pounds of high explosives to an outpost of Marines along the DMZ. It was an eventful flight. We took off and fol-

lowed Route 1 north because there was no instrument approach and we had to stay below the clouds, which were between 300 and 500 feet, in order to find the field we were to land on. The problem was that everybody else was flying down there under this cloud layer. The fog and mist was full of helicopters and occasionally another C-130 dummy flying down there with us. Half the crew was in the cockpit looking out different sides of the plane calling out the location of other aircraft so we could dodge them.

To make our approach to the Marine outpost we had to overfly the DMZ. Charlie's antiaircraft positions were all around. About two miles out from the runway the ground fire started because they could see what we were planning to do. We had to make the approach low and slow and we began to get hit. You heard this noise like somebody slammed the front door real hard, and suddenly there was daylight where a bulkhead should be. You can't help yourself, you go ahead and take a peek, and sure enough you can see right through the other side. We were losing a lot of hydraulic fluid and finally there was so much damage the pilot told the crewmen to stop reporting it, just shut up so we could concentrate on trying to land.

Pilots know when the hydraulics are going because instead of barely moving one hand on the yoke with very little corrections, now you're shoving the wheel all the way over to the left and then all the way over to the right. The airplane yaws through the air rather than flying a straight and steady path to the runway.

We had two pairs of hands on the wheels, and both of us were stepping on the right rudder because we'd lost an engine by that time, the outboard left, number one, which meant the aircraft wanted to turn left because the right engines were pushing harder. The plane commander couldn't do it alone. His leg was already trembling from pushing, and he was too busy just trying to keep the thing aimed at the runway.

I shoved my seat forward, wedged my shoulder against the seat back, put my foot on the right rudder, and pushed as hard as I could. I had to curl way down in my seat and then shove with all my back and leg muscles to keep the right rudder pedal fully depressed. At the same time I was trying to keep my head

Albert (right) and Andrés Tijerina with their mother, Belia, in front of the capitol building in Austin, Texas, during a Texas A&M Corps trip in February 1965.

up enough so I could see what the hell my instruments and the plane commander were doing. By then we were getting sirens and had red lights flashing all over the panel. We had stopped looking at the hydraulic gauges because we knew what they said. Our main system was knocked out, and we had leaks in the back-up, and we were coming in hot and heavy onto a short runway—about 1,800 feet.

We managed to touch down at the very end of the runway, but we were faster than we wanted. We instantly reversed the two inboard engines but we were still barreling down that runway. The C-130 has antiskid brakes that keep the wheels from locking, but those four giant balloon wheels were putting tremendous friction on the steel runway matting. Suddenly we heard kaboom, boom, boom and could feel something bashing the underside of the aircraft. We were buckling the runway, and the dislodged matting was beating our landing gear doors off. By now the airplane was no longer going straight down the runway; at the midway point we were fishtailing. Our wing actually dipped below the level of the runway, and if that strip had been wider and had not had a drop-off at the edge we would not have survived. If either wing or the engines had hit the ground, the wing would have broken off and the aircraft would have exploded along with the 30,000 pounds of ammunition. There would have been nothing left. Finally we slid around the other way into a broadside skid and halted, our back wheels off the end of the runway.

As we taxied back onto the runway everybody started to tremble. When you talked your lower jaw quivered. The navigator wasn't talking at all; he was standing staring into space. Then the Communist mortars started coming in because they knew the plane was full of supplies. As we unloaded, a construction unit repaired the runway, and our engineer was able to get the number-one engine running again and patch up the back-up hydraulics. After an eternity we taxied back out to the end of the runway. When we had full power, we released the brakes and the plane jerked us back against the headrest. That 120,000 pounds of aircraft reached 100 knots in about ten seconds and then jumped off the ground at a forty-five-degree angle. We continued that high angle climb, spiraling up

over the base until, to our relief, at about 10,000 feet the aircraft popped out over the tops of the clouds and into the bright, hot sunlight.

When I left for Vietnam I remember my wife was crying so I told her, "Don't worry, they'll never get the kid." About eight months later I came through ferrying a C-130 from Taiwan to the Lockheed plant in Georgia. When my family took me back to the airport for the second half of my tour, my mother said, "Be careful, you could get killed." This time I said, "Yeah, I know."

Albert knew, too. While he was still in Ohio piloting B-52s Albert had a premonition about flying combat in Vietnam, and he wrote me about it in February 1968. "We go together at the O-Club to celebrate and while we were there the CO told us, don't any of you worry; every single one of you will be in Vietnam in F-4Cs. I promise you. Well, I didn't think much of it, but that night … I woke up in my room at about three in the morning. I was completely soaked in sweat, cold and shaking and scared out of my mind. I hadn't had a bad dream or anything, but my subconscious must have

Albert Tijerina in a CH-53 helicopter at Nakhom Phanom Royal Thai Air Force Base in 1971.

Colonel Lloyd C. Edwards, Jr. presents Albert Tijerina's posthumous Purple Heart and Distinguished Flying Cross to his family in the summer of 1971.

been doing some figuring and come to a conclusion because it woke me up and I knew only one thing. I knew it. Don't ask me how, but I knew I was going to go to Vietnam and get killed. I knew it just as I knew who I was."

With most people such thoughts might be dismissed, but ever since we were kids we knew in my family that Albert was extrasensory. Several times he sensed things that others could not, and the premonition stayed in Albert's mind. He alluded to it in another letter a month later when he told me why he selected to fly B-52s. "Remember I told you that it was important to both of us that we select an aircraft using our family values and our principles about not wanting to kill. Some guys in my class actually could not wait to go because they wanted to ride the fast planes and bomb people. They were hoping that the war wouldn't end and I didn't want to be any part of it. We were worlds apart.

"How far does a soldier go before he says, Is this right? How about the guys who serve with other purposes in mind: The guy who likes to kill, the one who likes to think of himself as a tiger, the guy who thinks war is glamorous, the guy who likes medals, the guy who wants to get away from his wife, the guy who wants to be general, the guy who wants to prove something to himself. Are they just as right as the one who merely wants to do his duty? I thought of all this when I chose B-52s. And, lastly, if I do end up going over and getting killed, I'll have lived just this much more with Mandy and Albert Anthony."

My brother was supposed to have left the air force before he was transferred to Vietnam. Albert's time was up, he had plans to go back to school, and he was already preparing to move back to Texas. But when he submitted his papers for separation, his commander informed him he was getting a three-year extension. The CO said his approved application for release could not be returned from air force headquarters in time. For that reason alone Albert was extended and transferred to fly CH-53 helicopters. Rightfully, he should have been released and never had the last tour.

When my brother left his family the last time, he cried openly. Not because he was afraid, but because he felt in a very real way that he was never going to see

them again and that it was his final good-bye. But, he said, it was something we both had to do. "You did yours, now it's my turn."

Albert was sent to Nakhon Phanom Royal Thai Air Force Base in December 1970 and attached to the 21st Special Operations Squadron. In the last letter he wrote to me, in March 1971, his bitterness was very apparent. "I've been with my darling family for about five years now, and it's like ripping my heart out to be away from them. I'm such a weakling in these matters. I wish so badly I could see them and hold them. Andy, get out of the air force as fast as possible. Get out of flying if you can. I just can't imagine that before you get out, they won't think of some TDY [temporary assignment to combat flying] somewhere for you. I can't say much about our flying except that we fly places you wouldn't believe if I told you. It is so sorrowful to see some of the young Laotian soldiers that we carry. I cry inside when I smile at them. I hate the whites even more than I ever have before. Not just because of the war, but because they are so hateful about everything. I can't understand them."

Don't misunderstand, Albert did not hate all white people, but he did see around him the effects of an insensitive bureaucracy with Anglo-Saxon values that dismissed the Laotians and other Orientals as inconsequential. My brother could relate to the plight of those young soldiers because he felt they were victims of the same racism that had blighted his own childhood.

On March 1, Albert was flying a CH-53 on a clandestine mission taking Laotian soldiers into combat. The official report said that he was in the lead aircraft of a flight of three whose mission was to transfer ground troops from a friendly operating location deep in hostile territory to a forward base camp in northern Laos. Albert was flying copilot. We learned from his squadron mates that as they were approaching the battle zone they came over a ridge and took heavy ground fire. Albert's helicopter lost an engine, and the second one began faltering. They began to lose altitude but avoided a concentration of enemy troops and crash-landed into a friendly landing zone. The helicopter smashed into the trees, which crushed the front end and killed the pilots. The craft exploded, but the landing al-

lowed most of the passengers and crew to escape into friendly hands. As the battle continued, the Communists occupied the crash site, and it was not until a few days later that the bodies were recovered from the crash area.

What I saw within a year after he was killed was that something had ended in my family. Albert and I used to sing sad songs and Mexican songs while our grandmother and all of our uncles would gather around us on the front porch and listen. We all felt together. But I tried singing once by myself and they wouldn't let me. Just as my own life was traumatically altered, so was that of my entire extended family. We could no longer get together on the front porch and sing or drink beer. Some uncle would start crying and it would ruin the party. My mother's personality actually changed. You couldn't say anything about Albert because it would just end the conversation, it would end the evening, she would just walk away. So after awhile we didn't get together anymore.

But our service resulted in one thing that Albert and I wanted as Mexican-Americans. Society had to accept us as veterans. My brother lost his life, but when I came back, I came back to a San Angelo that treated me as an equal in employment, education, and socially. We Mexican-Americans still have big needs and I'm not saying that there are not inequities. There are. But I am saying the gross blatant abuse of personal and civil liberties is gone. It was not there after we came back from Vietnam, and it's not facing Albert's nor my children. They are not oblivious to the discrimination that we felt. They know about those things. But they don't relate to them very strongly. If someone called them a dirty Mexican, they'd be shocked. It's just never happened to them.

And the children are helping the family to start anew. My kids are growing up close to Albert's kids and Sylvia's children come from California to visit here. They are all doing well establishing a firm foundation for their own lives. They're good kids and outstanding achievers as well. Looking at the home situation, I feel that our part of America grew the way we wanted it to.

After fourteen years, my mother has been able to return to San Angelo to live and reestablish our family's roots. Picking up the pieces has been extremely difficult, but one recent piece was my nephew Albert Anthony's admission to Texas A&M. The day he graduated from high school we all applauded when he walked into the house, and my mother presented him with Albert's Aggie beer mug. She had kept it because my brother had asked her to save it.

In July 1985 the air force dedicated a dormitory at Goodfellow Air Force Base in San Angelo and named it Tijerina Hall in honor of Albert. This event brought my entire family back together again as it had not been for fourteen years. Much of the extended family was there, all the uncles and aunts; my mother; Sylvia; Albert's wife, Amanda; and all our children. There were some very powerful moments. When we came onto the base, I was driving and my son said, "There it is dad, it's Tijerina Hall." My truck stopped all by itself and everyone became silent. The building with Albert's name on it was a very moving thing for my family to see. It will never change the sorrow in our hearts, but this dedication gave us a way to express a pride in our memory of Albert. And it was more than just us. It was society, it was our government, recognizing him. It doesn't change the fact of the sacrifice, but at least it is recognized and a positive value has been placed on the sacrifice that Albert made. It's our emotional watershed.

Later when the whole family got together it was a very happy occasion, and we were able to think about Albert and talk about him without crying and feeling sad. We went home that night, and there must have been twenty of us sitting in his widow's living room watching old films of the whole family from back in the fifties and sixties. Albert was in them, and we watched and laughed and admired a lot of things about Albert and talked about him. Not once did my mother cry. We were able to convert our sorrowful feelings to a proud, positive emotion.

I'm still bitter about what happened to Albert, but I don't blame the country. I don't blame the nation. I do blame a big blind bureaucracy that has goals other than the welfare of their men in mind. I've worked real hard at holding up my end of the bargain with Albert, but it's like one horse pulling a wagon that was designed for two. I love my wife and my three teenage sons, and I give myself to my community. I'm not an empty person. But compared to what I should have been, and feel I should be, less than half of me is really there.

I have a recurring dream. I call it my trick dream. It's always in the present, and it's always the same scenario. Albert and I are sitting on the front porch, my mother and our wives are in the house, and we're talking about going somewhere or doing something. Then he has to leave for a moment, and he walks around the corner. I sit there for several minutes and then it strikes me. He's not coming back, and I know it's that damned dream. I'm sitting there like a dummy, waiting and smiling, tricked again.   ■

"It will never change the sorrow in our hearts. But this dedication [July 3, 1985] gave us a way to express a pride in our memory of Albert. . . . We were able to convert our sorrowful feelings to a proud, positive emotion."

A letter from home. FSB Fuller, January 1970.

Names, Acronyms, Terms

Agent Orange—a chemical defoliant widely used in Vietnam to deny jungle cover to the enemy. Named after the color-coded stripe painted around the barrels in which it was stored.

AID—Agency for International Development.

AIT—Advanced Individual Training. After eight weeks of basic training, each army recruit goes on to AIT to receive field training in one of many specialties, from combat arms to cooking.

AK/SKS—designations for Soviet-built automatic and semiautomatic rifles used by the North Vietnamese and Vietcong infantry.

Americal Division—U.S. 23d Infantry Division.

American Legion—an organization of honorably discharged U.S. veterans.

amtrac/amtrack—amphibious armored vehicle (tractor) used to transport troops and supplies, armed with a 7.62MM machine gun.

Amvets—an organization of American military veterans who served since 1940.

AO—Artillery Observer.

APC—armored personnel carrier. A track vehicle used to transport troops and supplies, usually armed with a .50-caliber machine gun.

ARVN—Army of the Republic of Vietnam, the South Vietnamese regular army.

AWOL—absent without leave.

BOQ—Bachelor Officer Quarters.

Charlie/Victor Charlie—see VC.

Chicom—Chinese Communist.

Chieu Hoi—the GVN "open arms" program promising clemency and compensation to VC guerrillas and NVA regulars who defected to live under South Vietnamese government authority.

CINCPAC—Commander in Chief, Pacific.

click/klick—a kilometer.

CO—commanding officer.

COMUSMACV—Commander, United States Military Command, Vietnam.

DMZ—demilitarized zone. Established by the Geneva Accords of 1954, provisionally dividing North Vietnam from South Vietnam along the seventeenth parallel.

DRV—Democratic Republic of (North) Vietnam. Since 1975, the designation for all Vietnam.

Five O'Clock Follies—daily press briefings by U.S. military officials at MACV headquarters, Saigon.

IV Corps—fourth allied military tactical zone encompassing the Mekong Delta region.

free fire zone—territory designated by the GVN to be completely under enemy control, thus permitting unlimited use of firepower against anyone in the zone.

Freedom Bird—common term for any airplane used to take U.S. military personnel out of Vietnam.

Geneva Agreements (Accords)—signed by the French and Vietminh on July 21, 1954, the accords marked the end of the French Indochina War and established a provisional boundary at the seventeenth parallel between the Democratic Republic of Vietnam (North) and the new Republic of Vietnam (South).

Green Beret—see Special Forces.

grunt—most popular nickname for an infantryman. Supposedly derived from the sound one made by lifting up his rucksack.

GVN—U.S. abbreviation for the government of South Vietnam. Also referred to as the Republic of Vietnam.

Hanoi Hilton—Hoa Lo Prison, Hanoi, North Vietnam, used for American prisoners of war.

JCS—U.S. Joint Chiefs of Staff.

JGS—Joint General Staff. South Vietnamese counterpart of the JCS.

JUSPAO—Joint United States Public Affairs Office.

KIA—killed in action.

Kit Carson Scout—a defected VC or NVA soldier employed by U.S. units as a scout.

LAW—M72 light antitank weapon. A shoulder-fired 66MM rocket with a one-time disposable fiber glass launcher.

lifer—any officer or enlisted person who serves beyond an initial tour of duty.

LSO—landing signals officer.

LZ—landing zone. A "hot" LZ was a landing zone under enemy fire.

MACV—Military Assistance Command, Vietnam.

medevac—medical evacuation of wounded or ill from the field by helicopter or airplane. Also name given to the evacuating aircraft.

montagnard—a member of any of the mountain tribes of Vietnam, Laos, or Cambodia.

Moratorium—the October 15, 1969, nationwide nonviolent demonstrations against U.S. involvement in Vietnam planned by the Vietnam Moratorium Committee. On November 13-15, 1969, the VMC joined with the New Mobilization Committee to stage Moratorium activities followed by a march on Washington.

MOS—Military Occupational Specialty.

MP—Military Police.

NLF—National Liberation Front. Officially the National Front for the Liberation of the South.

NVA—North Vietnamese Army. Also called the People's Army of Vietnam (PAVN) and Vietnam People's Army (VPA).

OCS—Officers' Candidate School.

I-A—Selective Service classification. Available for military service.

I Corps—"Eye" Corps. First allied tactical zone encompassing the five northernmost provinces of South Vietnam.

PBR—Patrol Boat, River.

PIO—Public Information Officer.

POW—prisoner of war.

PRG—Provisional Revolutionary Government. Established in 1969 as the Government of the NLF.

Project 100,000—a program introduced by Secretary of Defense McNamara in 1966 to provide special military training primarily for men of low-income or minority backgrounds.

Prov Corps—Provisional Corps, Vietnam. An intermediate command established between III MAF (Marine Amphibious Force) in I Corps and MACV in Saigon, designed to facilitate coordination between army and Marine units.

psyops—psychological warfare operations.

PTSD—Post-Traumatic Stress Disorder. Psychological syndrome of delayed reaction to unusually stressful events.

Puff the Magic Dragon—a C-47 cargo plane converted to a gunship by the addition of rapid-firing machine guns. Subsequent improvements included the Spooky, outfitted with Gatling guns and illumination flares, and the Shadow, an AC-119.

PX—post exchange.

R&R—rest and recuperation.

RF/PF—South Vietnamese Regional and Popular Forces. Paramilitary units organized to provide provincial and rural defense. The U.S. nickname Ruff-Puffs is derived from this abbreviation.

RPG—rocket-propelled grenade.

RVN—Republic of (South) Vietnam.

sapper—a VC or NVA commando, usually armed with explosives.

SDS—Students for a Democratic Society.

seventeenth parallel—temporary division line between North and South Vietnam established by the Geneva Accords pending unification elections scheduled for 1956. Elections were never held and the division remained until 1975.

SK/SKS—see AK.

slick—lightly armed transport helicopter.

Special Forces—U.S. soldiers, popularly known as Green Berets, trained in techniques of counterinsurgency warfare.

starlight scope—an image intensifier using reflected light to identify objects at night.

tac air—tactical air support.

TDY—temporary duty.

Tet offensive—a series of coordinated attacks by the VC and NVA against military installations and provincial capitals throughout South Vietnam at the start of the lunar New Year in late January 1968.

TF—task force.

III Corps—third allied military tactical zone encompassing the northern Mekong Delta to the southern central highlands.

TOC—tactical operations center.

II Corps—second allied military tactical zone encompassing the central highlands and adjoining coastal lowlands.

II-S—Selective Service classification. Registrant deferred because of activity in study.

USIA—United States Information Agency.

USO—United Service Organization.

VA—Veterans Administration.

VC—an abbreviation for Vietcong, which was, in turn, a contraction of Vietnam Cong San (Vietnamese Communist). VC, and its derivatives, Victor Charlie and Charlie, originally referred to members of the NLF but were eventually generalized to signify all enemy guerrilla troops.

VFW—Veterans of Foreign Wars.

Vietminh—the coalition, founded by Ho Chi Minh, that ruled the DRV. Absorbed by the Lao Dong (Communist) party in 1951.

Vietnamization—term given to President Nixon's phased withdrawal of U.S. troops and transfer of their responsibilities to the South Vietnamese.

VVAW—Vietnam Veterans Against the War.

xeon light—special high-illumination searchlight.

XO—executive officer. Second in command of a military unit.

Photography Credits

Map Credits